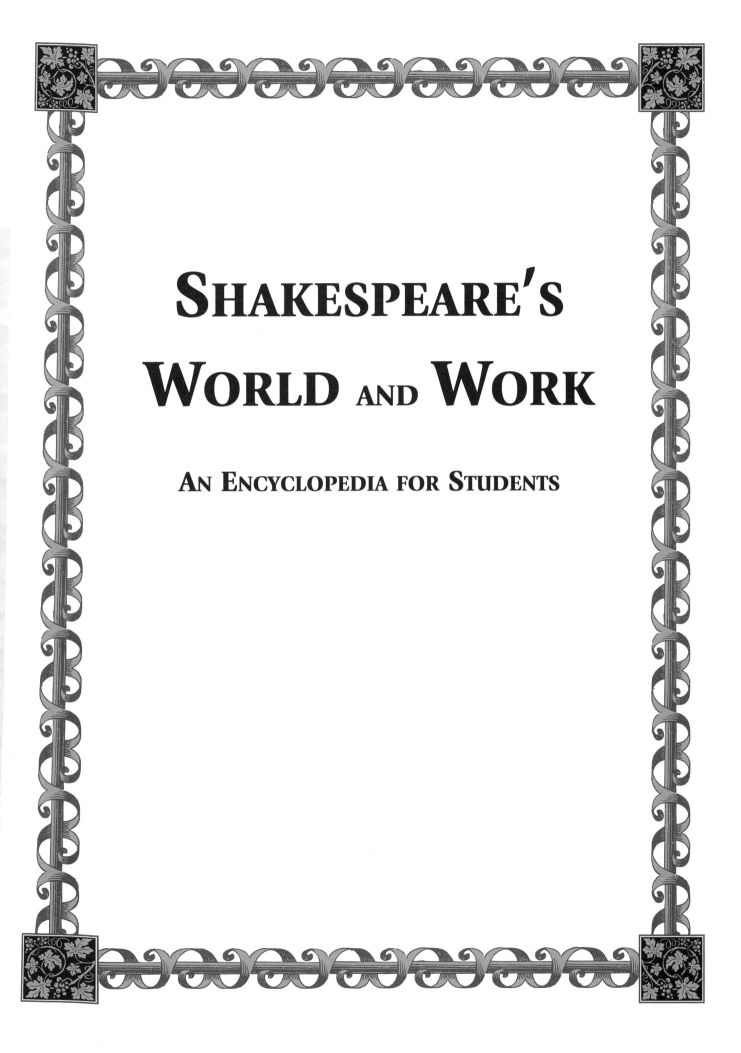

SHAKESPEARE'S WORLD AND WORK

AN ENCYCLOPEDIA FOR STUDENTS

JOHN F. ANDREWS
The Shakespeare Guild
Editor in Chief

WILLIAM M. HILL
The Peddie School
Associate Editor

CONTRIBUTORS

JUDITH ACKROYD
University College
Northampton, U.K.
Characters in Shakespeare's Plays;
Dramatic Techniques;
Plays: The Histories;
Plays: The Tragedies

RALPH BERRY
Stratford-upon-Avon, U.K.
Costumes; Directors and
Shakespeare; Measure for
Measure; Troilus and Cressida;
Twelfth Night

WILLIAM C. CARROLL
Boston University
Love's Labor's Lost

KENT CARTWRIGHT
University of Maryland
Macbeth; Macbeth, Lady

SUSAN CERASANO
Colgate University
Acting Profession;
Globe Theater

MAURICE CHARNEY
Rutgers, The State
University of New Jersey
Julius Caesar

ROBERT CLARE
Oxford, U.K.
Prose Technique

ERIC COLLUM
George Washington University
Gender and Sexuality;
Plays: The Comedies

CHARLES FREY
University of Washington
Teaching Shakespeare

WERNER HABICHT
University of Würzburg, Germany
Translations of Shakespeare

JAY L. HALIO
University of Delaware
Hamlet; King Lear;
Merchant of Venice,The;
Romeo and Juliet;
Settings

JOAN OZARK HOLMER
Georgetown University
Morality and Ethics

IVO KAMPS
University of Mississippi
Shakespeare's Works,
Changing Views

KATE D. LEVIN
The City College of New York
Language

PAMELA MASON
Shakespeare Institute
Much Ado About Nothing

MICHAEL OUELLETTE
Massachusetts Institute of Technology
Music Inspired by Shakespeare

LOIS POTTER
University of Delaware
Othello

JOSEPH PRICE
Pennsylvania State University
Shakespeare's Reputation;
Literature Inspired by Shakespeare

JEANNE ADDISON ROBERTS
The American University
Feminist Interpretations;
Taming of the Shrew, The

IAN SPIBY
University College
Northampton, U.K.
Characters in Shakespeare's Plays;
Dramatic Techniques; Plays: The
Histories; Plays: The Tragedies

ALDEN T. VAUGHAN
Columbia University
Tempest, The

VIRGINIA MASON VAUGHAN
Clark University
Tempest, The

GARY JAY WILLIAMS
The Catholic University of America
Midsummer Night's Dream, A;
Timon of Athens

SUSAN WILLIS
Auburn University
Television and Shakespeare

GEORGE WRIGHT
University of Minnesota
Poetic Technique

DAVID YOUNG
Oberlin College
Love; Plays: The Romances

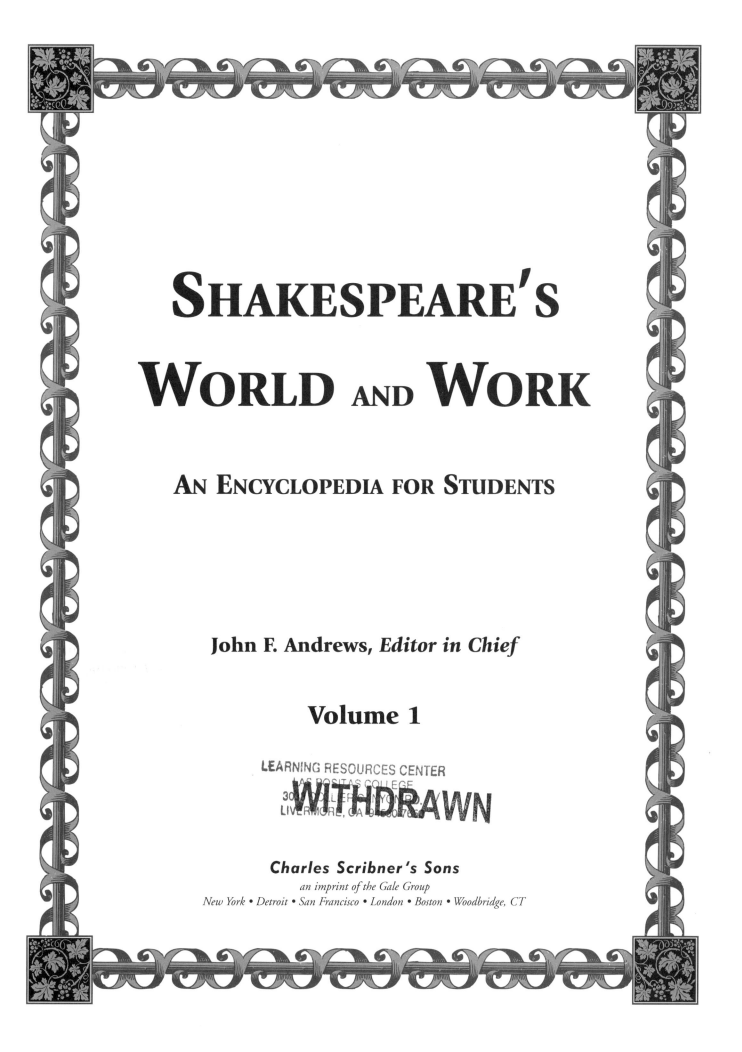

SHAKESPEARE'S
WORLD AND WORK

AN ENCYCLOPEDIA FOR STUDENTS

John F. Andrews, *Editor in Chief*

Volume 1

Charles Scribner's Sons
an imprint of the Gale Group
New York • Detroit • San Francisco • London • Boston • Woodbridge, CT

Developed for Charles Scribner's Sons by Visual Education Corporation, Princeton, N.J.

For Scribners
PUBLISHER: Karen Day
EDITOR: John Fitzpatrick
COVER DESIGN: Jennifer Wahi

For Visual Education Corporation
PROJECT DIRECTOR: Jewel G. Moulthrop
WRITERS: Guy Austrian, Jean Brainard, John Haley, Mark Mussari, Rebecca Stefoff
EDITORS: Amy Livingston, Joseph Ziegler
COPYEDITING SUPERVISOR: Helen Castro
COPY EDITORS: Marie Enders, Eleanor Hero
INDEXER: Sallie Steele
PHOTO RESEARCH: Martin A. Levick
PRODUCTION SUPERVISOR: Paula Deverell
PRODUCTION ASSISTANTS: Susan Buschhorn, Brian Suskin
INTERIOR DESIGN: Maxson Crandall
ELECTRONIC PREPARATION: Fiona Torphy, Christine Osborne
ELECTRONIC PRODUCTION: Rob Ehlers, Lisa Evans-Skopas, Holly Morgan

Library of Congress Cataloging-in-Publication Data

Shakespeare's world and work : an encyclopedia for students / John F. Andrews.
    p. cm.
   Includes bibliographical references and index.
    ISBN 0-684-80629-0 (set) — ISBN 0-684-80626-6 (v.1) —
ISBN 0-684-80627-4 (v.2) — ISBN 0-684-80628-2 (v. 3)
    1. Shakespeare, William, 1564–1616—Encyclopedias. 2. Dramatists, English—
Early modern, 1500–1700—Biography—Encyclopedias. I. Andrews, John F.
(John Frank), 1942–

PR2892 .S56 2001
822.3'3—dc21
[B]

00-068743

TABLE OF CONTENTS

COLOR PLATES

VOLUME 1
Color plates for Elizabethan Life

VOLUME 2
Color plates for The Plays

VOLUME 3
Color plates for People

VOLUME 1

Table of Contents

VOLUME 2

VOLUME 3

Table of Contents

PREFACE

In 1985, under the auspices of the gracious and visionary Charles Scribner, Jr., one of the world's most respected publishing houses issued a three-volume reference set about the dramatist Samuel Taylor Coleridge described as "the greatest man that ever put on and off mortality." This collection, *William Shakespeare: His World, His Work, His Influence,* featured sixty articles by noted interpreters of the writer a famous contemporary, Ben Jonson, had declared "not of an age, but for all time."

Happily, the set was greeted with enthusiastic applause—so much so, in fact, that teachers, librarians, and parents soon began asking for a new collection of Shakespeare-related information that would be organized and attractively presented for the enjoyment and edification of young people. In response, thanks in no small measure to the resourcefulness and perseverance of publisher Karen Day, Scribners is now delighted to issue another title, *Shakespeare's World and Work,* that combines the breadth of its predecessor with an accessible, lively format that should make it appealing both to youthful browsers and to a considerably broader audience than the parent work.

Among the details that distinguish this student encyclopedia from its precursor are *(a)* the alphabetical arrangement of its topics, *(b)* time lines that place significant dates and developments in historical context, *(c)* sidebars that illuminate and provide further insight into major subject areas, *(d)* brief definitions that appear in the margins of most articles to explain any terms or concepts that might pose special difficulties, and *(e)* cross-references that direct readers of each discussion to related entries elsewhere in the anthology. The result—beautifully enhanced by more than 200 illustrations, many of them in color—is a vivid and multifaceted introduction to the personalities, settings, and events that made Renaissance England so rich and diverse a backdrop for the poems and plays that have established Shakespeare as our most reliable guide to the mileposts of life.

As editor I'm honored to welcome back several of the eminent contributors who graced our previous endeavor. I think, for example, of Ralph Berry, Maurice Charney, Werner Habicht, Joseph G. Price, George T. Wright, and David Young. I'm pleased to observe, moreover, that we've been able to attract a stellar company of their academic colleagues, among them Judith Ackroyd, William C. Carroll, Kent Cartwright, Susan Cerasano, Robert Clare, Eric Collum, Charles Frey, Jay Halio, Joan O. Holmer, Ivo Kamps, Kate Levin, Pamela Mason, Michael Ouellette, Lois Potter, Jeanne A. Roberts, Ian Spiby, Alden and Virginia Vaughan, Gary Williams, and Susan Willis.

To coordinate all the efforts that went into this ambitious undertaking, and to supervise a capable staff of research professionals and freelance writers under the aegis of the Visual Education Corporation in Princeton—a team that included Amy Livingston, Paula Deverell, and Joseph Ziegler—we've been blessed with a splendid, indefatigable Senior Project Editor, Jewel Moulthrop. Jewel and her associates can take pride in another handsome addition to a Scribners library that already boasts such highly regarded compilations as *Ancient Greece and Rome, Latin America: History and Culture,* and *North America in Colonial Times.*

As these remarks go to press, an author who might once have been dismissed, in the parlance of modern show business, as a 436-year-old has-been is enjoying another winning streak as Hollywood's hottest screenwriter. It may be worth recalling, then, that Shakespeare was already being recognized in his own lifetime as the "soul of the age" his works reflected and adorned. During the 18th century one of the playwright's greatest editors and commentators, Samuel Johnson, was fully prepared to confirm the accuracy of his forebears' judgments. "This therefore is the praise of Shakespeare," Johnson observed, "that his drama is the mirror of life." Within a few years the most prominent actor of the mid-1700s was speaking in even more emphatic terms. "Shakespeare had a genius," argued David Garrick, "perhaps excelling anything that ever appeared in the world before him."

By the mid-19th century, America's leading man of letters, Ralph Waldo Emerson, was ready to accord the Stratford sage a unique position in the pantheon of history's deepest thinkers. "He was inconceivably

Preface

wise," asserted Emerson, "the others conceivably." Owing in part to George Bernard Shaw's skepticism about such Bardolatry, our most recent century has been somewhat less hyperbolic in its critical estimate of the foremost Renaissance dramatist. But this has not discouraged such testimonials as those of James Joyce, the author who gave us several monuments of the modern sensibility, among them *Dubliners, A Portrait of the Artist as a Young Man, Ulysses,* and *Finnegans Wake.* Joyce referred to the creator of Hamlet and Prospero as the man who "wrote the great folio of the world," and his preferred nickname for this peerless artist was "Shapesphere."

No other dramatist, in English or in any other language, can approach Shakespeare's unique eminence as poet, psychologist, and philosopher; and no one else in any humanistic endeavor has afforded us a perspective as comprehensive or has commanded an influence as all-pervasive. Shakespeare's phrases and cadences have become so familiar that it is sometimes with a start when we realize how many of our everyday expressions were first minted in his fertile mind. Every time we utter a cliché like "one fell swoop," for example, or misapply a sentiment such as "more honored in the breach than the observance," whether we realize it or not, we are speaking Shakespeare. When we attend a stage performance or watch a cinematic version of *Kiss Me Kate* or *West Side Story* and participate vicariously in the lives that Shakespeare's characters continue to have outside the dramatic settings in which they first moved and breathed, we are benefiting from just a few of the ways in which the "sweet Swan of Avon" has enlarged our cosmos by imitating it.

No matter where we turn—whether we find ourselves chuckling over a *New Yorker* drawing in which a queen asks her husband, "You gave your kingdom for a what?" or pausing for a double take at a Superbard T-shirt—we are continually reminded of the ubiquity of Shakespeare. In nearly every nation that has a theatrical or literary tradition, he turns out to be the playwright whose works are most frequently performed, the poet whose writings furnish the most convenient and memorable source of allusion. And because he is so central to our lives, sooner or later we're almost bound to feel a desire to know and understand him better.

That, of course, is the reasoning behind this publication. Appropriately, many of its articles elicit as many queries as they provide answers, because it is not the purpose of *Shakespeare's World and Work* to attempt definitive solutions to any of the problems the study of so inexhaustible a subject occasions. As Matthew Arnold reflected in a celebrated sonnet about the author he most admired, "Others abide our question. Thou art free."

These volumes will have achieved their aim if each reader emerges from them with an enhanced awareness of the complexity of Shakespeare's world and an expanded appreciation of the playwright's incomparable mastery of the means to immortalize it through the prose and verse for which we continue to gravitate to him. Meanwhile, it is our hope that those who peruse these pages will be helped to the same discovery that has thrilled millions of previous adventurers—that one of the most liberating experiences a person can enjoy is the privilege of falling under the spell of William Shakespeare.

John F. Andrews
Washington, D.C.

SHAKESPEAREAN CHRONOLOGY

Note: The dating of Shakespeare's plays is often uncertain. For simplicity, we have listed the *earliest* dates accepted by *The Riverside Shakespeare*, 2nd ed., 1997.

YEAR	EVENTS
1532	King Henry VIII breaks with the Catholic Church to marry Anne Boleyn.
1533	The future Queen Elizabeth I is born to King Henry VIII and Anne Boleyn.
1534	King Henry VIII becomes head of the Anglican Church.
1536	Anne Boleyn is executed.
1547	King Henry VIII dies. Edward VI is crowned.
1553	King Edward VI dies. Mary I assumes the throne and begins to reestablish Catholicism.
1555	Roman Catholicism is officially reestablished. Persecution of Protestants begins.
1558	Queen Mary I dies. Elizabeth I is crowned.
1559	Elizabethan Settlement reforms the Anglican Church. Strict sumptuary laws prohibit Elizabethans from wearing clothing above their station.
1564	William Shakespeare is born to John and Mary Shakespeare. Christopher Marlowe is born.
1566	John Shakespeare is appointed an alderman of Stratford-upon-Avon. King James VI of Scotland is born. Edward Alleyn is born.
1567	Richard Burbage is born. Thomas Nash is born.
1568	John Shakespeare is elected mayor of Stratford-upon-Avon. Mary, Queen of Scots, takes refuge in England.
1570	Pope Pius V excommunicates Queen Elizabeth I.
1571	John Shakespeare is elected chief alderman.
1572	Ben Jonson is born.
1573	Henry Wriothesley, 3rd earl of Southampton, is born.
1576	The Theater playhouse opens.
1577	The Curtain opens. Raphael Holinshed's *Chronicles* is published.
1579	John Fletcher is born.
1580	Sir Francis Drake completes circumnavigation of the world.
1582	William Shakespeare marries Anne Hathaway.
1583	A daughter (Susanna) is born to William Shakespeare and Anne Hathaway. The Queen's Men acting company is formed.
1585	Anne Hathaway gives birth to twins, Judith and Hamnet. First English colony is established in North America.
1586	Queen Elizabeth I outlaws printing presses outside of London, Cambridge, and Oxford. Philip Sidney dies.
1587	The Rose opens. Mary, Queen of Scots, is executed.
1588	Spanish Armada is defeated. Richard Tarlton dies.
1589	Shakespeare writes *Henry VI, Part 1*. Thomas Kyd writes *The Spanish Tragedy*. King James VI of Scotland marries Princess Anne of Denmark.

1590   Shakespeare writes *Henry VI, Part 2* and *Part 3*. Edmund Spenser's *The Faerie Queene* is published. Thomas Lodge's *Rosalynde* is published.

1591   Shakespeare writes *Richard III*. Philip Sidney's *Astrophel and Stella* is published.

1592   Shakespeare writes *The Comedy of Errors*. Robert Greene's *Groatsworth of Wit* is published. Philip Henslowe begins his *Diary*.

1593   Shakespeare's *Venus and Adonis* is published. Shakespeare writes *Titus Andronicus* and *The Taming of the Shrew*. Christopher Marlowe is killed in a tavern brawl. Theaters are closed throughout the year due to plague.

1594   Shakespeare's *The Rape of Lucrece* is published. Shakespeare writes *The Two Gentlemen of Verona, Love's Labor's Lost,* and *King John*. The Chamberlain's Men acting company is formed. Thomas Kyd dies.

1595   Shakespeare writes *Richard II, Romeo and Juliet,* and *A Midsummer Night's Dream*. William Shakespeare is named as one of the players paid for performing for Queen Elizabeth I. The Swan opens.

1596   Hamnet Shakespeare dies. John Shakespeare is granted a coat of arms. William Shakespeare writes *Henry IV, Part 1; Henry IV, Part 2;* and *The Merchant of Venice*.

1597   William Shakespeare purchases New Place in Stratford-upon-Avon. Shakespeare writes *The Merry Wives of Windsor*. Performance of *The Isle of Dogs* at the Swan theater results in the imprisonment of the playwrights and the temporary closing of all theaters. The Poor Law is passed.

1598   Shakespeare writes *Much Ado About Nothing*. War of the Theaters begins. Shakespeare acts in Ben Jonson's *Every Man in His Humour*. The Theater is dismantled.

1599   Shakespeare writes *Henry V, Julius Caesar,* and *As You Like It*. Robert Devereux, Earl of Essex, fails to quell rebellion in Ireland. The Globe opens. Edmund Spenser dies.

1600   Shakespeare writes *Hamlet*. The Fortune opens.

1601   John Shakespeare dies. Shakespeare's *The Phoenix and Turtle* is published. Shakespeare writes *Twelfth Night* and *Troilus and Cressida*. The Chamberlain's Men are hired to perform *Richard II*. Robert Devereux, Earl of Essex, is executed for revolting against Queen Elizabeth I.

1602   William Shakespeare purchases land in Old Stratford. Shakespeare writes *All's Well That Ends Well*. War of the Theaters ends.

1603   Queen Elizabeth I dies. King James VI of Scotland is crowned King James I of England. The Chamberlain's Men become the King's Men. Theaters are closed due to plague.

1604   The King's Men participate in King James I's coronation procession. King James ends war with Spain. Shakespeare writes *Measure for Measure* and *Othello*. Theaters reopen.

1605   William Shakespeare buys an interest in Stratford-upon-Avon tithes and writes *King Lear*. Gunpowder Plot is discovered. The Red Bull opens.

1606   Shakespeare writes *Macbeth, Antony and Cleopatra,* and *Pericles*. John Lyly dies.

1607   Susanna Shakespeare marries John Hall. Shakespeare writes *Coriolanus* and *Timon of Athens*. Jamestown, Virginia, is settled. Theaters are closed for three months due to plague.

1608   Mary Shakespeare dies. The King's Men lease Blackfriars.

1609   Shakespeare's *Sonnets* and *A Lover's Complaint* are published. Shakespeare writes *Cymbeline*. Theaters temporarily close due to plague.

1610   Shakespeare writes *The Tempest*. Ben Jonson writes *The Alchemist*.

1611   Shakespeare writes *The Winter's Tale*. The King James Bible is published.

1613   William Shakespeare buys Blackfriars Gatehouse and writes *Henry VIII* and *The Two Noble Kinsmen*. The Globe burns down. The Hope opens.

1616   Judith Shakespeare marries Thomas Quiney. William Shakespeare revises his will and dies.

1623 John Heminges and Henry Condell produce the First Folio. Anne Shakespeare dies. Sometime prior to this date a monument to William Shakespeare is placed in the Holy Trinity Church of Stratford-upon-Avon.

1625 King James I dies. Charles I is crowned.

1642 English Civil Wars begin. Puritans seize control of government. London theaters are closed.

1660 Ban on theaters is lifted. Women appear in plays on the English stage. Samuel Pepys begins his *Diary*.

1674 William Davenant produces a musical adaptation of *Macbeth*.

1709 Nicholas Rowe's edition of Shakespeare's works is published.

1725 Alexander Pope's edition of Shakespeare's works is published.

1729 Voltaire translates Shakespeare's works into French.

1730s Drury Lane and Covent Garden acting companies are granted theater monopolies in London.

1741 David Garrick debuts as Richard III.

1765 Samuel Johnson's edition of Shakespeare's works is published.

1769 Shakespeare Jubilee is held in Stratford-upon-Avon.

1803 First Variorum edition is published.

1807 Thomas Bowdler's *The Family Shakespeare* is published.

1823 Charles Kemble stages *King John* at Covent Garden.

1826 Ira Aldridge debuts as Othello.

1838 William Charles Macready restores the original text of *King Lear* to the stage.

1843 Monopolies on London theaters end.

1849 Astor Place Riot erupts in New York.

1883 Samuel Taylor Coleridge's *Lectures and Notes on Shakespeare and Other English Poets* is published.

1895 Elizabethan Stage Society is founded.

1899 A scene from a Shakespeare play is captured on film for the first time.

1910 Herbert Beerbohm Tree stages an elaborate *Midsummer Night's Dream*.

1912 Harley Granville-Barker produces the first authentic Shakespearean production of modern times.

1920s Barry Jackson introduces 20th-century costuming in Shakespeare's plays.

1930s Theodore Komisarjevsky introduces mixed-period costuming.

1937 First production of a Shakespeare play is made for television.

1944 Laurence Olivier produces a film version of *Henry V*.

1948 Olivier's *Hamlet* is released, the first foreign film to win the Academy Award for best picture.

1957 Performances of Shakespeare's works begin in New York City's Central Park.

1961 Royal Shakespeare Company is founded.

1965 Peter Hall directs his influential production of *Hamlet*.

1970 Peter Brook directs a film version of *King Lear*.

1985 Akira Kurosawa directs *Ran,* a film based on *King Lear*.

1989 Kenneth Branagh directs and stars in a film version of *Henry V*.

1996 Baz Luhrmann directs *Shakespeare's Romeo + Juliet*.

1999 BBC audience survey names Shakespeare as Britain's "Man of the Millennium."

CHRONOLOGY OF SHAKESPEARE'S WORKS

Note: All dates are based on *The Riverside Shakespeare*, 2nd ed., 1997.

1 Henry VI	1589–92
2 Henry VI	1590–91
3 Henry VI	1590–92
Richard III	1591–93
Venus and Adonis	1592–93
The Comedy of Errors	1592–94
Sonnets	1592–1609
Titus Andronicus	1593–94
The Rape of Lucrece	1593–94
The Taming of the Shrew	1593–94
The Two Gentlemen of Verona	1594
Love's Labor's Lost	1594
King John	1594–96
Richard II	1595
Romeo and Juliet	1595
A Midsummer Night's Dream	1595–96
Henry IV, Part 1	1596
The Merchant of Venice	1596–97
Henry IV, Part 2	1596–97
The Merry Wives of Windsor	1597
Much Ado About Nothing	1598–99
Henry V	1599
Julius Caesar	1599
As You Like It	1599–1600
Hamlet	1600–01
The Phoenix and Turtle	1601
Twelfth Night	1601–02
Troilus and Cressida	1601–02
All's Well That Ends Well	1602–03
A Lover's Complaint	1602–08
Measure for Measure	1604
Othello	1604
King Lear	1605
Macbeth	1606
Antony and Cleopatra	1606–07
Pericles	1606–08
Coriolanus	1607–08
Timon of Athens	1607–08
Cymbeline	1609–10
The Tempest	1610–11
The Winter's Tale	1611
Henry VIII	1613
The Two Noble Kinsmen	1613

ACTING COMPANIES, ELIZABETHAN

* *guild* association of craft and trade workers that set standards for and represented the interests of its members

* *farce* light dramatic composition that features broad satiric comedy, improbable situations, stereotyped characters, and exaggerated physical action

* *elite* best of its kind

PLAYING THE FOOL

Richard Tarlton, mainstay of the Queen's Men and probable model for Hamlet's Yorick, was a favorite of Queen Elizabeth I. According to Tarlton's biographer, John Fuller:

When Queen Elizabeth was serious . . . and out of good humour, he could *undumpish* (cheer) her at his pleasure. . . . [H]e told the Queen most of her faults more than her chaplains, and cured her melancholy better than all her physicians.

The acting companies of Shakespeare's day developed from the medieval trade guilds* that staged performances based on Bible stories and the lives of saints. Eventually players began to roam about the countryside, performing in towns and villages. During their travels they met other entertainers—such as jugglers, acrobats, and magicians—whose performances were livelier than their own and appealed to larger audiences. To compete with these performers, the acting companies began to include lighter fare, such as farces*, in their programs. Such plays, however, often included obscene words and gestures that offended some people.

In time, traveling performers acquired the same notoriety as ordinary VAGABONDS. Accused of purse snatching and other thievery, players were unwelcome in many places. Their wandering lifestyle and apparent lack of responsibility offended so many people that in 1531 King Henry VIII passed a law requiring anyone without property, a master, or a craft to be whipped by the local mayor or justice of the peace. It was in this environment that the first professional acting companies were organized.

THE GROWTH OF ACTING COMPANIES. The first Elizabethan acting companies consisted of boys. They came from music schools sponsored by royal chapels, cathedrals, and colleges. Talented and enthusiastic masters staged the performances. Adult acting companies, by contrast, often featured poorly written plays and low-budget productions. This was due, in part, to the lack of permanent theaters in England. With no fixed bases from which to work, adult companies had difficulty earning enough money to finance high-quality work.

The situation changed dramatically after the construction of the first permanent public theaters in London in the 1560s and 1570s. By 1578 London boasted eight public theaters and several adult companies. Most of these were named for their royal patrons, or sponsors, such as the earl of Leicester. Six companies were allowed to perform before the royal court: Leicester's Men, Warwick's Men, Sussex's Men, Essex's Men, the Children of the Chapel, and the Children of Paul's. The boy companies declined in popularity as the most important playwrights began to write for adult companies that performed at court.

In 1583 Queen ELIZABETH I took the best adult players from several companies and formed an elite* company, which became known as the Queen's Men. The most popular company of the day, it made 21 appearances before the royal court. Until the death of its leader and best actor, Richard Tarlton, in 1588, no other company could seriously compete with the Queen's Men.

From 1589 to 1594, outbreaks of the plague closed the theaters for long periods. When they reopened, two companies dominated the theater scene: the Admiral's Men and the Chamberlain's Men, whose members included Shakespeare himself. In 1603 King JAMES I became the sponsor of the Chamberlain's Men, and thereafter it was known as the KING'S MEN.

FINANCES AND ORGANIZATION. To join an acting company, each member bought a share in the company, which entitled him to a percentage of the profits from the performances. The price of a share in a successful

The gowned figure in this scene from the play *Roxana* (1632) is actually a boy in women's clothing. Until 1660 women were forbidden to appear on stage, and all acting companies included boys to play female roles.

company was quite high. For example, the cost of Shakespeare's share in the Chamberlain's Men was only slightly less than the cost of his house in Stratford-upon-Avon, which was one of the finest in the town.

Although an actor could make a comfortable living, it was the theater owner who profited the most. Few acting companies owned the theaters in which they played, and they often struggled to make money after their landlord took his share of the admission receipts. The landlord typically paid for the costumes, purchased the plays to be performed, and paid the actors' wages. From the performance receipts, the landlord deducted his profits and the company's share of production costs. With little or no control over their finances, many companies folded. New companies occupied theaters as old companies went out of business. The Chamberlain's Men owed their long financial success partly to the fact that they owned their own theater, the Globe.

Elizabethan acting companies had from 6 to 12 regular, share-owning members and several hired men who were paid wages for their work. Companies also had one or two boys to play women's roles; they usually received no pay but were given room and board while they learned their craft. Companies performed six days a week, often staging a different play every day and adding a new one every two weeks. An actor might have to remember up to 30 parts at a time. The best actor took all the leading roles, which meant remembering up to 800 lines per play, some 5,000 lines each week—more lines than *Hamlet* has altogether. Other actors were usually typecast, playing the parts for which they were best suited. For example, some actors routinely played clowns or soldiers. Stage directions were only roughly indicated in the scripts. As a result, in addition to speaking his lines, an actor frequently guided his own actions onstage, relying on his experience or on spoken directions from the playwright or the senior actors.

The government censored most plays to remove foul language, immoral content, or anything that might be considered offensive to the crown. In 1624 a scandal erupted over a performance of *A Game at Chess*, which contained scenes that insulted the Spanish crown, whose powerful ambassador was at the English court. The ultimate act of censorship occurred after the overthrow of King James I in 1642, when Parliament closed all the theaters in London. (*See also* **Acting Companies, Modern; Acting Profession; Actors, Shakespearean; Censorship, Licensing, and Copyrights; Children's Companies; Elizabethan Theaters; Guilds; Patronage of the Arts; Vagabonds, Beggars, and Rogues.**)

ACTING COMPANIES, MODERN

Performances of Shakespeare's works in the modern era are dramatically different from the performances of Shakespeare's time. The most significant change may be the presence of women on the stage, rather than the boy actors who formerly played the female roles. In addition, directors play a large role in modern productions, whereas Elizabethan productions generally had little or no direction. New technology and changing conventions* of stage production have

* *convention* established practice

* *monopoly* exclusive right to engage in a particular type of business

* *adaptation* literary composition rewritten into a new form

* *apron* part of a stage that is in front of the proscenium arch, which frames the main portion of the stage

also altered the way in which modern companies of actors present Shakespeare's plays.

From the mid-1730s until the mid-1800s, the acting companies at Drury Lane and Covent Garden enjoyed a monopoly* over London theater. Their Shakespeare productions tended to emphasize individual actors and the roles they played, rather than the play as a whole. The scripts were often greatly altered from what Shakespeare had written—their plots and their LANGUAGE changed to make them more appealing to the audience. Beginning around 1800, costumes and scenery grew steadily more elaborate, to such an extent that lavish stage effects often distracted the audience from the action of the play.

In 1843 the Act for Regulating the Theaters allowed many newer, smaller theaters to open. Shakespearean actors took over the management of many of these venues and established their own acting companies. One of the best actor-managers was John Phelps of the Sadler's Wells Theater. His productions shifted the emphasis from individual actors to ensemble performances, in which the entire cast works together as a whole. He was also one of the first stage managers to restore Shakespeare's plays to their original form instead of using the adaptations* of the previous century.

Techniques of production varied from company to company. Charles Kean, son of the legendary actor Edmund Kean, devised performances at the Princess Theater that went to extremes to create historically accurate costumes and sets. His stage furnishings were sometimes so elaborate that long intermissions were needed to change from one scene to the next. Henry Irving of the Lyceum Theater used sets that were carefully designed to "heighten the effects" of the drama without slowing its action. William Poel founded the Elizabethan Stage Society to promote a production style similar to that of Shakespeare's time: on an apron* stage thrust out into the audience, with little or no scenery. All three of these directors, however, performed Shakespeare's plays in adapted forms. Harley Granville-Baker of the Savoy Theater reversed this trend by focusing on the text, not on the staging. His productions of Shakespeare followed the plays in their original form, with the actors encouraged to speak their lines quickly and naturally.

In the 1900s, acting companies experimented with new approaches to Shakespeare. Directors began to explore modern themes and stage the plays in a way that related the action to current events and concerns. Barry Jackson of the Birmingham Repertory Theater started a popular trend by performing Shakespeare's plays in modern dress. In London, the Princess Victoria Theater—known as the Old Vic—dominated the theater scene from the 1930s through the 1950s, showcasing such star performers as Laurence Olivier, John Gielgud, and Edith Evans. In 1963 the Old Vic was turned over to the National Theater Company, under Olivier's direction.

Since the 1960s, the ROYAL SHAKESPEARE COMPANY in STRATFORD-UPON-AVON has been the leading group of Shakespearean performers in Britain, with the National Theater Company as its primary challenger. In the United States, most modern Shakespeare productions are performed by

SHAKESPEARE FESTIVAL organizations, which thrive throughout the country. In New York City, director Joseph Papp and his successors have produced performances of Shakespeare's plays in Central Park since 1958—staging every Shakespearean play at least once, with tickets available at no charge. In addition, countless film and TELEVISION productions have helped bring Shakespeare to wider audiences. (*See also* **Acting Companies, Elizabethan; Actors, Shakespearean; Directors and Shakespeare; Shakespeare on Screen; Shakespeare's Works, Adaptations of; Shakespeare's Works, Changing Views.**)

ACTING PROFESSION

* *guild* association of craft and trade workers that set standards for and represented the interests of its members

During Shakespeare's lifetime the acting profession was organized around playing companies, which consisted of groups of adult actors who performed together regularly and shared expenses. Before the construction of the public playhouses in the 1560s and 1570s, acting companies were itinerant; that is, instead of performing in a fixed location, they toured from place to place, acting in guild* halls, INN YARDS, or wherever else they could. Other elements of their organization were informal as well. For example, in order to collect money, the actors simply passed a hat among the spectators. Once the players began to perform in permanent structures where they could collect an admission fee from each spectator, the nature of playing altered significantly. By the mid-1590s, when two prominent companies dominated the London theater scene, the actors worked within well-established professional, performance, and financial structures.

THE COMPANY. While the early companies tended to be groups of 5 or 6 adult players, the companies with which Shakespeare performed were larger. In general the London companies consisted of 12 adult men and 2 or 3 boy players to enact the female roles. The adult actors were referred to as masters, shareholders, or sharers, both because they were the best players and because they each contributed money to purchase a portion of the company. The funds they made available were used to pay for ordinary expenses such as purchasing plays, costumes, and props. In some cases the shareholders' contributions were also used to pay rent to the owner of the playhouse.

Sharers assumed major responsibility for the company's business, both on stage and off. Several sharers managed the company's financial affairs—counting money and collecting fees for performances. Some heard readings of new plays before purchasing them. Others supervised rehearsals, while still others coordinated costumes or travel arrangements for court performances. In return for their work and financial investment, the sharers collected a portion of the returns from each performance, and some enjoyed substantial incomes. Richard Burbage, the leading actor and a sharer in Shakespeare's company, was reported to be worth £300—a considerable fortune—at the time of his death. Shakespeare himself was able to purchase the second grandest home in STRATFORD-UPON-AVON,

using the proceeds from his share as an actor and his earnings from the sale of his plays to the company.

THE PLAYERS. In addition to their financial investments and duties, sharers also trained apprentice* players. These boys could be as young as 10 or as old as 20 years of age. Sharers also enlisted the services of hired men, who worked for the company on a temporary basis, as they were needed.

The size of a company seems to have varied, depending on whether it was performing at home in London (which called for a larger group) or on tour in the countryside when plague* forced the closing of the metropolitan theaters (in which case a smaller group would be employed). Many of the plays that were written at the time were for a company that was able to accommodate approximately 20 roles. Among the 12 adult players, several performed the major roles, while 1 or 2 specialized as professional clowns.

Some actors were versatile enough to take on two or even three roles in the same play. This practice, which is called doubling, is the focus of much critical debate. Some theater historians hypothesize that actors who performed multiple roles were assigned parts that were related thematically within the play. For example, in *Hamlet,* after the foolish old counselor Polonius is killed, many critics suggest that the actor returned to play the First Grave-digger, with the humorous consequence that the actor playing Polonius seems to have dug his own grave. Other historians are less convinced that an actor's multiple roles were normally related. Instead, they suggest that actors shifted among several parts merely for the sake of convenience. According to this view, minor parts were performed by whichever players were free to go on stage at a particular time. Still other historians maintain that a combination of thematic doubling and convenience was at work. In any event, one thing is clear: players who were clothed as women, who wore elaborate costumes, or who were onstage for long stretches of time were unlikely to have taken on more than one role.

ELIZABETHAN STAGE PRACTICES. There is much speculation about stage practices during Shakespeare's time. Because there were no acting schools, it is uncertain how the majority of actors received their training. While boy players were clearly apprenticed to master actors, many actors joined playing companies as adults. In addition, historians have noted that while some actors used highly formal speech and gestures, others favored a more naturalistic approach. Consequently, the exact sound and feel of a Shakespearean performance cannot be known or reproduced.

Fortunately, other aspects of Elizabethan productions seem more certain. For example, only the lead actors were specially costumed for each performance. Other players borrowed from the company wardrobe or, in some cases, wore their own clothing onstage. Those actors who played clowns seem to have had great talent for improvisation*. Consequently, their roles, as they are recorded in dramatic texts, are probably greatly simplified. There is no record of any woman ever acting on the

One of the leading actors of Shakespeare's day was Edward Alleyn of the Admiral's Men. Alleyn became famous for his performances of leading roles, such as Christopher Marlowe's Doctor Faustus.

Acting Profession

* *puritanical* characterized by rigid morality
* *patent* official document granting a right or privilege

Elizabethan public stage. Boy players acted the roles of young women and children, and perhaps minor roles, such as messengers. An older boy or a young adult male actor might well have played older female characters, such as Lady Macbeth.

The repertory system—in which the same company performed many different plays in a season, with perhaps several different plays onstage each week—imposed many requirements for performers. In such a system it was necessary for actors to learn their roles quickly and to be exceptionally skilled and adaptable. Because players often remained with the same company for their entire careers (another feature affecting the repertory system), the actors' performances would have been well polished, and their interactions familiar, both to one another and to the audience. One can only imagine the quality of a performance by seasoned players who know the text and one another so thoroughly that they can anticipate each other's every move.

VIEWING THE PROFESSION. John Heminges and Henry Condell, the two players who coordinated the printing of the FIRST FOLIO of Shakespeare's plays in 1623, considered the actors who had brought the plays to life to be so important that they included a list of 26 "Names of the Principall Actors in all these Playes." First among these actors was William Shakespeare, who performed with the same company—originally known as the Chamberlain's Men and after 1603 as the King's Men—from 1594 until he retired. Unfortunately, no evidence exists about which roles he played or about whether he preferred writing plays to acting in them. Still, historians are fairly certain that he would have experienced the same social complications as did other players.

While aristocratic audiences and many ordinary theatergoers valued the acting companies, players encountered a fair amount of hostility throughout the history of the Shakespearean stage. Because the actors did not belong to a formal guild, their puritanical* opponents regarded them as no better than rogues and vagabonds. Some church officials questioned the idea that acting could have the status of a profession. As a result the London authorities kept a close watch on the playhouses and periodically closed them. Serious violations, such as playing without a license from the master of the revels or performing a play containing inflammatory material, were punishable by imprisonment. By 1600 legislation stated that no more than two companies could operate in London. Until 1603 wealthy aristocrats supported the acting companies, allowing the players to operate as "household servants" under their patronage. After this date royal patents* legitimized three companies under the patronage of King James, his wife (Queen Anne), and his son (Prince Henry). Ultimately, the players enjoyed patronage that was more powerful than that of any city authority, and their aristocratic connections opened the door to performances at court during the great festivities that took place there during the Christmas holidays and during the week following Easter. (*See also* **Acting Companies, Elizabethan; Acting Companies, Modern; Actors, Shakespearean; Elizabethan Theaters; Fools, Clowns, and Jesters.**)

ACTORS, SHAKESPEAREAN

See color plate 12, vol. 3.

In the four centuries that have passed since Shakespeare wrote his first play, thousands of actors have taken on Shakespearean roles not only in England but in dozens of other countries. The qualities of a successful Shakespearean actor have changed over time, often as a result of a particular actor's influence.

SHAKESPEARE'S ACTORS. The leading actor in Shakespeare's own company, the KING'S MEN, was Richard Burbage. He was most widely acclaimed for his portrayal of tragic roles, especially the title roles in *King Lear*, *Othello*, and *Hamlet*. It is likely that Shakespeare wrote these roles specifically for this popular actor.

Another member of Shakespeare's acting company, Will Kempe, gained international fame for his portrayal of Shakespeare's broad comic roles, such as Dogberry in *Much Ado About Nothing*. A clown even offstage, Kempe is also known for agreeing, on a bet, to dance all the way from London to Norwich, a town that is about 100 miles away. After completing the trip, Kempe proclaimed, "I have danced myself out of the world."

CHANGES IN THE THEATER. The King's Men continued to perform Shakespeare's plays until 1642, when the English government closed down all the public playhouses. When the ban was lifted in 1660, the English theater that emerged was noticeably different from that of Shakespeare's day. One major change was the introduction of actresses to play the women's roles, which until that time had been performed by boys. Another was that there were only two licensed acting companies: the King's Company, run by Thomas Killigrew, and the Duke's Company, run by William Davenant.

Davenant's company boasted the greatest Shakespearean actor of this period, Thomas Betterton. Betterton was said to have superb vocal control and an extraordinary ability to hold his audiences spellbound. He was best known for the role of Hamlet, which he started playing as a young man and continued to do into his 70s. In addition to Hamlet, Betterton played other tragic roles, including the title role in *Othello* and BRUTUS in *Julius Caesar*, and such comic roles as FALSTAFF and Sir Toby Belch in *Twelfth Night*.

Further changes occurred in the mid-1700s, influenced by David Garrick. The most famous English actor of his day, Garrick probably did more than anyone else to popularize Shakespeare. He introduced a new, more natural way of acting that replaced the formal style used in the past, and he is said to have had a hypnotic effect on his audiences. From Garrick's time until the mid-1800s, great actors, rather than great plays, became the focus of the theater.

Garrick eventually became the manager of his acting company and was as successful a producer as he had been an actor. Because he idolized Shakespeare, he tried to produce as many of Shakespeare's plays as he could, eventually staging 24 of them. He played a decisive role in restoring the original texts of works that had for many years been produced in adapted forms. In addition, Garrick was a playwright, a Shakespearean

scholar, and the organizer of the first SHAKESPEARE FESTIVAL, in 1769 at STRATFORD-UPON-AVON.

See color plate 15, vol. 3.

AUDIENCE PARTICIPATION

In the 1700s the actor-manager David Garrick made an important reform in theater: he banned members of the audience from the stage. Until then, audience members had often crowded onto the stage to get a better view. This unwanted "audience participation" not only interfered with the illusion the actors were trying to create but also restricted their movements. Actors—already burdened with heavy costumes and props—had to fight their way through crowds of spectators to make their way onto the stage. Once on stage, they had to be careful to avoid stepping on or tripping over the audience members.

THEATRICAL FAMILIES. In addition to Garrick, two families of actors dominated the English stage in the 1700s. The first, from about 1700 to 1750, was the Cibber family. The father, Colley Cibber, though famous for acting, was even better known for rewriting Shakespeare's plays for the stage. His adaptation of *Richard III* was so popular that it was the most commonly used version of the play for more than 200 years. Colley's son Theophilus, an unattractive man with a shrill voice, nonetheless became a popular Shakespearean actor because of his skill with such comic roles as Parolles in *All's Well That Ends Well*. His wife, Susannah, originally an opera singer, began acting in dramatic roles two years after her marriage to Theophilus. Her superior ability with such tragic Shakespearean roles as OPHELIA and Lady MACBETH made many critics view her as the ideal female counterpart to Garrick.

During the late 1700s, the most prominent Shakespearean actors in England were the members of the Kemble family. John Philip Kemble, the older of two brothers, was noted for the energy and intensity of his performances. His style, sometimes formal and stiff, was at other times strikingly natural. His death scene in *Coriolanus,* perhaps his finest role, was so lifelike that it prompted screams from audience members. A producer as well as an actor, John Philip staged 27 of Shakespeare's plays, sometimes in their original forms and sometimes in adaptations.

John Philip's younger brother, Charles Kemble, was also a respected Shakespearean actor, his best role being Mercutio in *Romeo and Juliet.* His wife Maria, who acted under the name of Mrs. Charles Kemble, and their daughter Fanny were two of the leading actresses of the day. Their talents, however, paled before those of Sarah Siddons, the sister of John Philip and Charles Kemble. Siddons is considered by many to have been not only the greatest English actress of the 1700s but also the greatest English tragic actress of all time. She studied her roles with great care and performed them with extraordinary emotion. As one reviewer said of her, "She was Tragedy personified." Siddons was best known for her portrayal of Lady Macbeth, which was so intense it prompted one audience member to remark, "I swear that I smelt blood!"

The greatest Shakespearean actor of the early 1800s was Edmund Kean, an English tragic actor who enlivened his performances by adding "points," bits of stage direction that expressed his view of a character. For example, his Richard III lost his sword and yet continued fighting without one. Samuel Taylor COLERIDGE remarked that watching Kean act was like "reading Shakespeare by flashes of lightning." Edmund's son, Charles Kean, followed in his father's footsteps. His early work was scorned by critics, but in later years he earned praise portraying many of the same tragic figures as his father. Unlike Edmund Kean, Charles acted in comic roles as well.

SHAKESPEARE IN AMERICA. In the early to mid-1800s, several famous British actors (including Charles and Fanny Kemble and Edmund Kean)

appeared on stage in the United States. The first noteworthy Shakespearean actor to make his home in the United States was Junius Brutus Booth, who emigrated from England in 1821. While some criticized Booth as merely an imitator of Edmund Kean, others emphasized his ability to sustain a complete character rather than offer the audience a series of disconnected points. Alcoholic and emotionally unstable, Booth was probably best known for villainous roles, including Richard III, IAGO, and SHYLOCK.

Booth's eldest son, Junius Brutus Booth, Jr., performed alongside his father in two productions, but his chief role was as a manager and producer. More noteworthy for their acting were his other sons, Edwin and John. Edwin Booth, an accomplished actor famous for his beautiful speaking style, played Shakespearean roles ranging from Hamlet to Shylock. His younger brother, John Wilkes Booth, was a talented Shakespearean actor as well, performing with a passion that made up for his sloppy diction. Eventually, he became notorious when he assassinated President Abraham Lincoln in 1865.

William Charles Macready, the most famous English Shakespearean actor of the mid-1800s, toured in America to enthusiastic audiences. His acting style was not as electrifying as Garrick's or Kean's, but he was conscientious and consistent. His American tour came to an abrupt end, however, when a riot broke out at the Astor Place Opera House during his appearance as Macbeth. As manager of the Covent Garden theater in London, Macready restored to the stage the original version of *King Lear*, which had been passed over for more than 150 years in favor of a 1681 adaptation with a happy ending.

See color plate 5, vol. 3.

Other noteworthy English actors who toured America in the late 1800s were Henry IRVING and Ellen Terry. In their production of *Much Ado About Nothing*, Irving's Benedick was overshadowed by Terry's enchanting Beatrice. Irving was far stronger in the role of Shylock, which he played more than a thousand times during his career. Despite a peculiar speaking style, he entranced his audiences with his wonderfully expressive features, sense of humor, and great dignity. Irving was also acclaimed as a theater manager whose productions were often spectacular. For one production he actually built a real stream and used live animals onstage.

THE 20TH CENTURY. Some of the best-known Shakespearean actors in the early 1900s were members of an American family, the Barrymores. The father, Maurice Barrymore (originally named Herbert Blythe), began his acting career in London and later moved to the United States, playing such Shakespearean roles as Romeo and ORLANDO. His three children—Lionel, Ethel, and John—all became well-known Shakespearean actors. John Barrymore, probably the most famous actor in the family, was even better known for his good looks, personal flair, and unstable disposition. His gentle and courtly Hamlet was perhaps the most widely acclaimed American representation of this character.

In England around the same time, two of the best-known Shakespearean actors were John Gielgud and Laurence Olivier. Both acted in

See color plate 5, vol. 3.

films as well as on stage, and both were knighted for their contributions to the English theater. Gielgud, who first gained renown with his 1930 portrayal of Hamlet, had an exquisitely expressive voice that served him well in such roles as Richard II, Benedick, and PROSPERO. Olivier, who began acting in Shakespeare's plays as a boy in the early 1920s, was a more physical actor, in the style of Garrick and Kean. Olivier also directed and starred in film versions of several of Shakespeare's plays, including *Richard III, Othello, Hamlet,* and *Henry V.* In 1935 Gielgud and Olivier alternated performances as Romeo and Mercutio in a production of *Romeo and Juliet,* which gave each actor the opportunity to show off his unique acting style.

Noteworthy Shakespearean actresses of this period were Edith Evans, Peggy Ashcroft, and Judith Anderson. Acting in films and on television as well as on stage, all three actresses were honored as Dames of the British empire (the female equivalent of being knighted). Evans and Ashcroft were both English and performed mostly in England; the Australian-born Anderson acted in both England and the United States. Evans, a versatile actress, was successful in such tragic roles as Cleopatra but performed even more often in comedies, playing most of Shakespeare's comic heroines during her long career. Ashcroft, superb in both comic and tragic roles, was best known for her outstanding portrayal of Juliet in Gielgud's 1935 production. Anderson was known for playing passionate and ruthless heroines, such as Lady Macbeth, a role she re-created many times throughout the 1920s and 1930s. In 1971 at the age of 73, she took on the role of Hamlet.

Judi Dench made her stage debut in 1957 as Ophelia. She soon began to specialize in Shakespearean works, both on stage and on television, and has won many awards for her performances. In 1988 she was made a Dame of the British empire for her work. Ian McKellan won popular and critical acclaim for his portrayal of Richard II in the 1960s. A versatile actor best known for his work with the Royal Shakespeare Company, Sir Ian has played a range of Shakespearean roles, including Iago, Macbeth, Coriolanus, and Richard III. British actor Kenneth Branagh is known for his magnetic and sometimes whimsical performances. Credited with bringing Shakespeare to the masses, Branagh has acted in and directed popular film versions of *Henry V* (1989), *Much Ado About Nothing* (1993), *Hamlet* (1996), and *Love's Labor's Lost* (2000). (*See also* **Acting Companies, Elizabethan; Acting Companies, Modern; Acting Profession; Astor Place Riot; Characters in Shakespeare's Plays; Directors and Shakespeare; Heminges, John; Shakespeare on Screen; Shakespearean Theater: 17th Century; Shakespearean Theater: 18th Century; Shakespearean Theater: 19th Century; Shakespearean Theater: 20th Century.**)

ADAPTATIONS

See *Shakespeare's Works, Adaptations of.*

AGRICULTURE

* *pastoral* relating to the countryside; often used to draw a contrast between the innocence and serenity of rural life and the corruption and extravagance of court life
* *game* wild animals hunted for food

* *steward* person who manages another person's household or estate

THE ENCLOSURE MOVEMENT

In the 1500s, population increases drove food prices up and created shortages. Many gentlemen and yeomen tried to increase the yield of their lands through enclosure. They traded their strips of land to form one large block, enclosed it with fences or hedges, and then plowed the balks between the strips to increase the amount of land under cultivation. Many enclosures were converted to pasture because sheep could be raised more profitably than grain products for much of the period. As landowners chose to keep control of more of their lands, they canceled tenants' leases, depending only on day laborers. As a result, unemployment rose and vagabonds became a major problem.

English agriculture in Shakespeare's day centered on sheep and grain. The woodlands in the north and west of England were mostly pastoral* regions. Lightly forested, with sections of meadow for pasturing sheep, these areas also provided game* and feed (such as acorns) for pigs and other animals. The population was scattered in tiny, isolated villages. In the lower and drier regions to the south and east, grain growing was the main agricultural activity. The population in these regions was denser, occupying larger villages and towns.

LANDHOLDINGS. A typical village would farm three large fields. Each year, two of the fields were planted and the third left fallow, or uncultivated. Alternating the fields that were cultivated from year to year helped to keep the land fertile. The fallow field was used as pasture for the village animals, whose manure, in turn, helped to fertilize it.

Most farmers did not own the lands they worked. The fields generally belonged to a squire, a gentleman whose estate was located near the village. Sometimes, however, the squire who owned the land lived in London and the land was managed by his steward*. The land might also belong to a nobleman who had acquired it through marriage or to a London merchant who had purchased the property as an investment. Landholdings were divided into half-acre strips, separated by grassy paths called balks. Each strip was one furlong in length—a unit of measure defined as the distance a team of oxen could pull a plow before needing to rest (about 220 yards). Due to the complications of MARRIAGE and INHERITANCE laws, strips of land owned by a squire might not be next to each other or even close together.

Most villagers were tenants of the squire, with a lease for the use of strips of land and a cottage in the village in exchange for rent payments. The leases extended for long periods of time, ranging from several years to a few lifetimes (meaning that the tenants could pass the land on to their heirs). This type of lease was called a copyhold. Other villagers held their land in freehold, meaning that they had most of the rights of ownership: they could use the land and pass it down to their heirs indefinitely. These villagers, known as yeomen, might choose to farm their land themselves or to rent out strips to tenant farmers.

Other villagers were cottagers—laborers employed by the squire, yeomen, or tenant farmers for day wages. They did not own or rent land, but paid rent to the squire for a cottage in the village. They did have the use of the land known as the village common—a section of land unsuitable for cultivation. Everyone who lived in the village was entitled to use the common for pasturing animals, gathering wood, and planting a small private garden.

FARM LABOR AND PRODUCTS. Farming was a cooperative effort. A team of oxen for plowing required eight animals, but villagers were unlikely to own more than one or two, so they had to combine their resources. Activities such as haymaking and harvesting also required many hands. The manorial court, a group composed of all the tenants and yeomen in the village and supervised by the squire's steward, met to

Most farmers in Elizabethan England rented their land from a local gentleman, or squire. The squire's fine house, visible in the distance, was often located near the village.

* *bran* edible outer coating of cereal grain

decide such matters as what crops to plant and when. Each year the court appointed an official called a reeve to coordinate the actual work in the fields.

Ordinarily two different crops were planted every year. One was planted in spring and gathered in late summer or fall, and the second was planted in early winter and gathered early the following spring. This method not only made work easier by spreading it over most of the year, but also helped to relieve food shortages if the country went through a bad growing season. In England, harvests might be threatened by both drought and excessive rains. Local areas had to be self-sufficient since poor roads meant that grain could not be transported from one place to another.

Wheat or rye was grown during the winter season and oats or barley in the summer. Sometimes legumes, such as beans or peas, might be planted instead because these plants have properties that nourish the soil. All types of grains were made into bread, but wheat flour was the most prized because it made the tastiest breads. Wheat was the most difficult crop to grow and was therefore scarce, making wheat bread a delicacy frequently reserved for the upper classes. Coarser and less expensive bread was made by including more bran* in the wheat flour or mixing it with other grains, such as rye. Oats were used to make bread or flat "cakes" similar to pancakes, while barley was used for bread and also for brewing ale.

Even in areas that focused on grain growing, some sheep were usually raised for their wool because the manufacture of woolen cloth was England's principal industry. Sheep were also an important source of milk. Villagers might also keep cows, pigs, and poultry. The butter, cheese, meat, and eggs they obtained from these animals were taken to a nearby town on market days to be sold along with grain products. (*See also* **Cities, Towns, and Villages; Country Life; Food and Feasts; Gardens and Gardening; Nature; Poverty and Wealth; Social Classes; Trade; Transportation and Travel.**)

ALL'S WELL THAT ENDS WELL

Shakespeare's comedy *All's Well That Ends Well* deals with the problematic romantic relationship between a nobleman and a commoner. The play is harsher than most of the playwright's other comedies in its view of human nature. The behavior of the main characters is often selfish and deceitful, and the ending leaves the audience with the uneasy feeling that, in real life, there may be no "happily ever after." Because the play blends its dark outlook with a humorous style, most scholars consider *All's Well That Ends Well* one of Shakespeare's "problem plays."

PLOT SUMMARY. The play begins in the home of the Countess of Rousillion and her son Bertram. Bertram and an older nobleman named Lafew are on their way to Paris to visit the king of France, who has been ill. Bertram bids farewell to his mother and her ward Helena, the orphaned daughter of a famous physician. After he leaves, Helena confesses to the Countess that she is in love with Bertram. She knows that she, being a commoner, has little hope of winning his affection. Nonetheless, she decides to follow the Countess's son to Paris, believing she can use her father's medical secrets to heal the king.

The action switches to the king's court in Paris, where several young nobles are leaving to fight in a war in Italy. Bertram wants to go too, but the king insists he stay behind because he is too young. Helena arrives and succeeds in curing the king's illness. As a reward, she asks to be married to Bertram. Although Bertram protests because of her lower social rank, the king forces him to wed her. Bertram then vows that although he is married to her, he will never sleep with her. Encouraged by his irresponsible friend Parolles, he then runs away to the Italian war.

Bertram sends the Countess a letter stating that he will not accept Helena as his wife until she wears his ring and bears him a child. Helena then decides to leave France and become a wanderer to avoid becoming a burden to Bertram. She travels to Italy, where she meets Diana, the daughter of a Florentine landlady. Helena learns that Bertram is in Florence and has attempted to seduce Diana. Helena engages Diana and her mother in a plan to trap Bertram: Diana will agree to meet him, but Helena will take Diana's place in bed before he arrives.

Diana meets Bertram and tells him he may come to her for one hour that night, but only if he does not speak to her. She persuades him to give her his family ring and promises to give him another ring in exchange when he meets her that night. Meanwhile, Bertram's comrades carry out a plan to prove to him that Parolles is a coward and a liar. Pretending to be

In the final scene of *All's Well That Ends Well,* Helena forces her reluctant husband, Bertram, to accept her as his wife by announcing that she is carrying his child. The king of France, in the foreground, concludes the play with the perhaps ironic observation, "All yet seems well."

A PROBLEMATIC HEROINE

Not all critics warmed to Helena's character or found fault with Bertram. Samuel Taylor Coleridge felt that Bertram was justified in resisting the king's order to marry Helena, whose only merit, as far as Bertram knew, was that she cured the king. Coleridge saw Bertram as a typical young nobleman whose pride and "appetite for pleasure" were only natural for his age. He also called Helena "not very delicate" and claimed that it took "all Shakespeare's . . . skill to interest us in her." Curiously, Edward Dowden later quoted Coleridge as calling Helena "the loveliest of Shakespeare's characters." If Coleridge actually said this, he must have had mixed feelings about this complex character.

enemy soldiers, they seize Parolles and blindfold him. Parolles agrees to reveal military secrets if they spare his life. They then remove his blindfold and expose him as a coward in front of his friend Bertram. Unashamed of his actions, Parolles says that since he has been shown to be a fool, from now on he will make his living as a court jester.

Helena, having succeeded in her plan to trap Bertram, starts a rumor that she is dead. Bertram, hearing this rumor, decides to return home to France. When he arrives, he finds the king at Rousillion. The king promises to pardon Bertram for abandoning Helena if he will agree to marry Lafew's daughter. Bertram offers Lafew a ring as a symbol of his acceptance. The king recognizes the ring as one he gave to Helena in Paris and promptly arrests Bertram as a suspect in Helena's untimely death. Diana then enters, claiming that Bertram seduced her and promised to marry her, and shows his family ring as proof of her claim. Bertram denies the charge, but Parolles, who has taken a position as jester to Lafew, confirms Diana's story. Diana then produces Helena, who reveals the trick she has played on Bertram. She reminds him that, since she has now worn his ring and carries his child, he must honor his promise to accept her as his wife. Bertram vows that if her story is true, he will "love her dearly, ever, ever dearly" (V.iii.316).

SOURCES AND HISTORY. Most scholars believe that Shakespeare wrote *All's Well That Ends Well* sometime around 1602 or 1603. They base this claim on its similarity to *Measure for Measure*, another problem play, which was written in 1604. The themes, the way the characters are drawn, and the use of LANGUAGE suggest that both plays were written around the same time.

All's Well That Ends Well is based on a portion of the *Decameron*, a work written by Giovanni Boccaccio in 1353. Shakespeare probably encountered an English translation of the story in William Painter's 1575 work titled *Palace of Pleasure*. Shakespeare added the characters of Lafew, the Countess, and Parolles, although Parolles may have been based on a character from Thomas Nash's *Unfortunate Traveller*. The play first appeared in print in the FIRST FOLIO, and the text printed there has many problems: Stage directions are confusing and parts of some speeches appear to have been assigned to the wrong speaker. The writing also seems less polished than in most of Shakespeare's plays. These flaws have led some scholars to conclude that the copy given to the First Folio printer was Shakespeare's uncorrected original draft, or foul papers.

All's Well That Ends Well has been performed less than almost any other Shakespearean play. The first production on record was in the early 1740s, nearly 140 years after the play was written. It gained some popularity for a time, mostly because of Henry Woodward's portrayal of Parolles. Productions in the late 1700s refocused the play on Bertram and Helena, but the comedy enjoyed little success throughout the 1800s. In 1832 an opera version that included songs taken from other Shakespeare plays was presented at Covent Garden.

Several revivals were staged in the early 1900s. In a 1920 production the actress playing Helena portrayed the character as a symbol of the

Edwardian referring to the reign of Edward VII, king of England from 1901 to 1910

newly liberated modern woman. In 1927 the Birmingham Repertory Theater staged a modern-dress version featuring Laurence Olivier as Parolles. A 1953 version directed by Tyrone Guthrie for the Shakesperean Festival Theater in Stratford, Ontario, set much of the action in the morally rigid world of Edwardian* England. This version appeared in Stratford, England, in 1959 and in a television production in 1968. From 1981 to 1983, the ROYAL SHAKESPEARE COMPANY staged a successful production, directed by Trevor Nunn with Peggy Ashcroft as the Countess, that was set in the same time period. This version was eventually produced on Broadway.

COMMENTARY. Audiences and critics have had mixed reactions to *All's Well That Ends Well* throughout its performance history. One common reaction is dissatisfaction with the characters. Bertram, though a nobleman, is hardly noble. While other characters praise Helena's fine qualities, Bertram rejects her simply because she is not an aristocrat. After the king forces him to marry Helena, Bertram abandons her and seduces another woman. He swears love to Diana and promises to marry her—a promise he obviously never intends to keep. In the final scene, when Diana accuses him of seducing her, he lies to the king about his entire affair with her.

The character of Helena, too, is problematic for some audiences. Not only is she obsessed with Bertram and willing to overlook his faults, but she continues to pursue him even though he has clearly rejected her. Moreover, the means she uses to achieve this goal—lying and trickery—have offended some observers. The audience enjoys her victory at the end more because it brings down Bertram than because they believe she will be happy as his wife. When the king says in the next-to-last line, "All yet seems well" (V.iii.333), it is by no means clear that the play's ending is truly a happy one.

Despite its problematic characters, *All's Well That Ends Well* does express two important ideas. Its main theme is that nobility comes from a person's spirit, not from social rank. Helena is a commoner but deserving of praise. Bertram and Parolles are nobles, but both are unworthy of the title. This is especially true of Parolles, who betrays his comrades and encourages his friend Bertram to behave badly.

The play also reflects another, deeper idea, summarized in its final line: "The bitter past, more welcome is the sweet" (V.iii.334). Life is both bitter and sweet, and both the good and the bad in human nature must be acknowledged. This is a theme that Shakespeare explores effectively in many of his plays. Despite his faults, the praise Bertram receives from other characters early in the play suggests that there is good in him, and accepting Helena as his wife at the end gives him a chance to live up to his potential. Even Parolles comes to admit his own failings and finds his proper place in life, earning Lafew's promise that "though you are a fool and a knave, you shall eat." (V.ii.53–54)(*See also* **Acting Companies, Modern; Actors, Shakespearean; Aristocracy; Morality and Ethics; Plays: The Comedies; Printing and Publishing; Royalty and Nobility; Social Classes.**)

ANALYSIS OF
SHAKESPEARE'S WORKS

See *Shakespeare's Reputation; Shakespeare's Works, Changing Views;* individual works.

ANTONY

See *Antony and Cleopatra.*

ANTONY AND
CLEOPATRA

* triumvirate form of rule in which authority
is shared by three people

One of Shakespeare's ten tragedies, *Antony and Cleopatra* is also one of his most complex plays. Written around 1607, relatively late in Shakespeare's career, *Antony and Cleopatra* dramatizes a love affair that took place between the Roman general Marc Antony and the Egyptian queen Cleopatra, who lived in the first century B.C. In his account of their ill-fated romance, Shakespeare explores the conflict that can arise between passion and duty.

PLOT SUMMARY. The play begins around 50 B.C., when the Roman republic was ruled by a triumvirate* consisting of Antony, Octavius Caesar, and Marcus Lepidus. Antony is living a self-indulgent life with Cleopatra. An urgent message arrives from Rome telling him that his wife, Fulvia, has died while rebelling against Caesar. Other messages bring news that the Roman general Pompey is leading a rebellion against the triumvirate and that Caesar is trying to gain sole control of Rome. Antony reluctantly leaves Cleopatra and returns to Rome to help defend the city against Pompey and repair his relationship with Caesar.

Caesar is angry with Antony for having stayed in Alexandria with Cleopatra when he was needed in Rome. Antony, in turn, is angry with Caesar for trying to become the sole ruler of Rome. During a meeting at Lepidus's house, Antony agrees to marry Caesar's sister, Octavia, in order to strengthen his ties with Caesar. Later, Antony is told by a fortune-teller that he will be successful only when he moves far away from Caesar. After hearing this prediction, Antony decides to return to Egypt. Back in Egypt, a messenger arrives and tells Cleopatra about Antony's marriage to Octavia. Enraged by the news, Cleopatra nearly kills the messenger. Her anger subsides, however, when the messenger describes Octavia as an unattractive woman of 30, with a round face and low voice.

Meanwhile, Antony and Octavia are traveling to Egypt, but relations between Caesar and Antony are still strained. Octavia returns to Rome to patch things up between her husband and her brother. When Antony reaches Alexandria, he declares himself and Cleopatra to be rulers of Rome's eastern provinces. Caesar views this as a personal betrayal as well as an act of war against Rome. In response, he challenges Antony to a naval battle. The battle commences and soon ends in Antony's defeat.

Antony is humiliated by the defeat but says it is worth losing everything for Cleopatra's love. He asks Caesar to allow him to live in Egypt or

Athens and to permit Cleopatra to continue ruling Egypt. Caesar replies that he will allow Cleopatra to remain queen, but only if she kills Antony or drives him out of Egypt. Cleopatra pretends to agree to Caesar's demand while assuring Antony that she still loves him. Antony is emboldened by Cleopatra's support and decides that he will continue fighting Caesar.

Antony marches to battle against Caesar. After the first day of fighting, he is victorious and returns to Cleopatra at night to plan the next day's strategy. During the sea battle that follows, however, Cleopatra's Egyptian navy deserts Antony. Believing that Cleopatra has betrayed him, Antony drives her away and threatens to kill her. After taking refuge in a monument, Cleopatra sends a messenger to tell Antony that she has committed suicide. In despair, Antony falls on his sword in a suicide attempt. However, he only wounds himself. Fearing that Antony will die, Cleopatra reveals to him that she has lied about her own suicide and summons him to her hiding place. Antony's servants carry him on a stretcher to Cleopatra, but he soon dies from his self-inflicted wound.

After learning of Antony's death, Caesar mourns him as a great man. Caesar then sends Cleopatra a message promising mercy and permission for her son to inherit the Egyptian throne. Cleopatra learns, however, that Caesar's real intention is to parade her through Rome's streets as a prisoner of war. Rather than face such humiliation, she allows two poisonous snakes—called asps—to bite her, and she dies. Following her death, Caesar orders that Cleopatra and Antony be buried together after a magnificent funeral to celebrate their great love.

TEXT AND SOURCES. Scholars believe that Shakespeare wrote *Antony and Cleopatra* sometime around 1608, the year it was registered with the Stationer's Guild—an association of printers who kept a record of works they intended to publish. However, it is unknown whether a printed version of the play was actually produced at that time. If it was, no copy has survived. The first known copy of the play appeared in 1623 in the FIRST FOLIO, the earliest collected edition of Shakespeare's plays. All later editions of the play have been based on the First Folio text, including the Second Folio edition, published in 1632.

The First Folio text probably was copied directly from Shakespeare's original manuscript and not from a PROMPT BOOK—a copy of an original play adapted by performers for use on the stage. Scholars believe this is likely for two reasons. First, the Folio text contains many misspellings and abbreviations that Shakespeare commonly used (most of which were corrected in the Second Folio edition). Second, the Folio text is long and contains elaborate stage directions, which would have been altered in a prompt book version.

Because *Antony and Cleopatra* tells the story of real people who participated in actual historical events, Shakespeare most likely consulted several historical sources. Many of the sources he used had been translated into English shortly before he wrote the play. Shakespeare's primary source was PLUTARCH'S LIVES. Plutarch was a Greek historian who wrote a collection of biographies of famous Greeks and Romans, including Marc

Cleopatra (played here by Judi Dench) is one of Shakespeare's most powerful heroines. Willful, intelligent, and passionate, she kills herself rather than allow Caesar to claim her as a prisoner.

Antony and Cleopatra

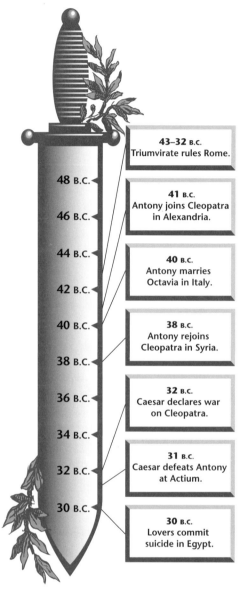

43–32 B.C.
Triumvirate rules Rome.

48 B.C.

41 B.C.
Antony joins Cleopatra
in Alexandria.

46 B.C.

44 B.C.

40 B.C.
Antony marries
Octavia in Italy.

42 B.C.

40 B.C.

38 B.C.
Antony rejoins
Cleopatra in Syria.

38 B.C.

32 B.C.
Caesar declares war
on Cleopatra.

36 B.C.

34 B.C.

31 B.C.
Caesar defeats Antony
at Actium.

32 B.C.

30 B.C.

30 B.C.
Lovers commit
suicide in Egypt.

*****ambiguous** unclear; able to be interpreted
in more than one way

Antony. In 1579 a writer named Thomas North translated Plutarch's work into English. It is clear that Shakespeare relied heavily on North's translation of Plutarch's writings about Antony. Many scenes from the play, and sometimes even the words themselves, were borrowed from North's translation.

Another possible source was Samuel Daniel's play *The Tragedie of Cleopatra.* Written in 1594, it continues Cleopatra's story beyond Antony's death, which is where Plutarch's tale ends. Shakespeare may also have used Daniel's poem "Letter from Octavia," which describes Antony's relationship with his second wife. Another probable source was the play *Marc-Antoine,* written in 1578 by the French playwright Robert Garnier and translated into English in 1590.

For information about ancient Egypt, Shakespeare may have relied on *A Geographical History of Africa,* translated in 1600 by the English writer John Pory. Information about ancient Rome most likely came from *Civil Wars,* written by the Roman historian Appian and first translated into English in 1578.

COMMENTARY. Since the early 1600s, many scholars and critics have addressed the basic conflict in the play and discussed how the play relates to Shakespeare's other works. The first act of *Antony and Cleopatra* clearly establishes the nature of its basic conflict—duty versus love. Antony has neglected his responsibility to defend Rome because he loves Cleopatra. It is only with great difficulty that he leaves her and returns to Rome when the city is threatened by Pompey's rebellion and Caesar's quest for absolute power.

Throughout most of the rest of the play, Antony is forced to choose between his role as a Roman general and his love for Cleopatra. In the end, neither love nor duty triumphs: Antony forsakes his country, and both Antony and Cleopatra die by their own hands. Thus, there is no clear resolution of the conflict. Because the issue is never resolved, *Antony and Cleopatra* is sometimes considered to be one of the "problem plays," in which the ending is ambiguous*.

Although the story of *Antony and Cleopatra* is tragic, the play contains elements that are found in many Elizabethan comedies. Like all of Shakespeare's comedies, *Antony and Cleopatra* deals with the foolish and crazy behavior of people in love—although the lovers' tragic deaths make the play unlike a comedy, which ends with a marriage. The play also resembles a comedy because most of the action moves back and forth between two different settings—Egypt and Rome—much as the action of *A Midsummer Night's Dream* moves between the forest and the royal court. In *Antony and Cleopatra,* Egypt represents the world of love and pleasure, while Rome symbolizes the world of duty and responsibility. In *A Midsummer Night's Dream,* the forest represents the enchanted world of love and fairies, while the royal court represents the logical world of society. *Antony and Cleopatra* also has scenes that are intended to make the audience laugh. For example, after Antony drinks too much wine, Cleopatra dresses the battle-hardened general in her clothes as she parades around wearing his sword. Because of this and other comic features,

Antony and Cleopatra is seen by some scholars as a mixture of tragedy, comedy, and history.

STAGE HISTORY. Scholars believe that *Antony and Cleopatra* was first performed at the BLACKFRIARS Theater in London in the early 1600s. Unlike many other Shakespearean plays, which were staged repeatedly in the decades after they were written, *Antony and Cleopatra* was not staged again until 1759. In that year it was revived by David Garrick, who played the part of Antony. Garrick was one of the most popular English actors of his day, and he spent much money on lavish costumes and sets. Nonetheless, the production was unsuccessful, and it ran for only six nights.

Antony and Cleopatra was revived several times during the 1800s, in the United States and Canada as well as in England. The scenery and special effects, such as the sights and sounds of battle, became more spectacular over time. However, the play continued to be poorly received by the public. One reason that productions of the play failed was that audiences preferred *All for Love*—another play about Antony and Cleopatra. Written in 1678 by John Dryden, *All for Love* continued to be popular until the late 1700s and was often revived after that.

Since about 1900, *Antony and Cleopatra* has become much more appreciated, and it has been staged successfully many times on both sides of the Atlantic. A notable production of the play was given at the Old Vic Theater in London in 1922. The action was presented on a nearly bare stage, a radical departure from the spectacular scenery and special effects of earlier productions. This simplicity of design enabled the director to present the play without interrupting the action. Subsequent approaches to the play have generally followed this example. Another notable production was given at the St. James Theater in London in 1951, starring Laurence Olivier as Antony and Vivien Leigh as Cleopatra. Set on a revolving stage, the action moved from one scene to another without delay, making for a speedier, more compelling production.

In addition to stage productions, several film versions of *Antony and Cleopatra* have been made. The best-known movie, produced in 1972, was directed by and starred Charlton Heston, who portrayed Antony. The play also has been produced for TELEVISION, most recently in a 1981 BBC Television Shakespeare production directed by Jonathan Miller. (*See also* **Directors and Shakespeare; History in Shakespeare's Plays: Ancient Greece and Rome; Play Structure; Plays: The Tragedies; Shakespeare's Sources.**)

AUTHOR! AUTHOR?

Samuel Daniel was a contemporary of Shakespeare who published a play called *The Tragedie of Cleopatra* in 1594. In 1607 Daniel published a revised version of his play that is very similar to Shakespeare's *Antony and Cleopatra*. Shakespeare probably wrote his play in 1607, but whether he composed it before or after Daniel's revision was published is unknown. So the question remains: Did Shakespeare copy Daniel, or did Daniel copy Shakespeare? Most scholars believe that Daniel, not Shakespeare, was the copier.

ARCHITECTURE

English architecture changed dramatically during the late 1500s, both in the types of materials used and in the designs of buildings. These changes were largely the result of a halt to the English civil wars in the late 1400s. Peace meant that nobles no longer needed to build homes with thick protective walls and narrow windows. Peace also

Architecture

* *Gothic* style of architecture characterized by pointed arches and high, thin walls supported by flying buttresses
* *Tudor* referring to the dynasty that ruled England from 1485 to 1603

See color plate 3, vol. 1.

* *wattle* twigs, reeds, or branches wrapped around poles and used for construction of walls or fences

* *lattice-work* an open framework made of strips of wood or other materials woven together

Many houses in London had shops on the ground floor. The shopkeeper's family lived on the upper floors (sometimes as many as three), which projected out over the street.

brought prosperity, which led many people to seek a more comfortable lifestyle as well as a way to show off their newfound wealth. Quite a few of them did so by making improvements to their old houses or by building newer, larger, and more elaborate ones. By the time of Shakespeare's death in 1616, the new Elizabethan style had largely replaced the old Gothic* and Tudor* styles that had previously dominated English architecture.

BUILDING MATERIALS. One of the most noticeable changes was the use of newer and sturdier building materials. For hundreds of years even relatively wealthy Englishmen built their houses out of wood and plaster. Only the richest lords could afford to erect stone castles or manor houses, and great quantities of wood were still used, even in the houses of wealthy nobles. The reason was simple: compared to stone, wood was abundant and cheap. Finer houses were made from sturdy oak, but most were built of lighter woods, such as willow. A Spanish visitor, commenting on the poor appearance of English dwellings of the early 1500s, remarked, "These English have their houses made of sticks and dirt." Indeed, many houses were little more than that.

Architecture during the late 1400s and early 1500s was dominated by half-timber construction—the use of wooden beams as a framework. The space between the timbers was filled with clay or wattle* and covered with a coat of plaster. Roofs were typically thatched—covered with sticks, straw, and other plant materials woven together. Glass windows were a luxury only a few could afford; most houses had either thin sheets of animal horn or lattice-work* shutters covering the windows. The interiors of these homes were often dark and damp.

By the late 1500s, brick and stone were being used as building materials, even in middle-class houses. Wood was still used, but cheaper materials—such as sticks and wattle—largely disappeared from all but the poorest of homes. Tiled roofs replaced thatched ones, providing greater protection from the rain and wind and reducing the risk of disastrous fires. Glass became increasingly common, and finer houses included large, colorful stained-glass windows. No longer desperate for basic shelter, many homeowners strove to build houses they could pass down to future generations.

MODEST HOUSES. Although both wealthy and modest homes used many of the same basic materials, there were differences in their design and construction. The poorest homes were simply timber frames filled in with clay-covered straw and a thatched roof. Their single room featured a dirt floor and an open hearth for cooking and warmth. Larger cottages had an attic or upper room reached by a ladder or crude winding staircase. These upper stories usually housed bedchambers for the family.

In wealthier cottages, an enclosed fireplace with a chimney to carry smoke outside the house was used instead of a hearth. Prosperous farmers or artisans* built two-story houses out of local materials, such as timber, brick, and stone. The downstairs typically consisted of an entry hall, a dining room, a living room, and a sitting room. The ground level also contained a kitchen, a pantry, and rooms for household tasks such as

20

making cheese and preserving meat. Bedrooms occupied the second level, with separate quarters for the servants. Many country houses included a courtyard bordered on one side by the house and on the remaining sides by outbuildings, such as horse stables, barns, chicken coops, and workshops.

City houses, in London for example, were two-story wooden or brick structures with tile or lead roofs, although some were as high as four floors. For many, the ground floor served as a shop. A porch, covered by a low roof, often extended the length of the house, and it was here that the owner displayed his goods for sale. The upper floors extended out over the street. Low walls enclosed gardens at the rear of the house. Wealthy city dwellers surrounded their houses with parks or large gardens. Those who could afford to do so rebuilt their existing houses, replacing wood with stone. Shakespeare himself rebuilt his home in STRATFORD-UPON-AVON in this fashion.

ESTATES AND MANORS. The houses of the wealthy included all of the new features of Elizabethan architecture. These grand mansions were built of the finest stone, which was decorated with intricate carvings. They featured massive rows of tall windows, enabling light to flood the rooms. Mansions were typically laid out in a plan resembling an *H* or an *E*, with the main entrance in the "crossbar" of the H or in the central projection of the E. Houses were designed to enclose one or more courtyards or formal gardens.

Visitors approaching the house often had to pass through a gatehouse where a porter guarded the property from beggars and other trespassers. The main entrance to the house usually led into the great hall, an element left over from the design of medieval* castles. In earlier days the entire household dined here, with the family seated at a table on a raised platform at one end of the room. By Shakespeare's day, wealthy families ate in private dining rooms, but servants and less important guests still ate in the great hall. This room typically contained a magnificent open staircase that replaced the narrow spiral staircases of the medieval castle. The most impressive room, however, was the gallery, an upstairs room that ran the entire width of the house and separated the family's living quarters from those of the servants. With its rows of tall windows, it was often the brightest room in the house. It was also often the most richly decorated, with carved woodwork and wall tapestries—handwoven fabrics decorated with colorful designs and pictures.

As in country houses, the downstairs was largely devoted to work rooms or common rooms, while bedrooms and private chambers were found above. Interestingly, the architecture of the day did not include hallways and corridors. Therefore, to reach a bedroom at the far end of the house, one had to walk through all the other bedrooms on the floor. Closed fireplaces were used instead of open hearths. A great house might have dozens of fireplaces, many of them in private bedrooms. Massed groups of chimneys sprouted from the roofs of such mansions, a popular look that hinted at the wealth of the owner. The new Elizabethan architecture thus offered the homeowner many opportunities to express

OUT OF THE FRYING PAN AND INTO THE FIREPLACE

The persecution of Catholics in Shakespeare's day led to an interesting addition to the homes of some Elizabethans. A law passed in 1584 made sheltering a priest an act of high treason, punishable by death. In order to continue practicing their faith, Catholics built into their homes a secret chamber called a priest hole. Often located in the chimney, the priest hole was reached by one or more hidden passages, typically disguised by fake panels or screens. If law officers were spotted approaching a house while a Mass was being held, the priest would dash into the priest hole, where he might have to hide for days to avoid capture.

* *artisan* skilled worker or craftsperson
* *medieval* referring to the Middle Ages, a period roughly between A.D. 500 and 1500

pride in his surroundings, whether he was a powerful lord, a prosperous merchant, or a common laborer with a little extra money. (*See also* **Households and Furnishings.**)

ARDEN, FOREST OF

The Forest of Arden is the primary setting for Shakespeare's play *As You Like It*. It is a peaceful place that enables characters to escape from their troubles, reflect on their lives, and devote themselves to love. In creating this setting, Shakespeare both drew on and made fun of the literary tradition known as PASTORALISM.

The historical Forest of Arden, or Ardennes, is located at the borders of present-day Belgium, France, and Luxembourg. Shakespeare's source for *As You Like It*, Thomas LODGE's *Rosalynde*, was also set in the Ardennes. This forest was familiar to Shakespeare's audience as the setting of Ludovico Ariosto's popular epic *Orlando Furioso*. However, Shakespeare's Arden is not a realistic European forest: characters encounter lions, snakes, and palm trees within its boundaries. Wildly improbable events can seem believable in this fantastical setting.

Interestingly, an ancient forest near Shakespeare's hometown of STRATFORD-UPON-AVON was also called Arden. The ancestors of Shakespeare's mother, Mary Arden, are thought to have taken their family name from this region.

The Arden of *As You Like It* is in some ways a typical pastoral* setting, peaceful and far removed from the cares of society. Shakespeare plays on the tradition, however, by showing that his Arden is not an idealized place. Those exiled to the forest find their lives less comfortable than they were at court; they are subject to the cold of winter and must hunt for their food. Arden's permanent residents, likewise, are not idealized. The shepherd lovers, Silvius and Phebe, are comically exaggerated versions of traditional romantic lovers. The shepherd Corin, by contrast, is a realistic image of a "true laborer"—honest, simple, and poor.

In retreating to the forest, the principal characters shed many of the trappings of position and wealth. They have the opportunity to interact with each other on a meaningful, personal basis, rather than according to the customs of the court. The quiet forest setting gives them the leisure to reflect on their lives and goals. Having resolved their problems in the fantasy realm of Arden, they are then free to return to the real world of the court with a deeper understanding of humanity.

ARISTOCRACY

In Shakespeare's England, SOCIAL CLASS was very important and relatively fixed. At the top of the social ladder sat the aristocracy, or nobility, the holders of hereditary titles of honor. Aristocrats controlled the majority of the nation's land, wealth, and political power. Below them were the gentry, or minor gentry—descendants of noble families who had smaller landholdings but still controlled a fair amount of wealth. Next came well-to-do farmers, known as yeomen, and tradesmen, known as citizens. The lowest of all were peasants, laborers, and servants, who made their living working for other people. Most people occupied the same social class throughout their lives, although it was sometimes possible for wealthy commoners to rise to the ranks of the minor gentry.

The highest-ranking aristocrat was the sovereign—the king or queen. Elizabethans believed in the principle of divine right, which held that the sovereign's power to rule was granted by God and was passed along to his or her children. The sovereign's children were known as princes and princesses. Brothers and other relatives of the monarch were lesser aristocrats with titles such as duke, marquess, earl, viscount, or baron.

Dukes typically ranked just below the sovereign and were usually close relatives of the king or queen. Next came the marquess, or marquis, a title often granted to someone who had gained the sovereign's favor. Both titles were first used in England in the 1300s. The title of earl was older, but earls ranked lower in the aristocracy than did dukes or marquesses. Even so, an earl usually controlled extensive landholdings and exercised significant influence. Viscounts ranked just below earls, and barons were the lowest order of aristocrats. The word *baron* was also used as a general term to refer to any member of the aristocracy. Together, the five highest ranks of aristocrats were called the peerage. Peers were entitled to participate in government by holding seats in the House of Lords.

On rare occasions, the king might promote a commoner to the lower ranks of the aristocracy. The title of knight was an honor granted for bravery in battle or for other services to the crown. Knighthood was an ancient tradition in England. The title of baronet, by contrast, was originally sold by King JAMES I in 1611 to raise money for his war against Ireland. A baronet, unlike a knight, could pass his title to his children, but he was not allowed to sit in the House of Lords.

The titles of Elizabethan aristocracy are still in use, although their purpose today is mostly social. Political power now rests primarily with the lower house of Parliament, the House of Commons. (*See also* **Government and Politics; Royalty and Nobility.**)

See color plate 2, vol. 1.

ARMS AND ARMOR

* *scenario* outline or synopsis of a play

The settings and scenarios* of Shakespeare's plays reflect the world of his time, a world that included much violence and many battles. From the emotional sword fights of *Romeo and Juliet* to the grand battle scenes of *Henry V* and *Macbeth*, the plays are filled with clashing weaponry. Elizabethan audiences were familiar with the weapons and armor of the time, but for the modern reader the references to arms and armor in the plays may become clearer with some background information.

* **medieval** referring to the Middle Ages, a
period roughly between A.D. 500 and 1500

TRADITIONAL ARMS AND ARMOR

Most of the weapons that are referred to or used in Shakespeare's plays have long histories. These were the blades, bows, and arrows of ancient and medieval* warfare, some of which were refined and made more deadly during Shakespeare's time. Soldiers and military leaders carried weapons and also wore protective armor of various styles and materials.

CROSSBOWS AND LONGBOWS. Developed in southwestern Europe around the 800s, the crossbow is mounted horizontally on a perpendicular beam of wood. The bowstring is held back by a mechanism; the arrow—known as a bolt—is fitted into place; and a mechanical trigger releases the string and launches the bolt.

The crossbow spread rapidly throughout northern Europe, where cramped and mountainous terrain made it ideal for short-range battle and hit-and-run attacks on superior forces. The crossbow was relatively inexpensive to produce or purchase, and it was easy to master. Effective against armored and mounted opponents, the crossbow was, nevertheless, less accurate and less powerful than the longbow. It also had a shorter range.

The English longbow was a mighty weapon, capable of piercing thick armor at up to 300 yards, a feature that ultimately contributed to the decline of armored cavalry* in Europe. The use of longbows was a key factor in the English army's defeat of the French in the battle of Agincourt, presented in Shakespeare's *Henry V.* The longbow's great disadvantage was that its effectiveness depended entirely on the user, who needed years of training and great strength to operate this weapon effectively. Many longbowmen were rural, landowning commoners, and as more Englishmen moved to cities and towns, the number of skilled longbowmen declined rapidly.

Meanwhile, craftsmen gradually improved the crossbow's accuracy and power, and its popularity spread. New mechanisms—such as levers, cranks, and pulleys—were devised to retract the bowstring. These devices increased the force of the bowstring's tension well beyond the user's own strength.

SLASHING AND PIERCING WEAPONS. Swords were the favored weapons of the nobility. Men of the upper classes normally owned a sword of fine quality, and they had the leisure time to invest in the training and practice required for skillful fighting. A swordsman might fight with a sword in one hand and a dagger in the other, or with a lance* if he were on horseback.

Soldiers from the lower classes, who were usually on foot, carried various long-handled weapons. The halberd, also called a bill, was a type of ax mounted on a six-foot-long wooden shaft. The large blade featured sharp spikes at the front and back, suitable for piercing armor or for pulling a horseman from his saddle. One disadvantage of the weapon was that when a soldier committed himself to a full, powerful swing of the halberd, he left himself vulnerable to a counterattack. Since the

* **cavalry** soldiers mounted on horseback

* **lance** weapon with a long wooden shaft
and a sharp metal tip

For many years the greatest advantage of the English military was its skilled bowmen. The longbow was more powerful than the crossbows favored by other nations, but it required strength and training to shoot accurately.

horseman's lance was longer, the soldier wielding the halberd was often unable to come close enough to strike.

The shortness of the halberd was remedied by the pike, a wooden spear about 12 feet long and with a 10-inch piercing point at the end. Groups of highly disciplined pike soldiers could swing their weapons in formation, protecting one another while penetrating the defenses of their mounted opponents.

ARMOR. Elizabethan soldiers wore armor to protect themselves against injury from handheld weapons and from flying objects, such as arrows. Some body parts required special pieces of armor, such as the codpiece for protecting the groin and the helmet for protecting the head.

Since the earliest days of recorded history, types of armor were made from leather, fabric, or both. Such armor had the advantage of being lightweight and fairly flexible, but its protection was limited against hard, sharp weapons driven with significant force.

Chain mail, a flexible mesh of interlocking metal rings, was popular in Roman times and remained so in medieval Europe. Although mail was typically fashioned into a shirt, some soldiers wore mail leggings and hoods. Mail's obvious advantages were its flexibility and the protection it provided against attacks from blade weapons. However, a powerful thrust from a sharp, pointed weapon could penetrate the rings and pierce the wearer's body.

Plate armor, made from pieces of solid metal of various sizes and shapes, gradually replaced mail as the most highly valued armor in Europe. From the 1200s to the 1600s, craftsmen continually improved and refined the design of plate armor. Sometimes mail was worn underneath the plates as protection where gaps existed between the plates. By the time of the Renaissance, interlocking plates fitted with straps covered the entire body of a man and some parts of his horse. A fine suit of decorated armor was the prized possession of many European noblemen. Unfortunately, plate armor was extremely heavy, and its wearer needed help to put it on and to remove it. He might also have needed help to stand if he were knocked off his feet or his horse. Plate armor could be penetrated by powerful longbows and crossbows, and also by the next major advance in weaponry—firearms.

FIREARMS

The introduction of gunpowder had a tremendous effect on warfare and weaponry. The first firearms were artillery—large guns that fired projectiles through the air. Handheld guns were a later development, and in Shakespeare's time they remained crude, unreliable, dangerous to use, and inaccurate. Nevertheless, the technological progress of firearms would eventually render traditional arms and armor obsolete.

GUNPOWDER. In the 800s, Chinese experimenters discovered the explosive properties of a mixture of potassium nitrate, charcoal, and sulfur. By the 1200s, the invention had spread to Europe. In its first form,

Arms and Armor

Arms in the Plays

In some of the history plays, Shakespeare has his characters use firearms in the battle scenes. Most of these references are historically inaccurate, however, since guns smaller than cannons were not employed in battle until about the mid-1400s. By placing these weapons in the hands of his characters, Shakespeare ignored historical accuracy for the sake of implements that were familiar to his audience. The use of these weapons enabled Elizabethans to recognize certain aspects of the characters' personalities, such as the hot-tempered Pistol in *Henry V,* who was likely to explode at any minute and injure whoever was standing nearby.

* *wrought iron* relatively pure iron that is shaped with hammers, producing a material stronger and more flexible than cast iron, but also more expensive

* *cast iron* mixture of iron and other materials that is melted, poured into molds, and hardened, producing a material cheaper and more brittle than wrought iron

* *rampart* broad embankment, usually with a wall on top, that serves as a barrier

* *siege* long and persistent effort to force a surrender by surrounding a fortress with armed troops, cutting it off from aid

gunpowder was a dry mixture of the ground elements. This mixture, called serpentine, was difficult to use for several reasons: the ingredients separated during travel, remixing the powders in battle was time-consuming, it had to be packed at just the right density, and it was unstable, making spontaneous explosions common.

In the early 1400s, people began to grind the ingredients with water and then allow the wet mixture to dry into cakes. This process held the powders together so they would not separate, making the mixture more stable and easier to transport.

ARTILLERY. The long tubular barrel of a cannon has an opening called a muzzle at the front end. The back, called the breech, is where the gunpowder is placed along with the projectile to be launched. The most common way to ignite the gunpowder is to insert a burning fuse through a small touchhole at the top of the breech.

The earliest type of cannon was made of wrought iron* and was called a muzzle-loader because the gunpowder and projectile were placed inside the muzzle and pushed down to the breech with a ramrod. The barrel of such a cannon was reinforced with wrought iron hoops that prevented the barrel from cracking or breaking apart during the explosion. A cap called a breechblock was fitted over the back end of the barrel to prevent gas and fire from exploding outward. Wrought iron muzzle-loaders of the late 1300s could fire stone cannonballs weighing more than 450 pounds.

The development of a wrought iron breechloader enabled soldiers to pack the gunpowder into a small chamber in the breechblock, which they then hammered onto the back end of the barrel before igniting the powder. Wrought iron artillery was known by several different names in England, including *bombard, lombard,* and *basilisk.* Artillery pieces were also named by the ratio of length of the barrel to its bore (diameter of the interior of the barrel): in decreasing order, *culverin, cannon-of-battery, pedrero,* and *mortar.*

Bronze and cast iron* replaced wrought iron in later cannon production. Engineers also designed wheeled carriages for transporting cannons and mounts for placing them on the decks of ships and the ramparts* of fortresses. Cannons also played a major role in sieges*, breaking down the walls of enemy cities.

GUNS. Guns were a natural progression from cannons in the development of firearms. They were smaller and lighter and could easily be carried by one man. The earliest guns were in fact small versions of cannons that required one soldier to hold and aim it and another to ignite the gunpowder. The first true handgun was developed with a trigger mechanism in which a small clasp held a burning fuse, called a match, and dipped it into the gunpowder chamber through a touchhole atop the barrel. This type of trigger was called a matchlock, and the most popular matchlock gun of the 1400s was the long harquebus.

The wheel lock trigger followed in the early 1500s. The trigger turned a wheel, which rotated against a piece of iron pyrite and created sparks that ignited the powder. A sturdier version of this, the flintlock, produced sparks from the friction of steel against flint. Flintlocks existed in the mid-1500s in the form of a musket. A shorter version of the musket was called the caliver. Pistols were shorter still, but in Shakespeare's time they were the least accurate firearm and the most likely to backfire and injure the user. (*See also* **Warfare.**)

ART INSPIRED BY SHAKESPEARE

* *engraving* print made from a design carved into a wooden block or metal plate

In the years since Shakespeare's death, his plays have inspired many visual artists. His characters and themes have provided material for an abundant supply of paintings, drawings, and engravings*. Illustrations for Shakespearean texts and designs for stage sets are also part of this body of artistic work.

EARLIEST ILLUSTRATIONS OF SHAKESPEARE. During Shakespeare's time, painting in England was largely limited to portraits. Very few English books had illustrations aside from a single engraving on the title page, often a portrait of the author. The early editions of Shakespeare's plays lacked illustrations, although the FIRST FOLIO contained an engraving on the title page that is the first known portrait of Shakespeare. A 1595 drawing by Henry Peacham of a scene from *Titus Andronicus* is the only known work of visual art about a Shakespearean subject that the playwright himself might have seen.

In 1709 Nicholas ROWE published the first illustrated edition of Shakespeare. The artists that the editor selected drew on stage productions of their day, in which some of the actors wore the clothing styles currently in fashion while others wore period costumes. Since all English theaters had been closed in the 1640s and 1650s, many of the plays had not been staged in many years. To illustrate these plays, the artists used their own ideas of how a scene might look. Following the custom of the time, they portrayed characters in typical stage poses rather than trying to convey action or emotion.

* *continental* referring to the European continent
* *classical* in the tradition of ancient Greece and Rome

The illustrators of Rowe's edition were inspired by the work of continental* artists—both the classical* style of the French Royal Academy of Painting and Sculpture and the simpler style of Dutch and Flemish painting. For example, the engraving for the title page of *Coriolanus* was an adaptation of a painting by the French artist Nicolas Poussin, showing the proud general's wife and mother begging him to spare Rome. This engraving, in turn, was adapted by the artist Francis Hayman in a later edition of Shakespeare's plays. Hayman's picture, with its grand setting and dramatic poses and gestures, was so influential that it became the model for a stage set at the Drury Lane Theater in 1807.

EXPRESSIVE SCENES. William Hogarth was the first painter to present a Shakespearean character in a real-life scene rather than a stage presentation. His 1728 drawing of FALSTAFF inspecting his troops (based on a scene in *Henry IV, Part 2*), though roughly sketched, is vivid and dramatic.

Art Inspired by Shakespeare

The figure of Falstaff is arrogant and careless, suggesting his sometimes corrupt nature. Hogarth also drew the other characters in a way that hinted at their personalities: Shadow is only a profile, Shallow has a stupid expression, and Silence communicates through gesture.

In the mid-1700s, it became fashionable for popular actors to have portraits painted of themselves in their best roles. These so-called conversation pieces attempted to capture the drama of a particular moment on the stage. Hogarth painted one of the earliest of these, a famous image of the great David Garrick as *Richard III.* Garrick was also painted as Romeo, Hamlet, and other Shakespearean characters by such major artists as Benjamin West and John Zoffany, the leading painter of conversation pieces. Engravings made from these theater paintings were very popular with the public.

As the Romantic* movement gained popularity in the late 1700s, painters of this school created scenes with natural settings that expressed the emotional and mental states of Shakespeare's characters. An example of this style is John Runciman's *King Lear in the Storm*, based on the third act of *King Lear.* The jagged lines of the cliffs and wind-tossed waves reflect Lear's grief, anger, and bewilderment rather than the actual setting of the scene in the play. The Romantic artist most influenced by Shakespeare was the Swiss-born painter Henry Fuseli. He based hundreds of drawings, engravings, and paintings on Shakespearean works, including a set of drawings for an edition of the plays.

THE SHAKESPEARE GALLERY. In 1786 John Boydell, a successful engraver and publisher, attempted to put together a collection of paintings in honor of Shakespeare. He hoped that this project would help establish an English school of historical painting that could rival the French Academy.

Boydell opened his Shakespeare Gallery with 34 paintings and added others over time, commissioning paintings from many of the most respected artists of the period. Sir Joshua Reynolds's *Death of Beaufort* and Benjamin West's *Ophelia* were painted in the classical style, which reflected the French Academy's goal of portraying humanity at its most glorious. Fuseli's works based on *Macbeth, Hamlet,* and *A Midsummer Night's Dream* were examples of the newer Romantic style. The works of other artists, like John Northcote's *Entry of Bolingbroke,* recalled the theatrical style of the mid-1700s. Many works in the gallery were reproduced as engravings for sale to the public.

The only major artist of the period not represented in Boydell's Shakespeare Gallery was Fuseli's good friend William Blake. A poet as well as an artist, Blake often drew on literature as a source of inspiration, but he focused more on the Bible and the works of John Milton than on Shakespeare. Nonetheless, the prints and drawings that Blake produced on Shakespearean subjects are vivid and insightful. Some of his works portray characters and scenes from the plays, while others explore Shakespeare's themes and IMAGERY. One of his most powerful and dramatic works is a series of prints and drawings based on Queen Katherine's dream from *Henry VIII.*

* ***Romantic*** referring to a school of thought, prominent in the 1800s, that emphasized the importance of emotion in art

One of the Romantic painters most interested in Shakespearean themes was Eugène Delacroix. His painting *Hamlet and Horatio in the Cemetery* shows the famous scene from *Hamlet* in which an encounter with a gravedigger leads the prince to muse on mortality.

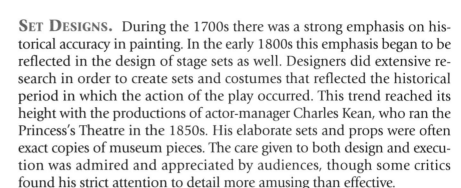

PORTRAITS OF SHAKESPEARE

The earliest known portrait of Shakespeare is the engraving created by Martin Droeshout for the title page of the *First Folio* in 1623. It is likely that this engraving was copied from an earlier drawing. Several other portraits have been presented as the possible original for Droeshout's engraving, but in some cases the date of the portrait is unknown, and in others it is not clear that the subject is Shakespeare. One image associated with many legends is the Chandos portrait, so called because it originally belonged to the duke of Chandos. At one time scholars believed that this portrait had been painted by the actor Richard Burbage.

See
color plate 13,
vol. 2.

SET DESIGNS. During the 1700s there was a strong emphasis on historical accuracy in painting. In the early 1800s this emphasis began to be reflected in the design of stage sets as well. Designers did extensive research in order to create sets and costumes that reflected the historical period in which the action of the play occurred. This trend reached its height with the productions of actor-manager Charles Kean, who ran the Princess's Theatre in the 1850s. His elaborate sets and props were often exact copies of museum pieces. The care given to both design and execution was admired and appreciated by audiences, though some critics found his strict attention to detail more amusing than effective.

By the late 1800s, designers began to abandon these excessively accurate sets, replacing them with sets that suggested the imaginary world of the play rather than the real world of the period in which the action took place. These simpler sets allowed the words and the acting to dominate the performance without being overshadowed by scenery. The move to greater simplicity carried over into the 1900s, with sets becoming increasingly spare.

CHANGING INTERPRETATIONS. The Romantic movement persisted into the mid-1800s, and Shakespeare's works continued to inspire English artists such as William Turner and Richard Bonington. John Constable's *Jaques and the Wounded Stag,* based on a scene in *As You Like It,* is an important work of the period. French artists also took an interest in Shakespeare—particularly Eugène Delacroix, who created a series of 16 lithographs based on scenes from *Hamlet.* His contemporary Jean-Baptiste Corot painted *Macbeth and the Witches,* using landscape techniques to great advantage.

A new painting style, that of the pre-Raphaelites, arose in the second half of the 1800s. Like the Romantics, the pre-Raphaelites were interested in portraying psychological states, but they conveyed emotion by focusing on telling details, posture, and expression rather than on dramatic landscapes. Their paintings on Shakespearean subjects abandoned the 18th-century concern with historically accurate settings, concentrating instead on portraying scenes and costumes in harmony with the overall mood. In the drawings and watercolors of Dante Gabriel Rossetti, for example, the figures often have a sad and dreamy look. Ford Madox Brown's *Lear and Cordelia* uses the characters' positions and gestures to convey the emotional impact of the moment when CORDELIA first sees her estranged father.

Interest in visually interpreting Shakespeare's works declined in the 1900s. A few modern artists, including Walter Sickert and Wyndham Lewis, have used Shakespearean subjects, but most art based on Shakespeare has been limited to set designs. John Piper's settings for Benjamin Britten's operatic version of *A Midsummer Night's Dream* are one striking example. Other set designs, by such artists as Eric Ravilious and Thomas P. Robinson, have been published in illustrated editions of the plays. Artists also continue to create sketches based on Shakespearean productions, such as Eric Griffiths' drawing of the opening scene from a 1983 production of *The Comedy of Errors.*

One of the most significant 20th-century works based on Shakespeare is a painting Josef Herman created for a "Shakespeare in Art" exhibition in 1964. It depicts King Lear alone and despairing in the foreground while the Fool plays a flute in the background. No scene like this actually appears in the play, but the image symbolically portrays the abandoned king's loneliness and despair. Regrettably, neither Herman nor any other modern artist has produced an extensive body of work based on Shakespeare. (*See also* **Quartos and Folios; Settings; Shakespearean Theater: 19th Century; Shakespearean Theater: 20th Century.**)

AS YOU LIKE IT

* *pastoral* relating to the countryside; often used to draw a contrast between the innocence and serenity of rural life and the corruption and extravagance of court life
* *convention* established practice
* *usurp* to seize power from a rightful ruler

S et mostly in a French forest that is more like a fantasy realm than a realistic woodland, *As You Like It* is Shakespeare's commentary on the pastoral* style that was popular in his day. Throughout the play, Shakespeare pokes fun at the conventions* of PASTORALISM, such as shepherds and silly romantic verses, but he also uses the strengths of the pastoral style to explore serious issues. The comedy contrasts idealism with reality and offers a humorous yet serious examination of what matters most in life.

PLOT SUMMARY. *As You Like It* begins at the court of Duke Frederick, who has usurped* power from his brother, Duke Senior. Duke Senior, with several of his courtiers, has gone into exile in the neighboring Forest of ARDEN. His daughter ROSALIND, however, has remained at court as companion to her cousin Celia, who loves Rosalind as a sister.

The friendship between the two women contrasts with the bitter relationship between Oliver and ORLANDO, the oldest and youngest sons of a dead nobleman who was once a friend to Duke Senior. When Orlando goes to Duke Frederick's court to take part in a wrestling contest, he meets Rosalind and the two are immediately drawn to each other. Orlando wins the wrestling match, but Duke Frederick sends him away after learning that Orlando is the son of his banished brother's friend. When Orlando returns home, he discovers that Oliver intends to kill him. With his old and faithful servant Adam, Orlando flees into the Forest of Arden.

Meanwhile, Duke Frederick tires of having Rosalind at court and decides to banish her. Celia promises to accompany her into exile and suggests that they go to the Forest of Arden to seek out Rosalind's father. Rosalind decides to disguise herself as a young shepherd boy named Ganymede, and Celia poses as Ganymede's sister Aliena. The young women take Touchstone, the court fool, as their traveling companion.

Orlando arrives in Arden and joins the company of Duke Senior and his courtiers. Rosalind and Celia also arrive in the forest, where they meet a shepherd named Corin. He helps them find food and a cottage to live in and introduces them to Silvius, a younger shepherd who is hopelessly in love with the shepherdess Phebe. Phebe, who scorns Silvius, is immediately smitten* with the disguised Rosalind.

* *smitten* romantically attracted

goatherd herder of goats

In Arden, Orlando indulges his love for Rosalind by hanging verses about her on the trees. When Rosalind, dressed as Ganymede, meets Orlando, she decides to test his true feelings. She proposes to cure him of his love by posing as Rosalind and having him woo her. Meanwhile Touchstone, although he has no illusions about love, also finds a prospective wife in the unattractive but honest goatherd* Audrey.

As the play progresses, the various characters now gathered in Arden encounter one another. They have clever and entertaining arguments about the nature of love, compare life in the country and at court, and discuss the purpose of human life. One of Duke Senior's courtiers, the melancholy Jaques, who has traveled widely and become convinced that there is little good in human nature, spends his time in self-indulgent expressions of pessimism. In the play's most famous speech, he observes that "All the world's a stage, / And all the men and women merely players"(II.vii.140), and implies that life is nothing but a long journey toward death.

Back at court, Duke Frederick begins to think that Rosalind and Celia have fled with Orlando. He seizes Oliver's lands and tells him to find and bring back his brother within a year or die. Oliver goes to Arden to look for them. Orlando finds him there, asleep, with a threatening lioness nearby. Overcoming his anger toward his brother, Orlando kills the lioness and is injured. Oliver wakes and sees that Orlando has saved him, and the brothers are reconciled. The wounded Orlando is too weak to meet with Ganymede as he has promised, so Oliver goes in his place to explain his brother's absence. He meets Celia, and they fall in love. Oliver decides to give his inheritance to Orlando so he can remain in Arden with Celia.

Orlando and Rosalind-as-Ganymede grow weary of playing games about love, and Rosalind determines to untangle all the confused relationships. She tells Phebe that "I will marry you, if ever I marry woman,

In one of Shakespeare's most humorous and complicated love stories, *As You Like It,* the shepherd Silvius is in love with the scornful shepherdess Phebe. Phebe, in turn, loves Ganymede, who is really a woman in disguise. This woman, Rosalind, loves and is loved by Orlando—although he does not know her secret identity.

and I'll be married to-morrow" (V.ii.113–14), then obtains Phebe's promise to marry Silvius if she does not marry Ganymede. Rosalind-as-Ganymede also assures Orlando that she can produce Rosalind. In the final scene, Rosalind reveals her true identity to the other characters and is reunited with her father. Hymen, the Greek god of marriage, appears and joins the four couples in marriage. To complete the happy ending, a brother of Orlando and Oliver arrives. He brings the news that, while on the way to Arden with an army to fight his brother, Duke Frederick was converted by a holy man and has decided to enter a monastery and return the dukedom to his brother. Jaques immediately vows to join him there, and the wedding festivities are thus able to proceed without the shadow his gloomy presence would have cast over them.

motif minor theme or subject

SOURCES AND HISTORY. The source of Shakespeare's *As You Like It* is Thomas LODGE's *Rosalynde*, a prose narrative published in 1590. Lodge himself had adapted *The Tale of Gamelyn,* a long narrative poem written in the 1300s about a young man mistreated by his older brother. Lodge introduced the female characters, the love plot, and the three shepherds. Shakespeare kept Lodge's principal characters and invented several new ones, notably Jaques and Touchstone. He also made Duke Senior and Frederick brothers, emphasizing the theme of discord between brothers. Shakespeare used most of Lodge's plot but changed the ending. In Lodge's version, Frederick is killed in a battle against Duke Senior's men.

Shakespeare borrowed motifs* from other writers as well. The poetic excesses of his lovers are derived from Sir Philip SIDNEY's *Arcadia* and from the works of John Lyly. By changing the name of Lodge's hero Rosader to Orlando, Shakespeare also referred to the hero of Ludovico Ariosto's hugely popular *Orlando Furioso.* The comparison of Duke Senior and his courtiers to Robin Hood and his Merry Men may have been drawn from a pair of successful plays about Robin Hood then being performed by the Admiral's Men, an ACTING COMPANY.

Scholars believe that *As You Like It* was written in 1599 or 1600, possibly for the opening season of the GLOBE THEATER in the fall of 1599. It was first printed in the FIRST FOLIO edition of Shakespeare's works, which appeared in 1623. Because speakers are clearly identified and stage directions given, the Folio version is thought to be based on a reliable copy taken from the PROMPT BOOK used for staging the play.

Little is known about how *As You Like It* was produced in Shakespeare's day. It appears to have been forgotten during the late 1600s. Then in 1723 an adaptation titled *Love in a Forest* appeared. The characters of Touchstone, Audrey, Corin, Phebe, and a few minor parts had all been removed. The play was fleshed out with parts of other Shakespearean plays, including the bloody history *Richard III.* Jaques replaced Oliver as Celia's lover, and a sword fight took the place of the wrestling match. The original version was revived in 1740 in a highly successful performance featuring Kitty Clive as Celia. The play became very popular during the 1800s, and the part of Rosalind has remained a great favorite of leading ladies, including Dorothea Jordan, Edith Evans, Peggy Ashcroft, Vanessa Redgrave, and Katharine Hepburn.

Not surprisingly, *As You Like It* is frequently performed outdoors. The 1900s saw a musical adaptation and a return to an all-male cast. Three silent film versions of the play were made, but so far the only film produced with a soundtrack has been the 1936 version with Laurence Olivier as Orlando. Several television productions have also appeared over the years. *As You Like It* continues to be popular among community theaters and school groups as well as professionals.

COMMENTARY. As its title implies, *As You Like It* has something for everybody. It offers the traditional plot devices of romantic comedy, a commentary on the pastoral style, and a spectacle complete with songs, dances, and stage wrestling. Meanwhile it presents a thoughtful discussion of life and love. It brings together opposing points of view and contradictory aspects of life, and shows how they can coexist.

Shakespeare both uses and plays upon the conventions of pastoralism. The shepherd lovers, Silvius and Phebe, are silly and unrealistic, but the contrasting character, Corin, is a simple laborer who is content with his lot. The forest is not so much a real place as an idea: a retreat from society that strips away the facades* of court life, forcing characters to interact in a meaningful way. It provides a rest from the ordinary routines of life and allows time for reflection and emotional growth. Shakespeare shows that although the ideals represented by pastoralism may be imaginary, they are also meaningful and desirable.

One of these ideals is that of romantic LOVE. The varied presentations of love include the blind devotion of Silvius to the hard-hearted Phebe, the joyful bantering of Rosalind and Orlando, and the purely physical appetites of Touchstone. Shakespeare also explores other kinds of love: the devotion old Adam shows to young Orlando, the sisterly affection of Rosalind and Celia, and the relationships between parents and children, as seen in the way the dukes treat their daughters and nieces. Love appears throughout as a powerful force for reconciliation. Phebe gains sympathy for Silvius when she herself falls in love, and for the feuding brothers, affection conquers hate and antagonists are reunited.

Much of the play involves a dialogue between those who keep themselves detached from life and those who are engaged in it. Touchstone's wit and Jaques's pessimism provide a commentary on the main characters' stories, highlighting the flaws and follies of their romantic ideals, but neither character offers a more desirable alternative. Moreover, their detachment prevents them from experiencing any depth of feeling. Meanwhile, the leading characters—Rosalind, Orlando, Celia, and Duke Senior—choose to be emotionally engaged in life, fully experiencing both its sorrows and its joys and showing respect for the worth of others. Their willingness to be committed emotionally to other human beings gives meaning and purpose to their lives.

At the same time, Shakespeare does not disregard the realities of life that interfere with emotional engagement. The audience can relate to Touchstone's declaration, as he arrives in Arden, that he would "care not for my spirits, if my legs were not weary" (II.iv.2–3). The sarcastic observations of Jaques and Touchstone are valid, even if they do not offer the

* *facade* artificial outward appearance

LITERARY DETECTIVE WORK

Although no records exist to show when *As You Like It* was written, scholars have gathered various strands of evidence that suggest Shakespeare wrote it in 1599 or early 1600. The play does not appear in a list of his plays that was published in 1598, yet it is one of four plays that the Chamberlain's Men formally registered, but withheld from publication, in August of 1600. Another clue is that in Act III, Phebe quotes Christopher Marlowe's *Hero and Leander,* which was not published until 1598. The fact that the play was kept out of print suggests that it was a new play and the Chamberlain's Men wanted to prevent other companies from staging it.

Astor Place Riot

* *malicious* spiteful or mean-spirited

most meaningful way of dealing with life. These two characters are sometimes disagreeable, but they are not malicious*, and their clever conversation is often enjoyable. In presenting these characters with their mixture of desirable and undesirable qualities, Shakespeare shows that contradiction is an unavoidable part of life. (*See also* **Actors, Shakespearean; Characters in Shakespeare's Plays; Fools, Clowns, and Jesters; Plays: The Comedies; Playwrights and Poets; Seven Ages of Man; Shakespeare's Works, Adaptations of.**)

On May 7, 1849, an angry mob surrounded the Astor Place Opera House in New York City to protest a performance of *Macbeth* by English actor William Charles Macready, a rival to the popular American actor Edwin Forrest. Police fired on the rioters, killing 23 people.

A performance of *Macbeth* at the Astor Place Opera House in New York City in 1849 led to a riot in which 23 people were killed and more than 100 were wounded. The riot had its origins in a rivalry between the English actor William Charles Macready and the American actor Edwin Forrest. Macready was unpopular in the United States because of his superior attitude toward Americans. Forrest, by contrast, had many supporters in the United States as well as numerous admirers abroad. When Forrest toured England in 1846, however, he received a poor reception from British audiences, which he blamed on Macready. In response, Forrest disrupted Macready's American tour by criticizing him in letters to the press.

On May 7, 1849, audience members loyal to Forrest threw apples, eggs, potatoes, and chairs onto the stage during Macready's performance at the Astor Place Opera House. Fearing for his safety, Macready left the stage during the third act. After being assured that he would be protected, he agreed to perform again two nights later. On the day of the show, however, more than 10,000 people gathered outside the opera house and 250 policemen were called in to protect Macready and the audience. The crowd began throwing stones and bricks and the National Guard was summoned. The soldiers fired warning shots with no effect and finally resorted to shooting into the crowd. Macready escaped to England, abandoning his earlier plans to settle in America. Many people blamed Forrest for the riot and, afterward, influential people in the theater business shunned him.

ASTRONOMY AND COSMOLOGY

The word *cosmos* refers to the universe, and *cosmology* is a set of beliefs about the structure and workings of the cosmos. The Elizabethans believed in an orderly, harmonious universe in which each thing fit naturally into its proper place. The order of the heavens, observed through astronomy, was thought to be reflected in the orderly arrangement of human societies on Earth.

MODELS OF THE UNIVERSE. The Elizabethan model of the heavens was based on the theories of the ancient Egyptian astronomer Ptolemy. In the Elizabethan scheme, earth stood at the center of the universe, fixed and unmoving. It was surrounded by a series of interlocking spheres containing the known heavenly bodies. The sphere closest to the earth contained the moon, while more distant spheres carried the sun, the planets, and the stars. The highest sphere of all was the supernatural realm in which God and the angels lived, and the movement of this sphere caused the rest to move as well.

The spheres above the moon were seen as perfect and unchanging. Below the moon, all was unstable. The earth was believed to be made up of four elements—fire, air, water, and earth—which were influenced by the movement of the spheres. Thus, the movements of stars and planets directly affected the fate of humans on earth. This idea was reflected in the practice of astrology, which involved plotting the positions of the stars and other heavenly bodies to determine how they would influence human events.

In Shakespeare's time this traditional cosmology was challenged by newer theories based on scientific observation. In 1543 the astronomer Nicolaus Copernicus published *On the Revolution of the Heavenly Spheres*, which proposed a radically revised view of the universe. In the Copernican system the sun, not the earth, was the center of the universe. The earth not only traveled around the sun, but also rotated in space. This view of the universe won the support of many Elizabethan philosophers. One of them, Thomas Digges, suggested in 1576 that the stars were not fixed in a single sphere but extended to the realm of God. In other words, the universe was infinite. Other writers also stepped up to challenge the traditional view of the universe. Sir Francis Bacon, for example, suggested that the planets travel around the earth in spiral-shaped orbits.

COSMOLOGY AND ELIZABETHAN SOCIETY. The new ideas about the structure of the universe had little impact on the beliefs of the average person. The Elizabethan worldview continued to be influenced by ancient ideas about astronomy and physics, even as those ideas were being disproved by newer ones. To many, it seemed perfectly reasonable to accept the new theories without rejecting the old cosmology. Regardless of whether the earth traveled around the sun or vice versa, the universe could still be interpreted as an orderly, structured arrangement with a proper place for every person and thing.

There were two central ideas in cosmology that influenced nearly every area of Elizabethan thought. The first was the concept of a divine plan. It was generally believed that God had created each thing in the universe for a specific purpose and that every event in the natural world was a reflection of God's will. Although humans were unable to fully grasp this divine plan, they could gain insight into it by studying the workings of the visible universe. This idea of a divine plan is expressed in *Julius Caesar* when Caesar's wife warns him that she has had a dream foretelling his death. Caesar refuses to change his plans for the day, arguing, "What can be avoided / Whose end is purpos'd by the mighty gods?" (II.ii.26–27).

The second idea, related to the first, was that the entire universe was arranged in a hierarchical* order, from the highest beings to the lowest.

Most Elizabethans believed that heavenly bodies affected human events. Many people attempted to predict the effects of the movements of stars and planets through astrology. The signs of the zodiac are shown here.

* *hierarchical* ordered according to rank

Every creature on earth was superior to some beings and inferior to others. Just as God and the angels were superior to humans, so humans were superior to animals, animals to plants, and plants to nonliving objects, such as stones. This ordered structure was sometimes described as a "great chain of being." The Elizabethan concern with rank and SOCIAL CLASS was linked to this idea. Elizabethans perceived the hierarchical arrangement of their society, in which noblemen were superior to citizens and citizens superior to peasants, as mirroring the hierarchy of the universe. In *Troilus and Cressida*, the character of Ulysses expresses this idea in a lengthy speech, declaring that "The heavens themselves . . . observe degree, priority, and place" (I.iii.85–86), and that when degree is ignored the world falls into chaos. (*See also* **Fate and Fortune; Magic and Folklore; Science and Technology.**)

AUDIENCES

See *Performances; Shakespearean Theater: 17th Century; Shakespearean Theater: 18th Century; Shakespearean Theater: 19th Century; Shakespearean Theater: 20th Century.*

AUTHORSHIP, THEORIES ABOUT

Since the mid-1800s, several readers have suggested that the plays and poems attributed to William Shakespeare were not in fact written by the man from STRATFORD-UPON-AVON. These skeptics have shared the conviction that the true author was a man of greater learning and higher social class than William Shakespeare. Some have proposed that the London actor named William Shakespeare served as a front for the real author, taking credit for the plays so that their actual writer could remain anonymous. The debate continues today, with passionate arguments being presented by several competing camps.

ISSUES IN THE CONTROVERSY. The question of authorship is open to uncertainty because so little physical evidence ties the plays and poems to William Shakespeare and so few historical records exist about the man's personal life. Armed with the possibility of doubt, various "anti-Stratfordian" investigators—some amateurs, others with professional training—have proposed other authors and have sought evidence to prove their theories.

A central issue of the debate is whether a man of William Shakespeare's background and education could have written poems and plays that many critics consider to be the best literary works in the English language. In addition to their great beauty and sophistication, these writings display a knowledge of the customs and practices of the highest classes in European society—royalty and nobility. The issue of social and economic class, therefore, is significant. Records show that Shakespeare's father was a glover* by trade and that young William grew up in a small

* *glover* one who makes or sells gloves

town far from the wealth and culture of London. Many anti-Stratfordians regard this figure with contempt, describing him as dull, rural, and uneducated. They are certain that only a distinguished nobleman would have had the time, education, and wealth to create such literary and dramatic masterpieces. Furthermore, they say, the nobleman who wrote the plays would likely have used a pseudonym*, because drama was then considered a low form of public entertainment.

In response to these arguments, Stratfordians (those who support the authorship of William Shakespeare) accuse their opponents of snobbery for their refusal to believe that a commoner could rise to such heights of eloquence and artistry. Stratfordians point out that Shakespeare's father became a civic official in Stratford and probably sent his son to the town's grammar school, where students received a broad education in the classical* literature that served as sources for many of the plays.

THE PROPOSED ALTERNATIVES. In the mid-1800s, the most popular candidate for the true authorship of Shakespeare's works was Francis Bacon, who lived from 1561 to 1626. Bacon was a philosopher, essayist, and lawyer who also became a knight and a nobleman. Enthusiastic supporters of the Baconian theory combed the plays for hidden clues and cryptic references to Bacon's identity. Other anti-Stratfordians have nominated the playwright Christopher MARLOWE; the earls of Essex, Derby, and Rutland; and even Queen ELIZABETH I.

Since the 1920s the primary focus of anti-Stratfordians has fallen on Edward de Vere, the 17th earl of Oxford. As a young nobleman at the court of Queen Elizabeth, Oxford won praise for his poetry, but he later earned the displeasure of some nobles for his involvement in theater, having operated a company of child actors. His reputation also suffered from his failing financial situation and from rumors of his HOMOSEXUAL-ITY. Scholars have noted the seemingly homosexual nature of Shakespeare's *Sonnets,* which express love for a handsome young nobleman. Some have suggested that the young man of the *Sonnets* is the earl of Southampton, to whom Shakespeare's poems *Venus and Adonis* and *The Rape of Lucrece* are dedicated. To supporters of Oxford's authorship, the *Sonnets* yield many other clues; like all literature, however, they have many possible meanings, too elusive to define with absolute certainty.

NEW DEFINITIONS OF AUTHORSHIP. Some theorists of literature have suggested in recent years that the question of the author's identity is less important than the controversy makes it seem. They point out that a literary work is as much a product of the society in which it was written as it is the creation of an isolated, individual genius. An author is a social being who, consciously or unconsciously, absorbs and responds to the influences, interests, and attitudes of his or her culture. According to this view, the culture of Elizabethan England is as responsible for Shakespeare's plays as is the man known as Shakespeare.

Another difficulty in identifying an individual author for Shakespeare's plays concerns the nature of theatrical writing. Any work produced on a stage involves more than one person. The actors, designers,

* *pseudonym* false name, especially a pen name

* *classical* in the tradition of ancient Greece and Rome

CELEBRITY ENDORSEMENTS

Those who argue over Shakespeare's authorship are not all historians and eccentric scholars. The controversy has often attracted the upper crust of society, especially in the United States. Famous actors, writers, artists, intellectuals, patrons of the arts—anyone who felt qualified—declared their opinions. The list of those who have questioned William Shakespeare's authorship in the past includes Walt Whitman, Mark Twain, Henry James, Ralph Waldo Emerson, Sigmund Freud, and Charlie Chaplin.

and spectators all play a part in creating the finished artistic work. Additional hands are involved in the copying and printing of the script. Given these complications, some critics have abandoned the search for a single inspired author and have concentrated instead on the writing itself and on the culture that gave rise to it. (*See also* **Playwrights and Poets; Shakespeare, Life and Career; Shakespeare's Reputation; Shakespeare's Works, Changing Views; Sonnets, The.**)

BACON, FRANCIS

See *Authorship, Theories About.*

BANKING AND COMMERCE

Elizabethan England had neither banks nor lending institutions to support trade and commerce. Despite the absence of such establishments, business (both domestic and international) thrived while banking and currency systems were still being developed.

MONEY AND BANKING. Money in Shakespeare's time consisted of coins, which came in a variety of types and denominations. Although the pound was the standard unit of exchange, no coin called a pound actually existed at that time. Instead, the pound was a measure of weight used to represent a sum of money—20 shillings. Paper money was nonexistent, probably because people did not trust money that was not made of precious metal.

Banks as we know them did not exist in Shakespeare's day. There were no places where one could open a savings account, establish credit, or arrange a loan. The lack of financial institutions made commercial activity difficult, especially for small businessmen. With no regular system of credit, almost all transactions had to be made in cash, which meant handling heavy, bulky bags of coins.

Large trading firms, however, were able to hire agents who arranged business transactions using bills of exchange. These were notes issued by private trading houses that could be redeemed for cash when presented by a creditor, thus making commerce easier. When dealing with foreign merchants, companies could usually arrange loans from moneylenders or even foreign governments.

Moneylending, as it existed in Shakespeare's time, was complicated by religious and ethnic issues. Many people believed that the Bible forbade Christians from charging each other interest on loans. By contrast, custom seemed to suggest that it was acceptable for JEWS to lend money and charge interest. As a result, Jewish moneylenders across Europe were the primary force behind the growth of international finance. The character of SHYLOCK in *The Merchant of Venice* is based on the popular Elizabethan image of Jewish moneylenders. Changes in moneylending practices occurred in England in the mid-1500s when Parliament allowed

London was the primary financial center of Elizabethan England. The Royal Exchange, which opened in 1571 (shown here as it looked in 1644), contained approximately 100 shops dealing in all types of goods.

interest-bearing loans as long as the interest rate did not exceed 10 percent. By 1571, all restrictions on moneylending had been abolished and an individual could lend money at whatever rate he chose. This loosening of regulations was a tremendous advantage to the growth of England's overseas commerce after 1600.

THE ENGLISH ECONOMY. During the 1500s and 1600s, Europe was overwhemingly agricultural, and so was England. Poor soil covered much of the high country of England, which made those regions better suited for the grazing of animals such as sheep. The widespread practice of raising sheep enabled England to establish a thriving wool industry. English merchants had been exporting wool to the cloth makers of Europe for some time, but by the mid-1400s, more and more woolen cloth was being made at home. The wool industry consisted of more than simply raising sheep and spinning wool. It also included such processes as weaving and dyeing, as well as the marketing and sale of the finished cloth, both at home and abroad. For some people, spinning and weaving wool supplemented the income they earned from farming. For many others, it was their main occupation. By Shakespeare's day, the wool industry had become so important to the English economy that an observer at the time called it "one of the pillars of our commonwealth."

Wool dominated the English economy, but it was not England's only industry. Although the Industrial Revolution was still some 200 years in the future, some of the industries that led to that dramatic changeover were already under way in England. Iron working was developing in regions where iron ore existed near the resources required to power blast furnaces, such as wood and flowing water. Tin had been

mined in Cornwall since ancient times, and lead was also mined and exported to Europe. Coal, which fueled the iron and soapmaking industries, was also replacing wood, which had been used for heating in most regions of England.

Despite the growth of mining, most English industries were still tied to agriculture, which was dependent on the weather. Droughts and floods not only killed crops but rendered windmills and waterwheels useless. A poor harvest meant hard times for most people, which in turn reduced the demand for manufactured goods.

TRADE. With around 600 market towns, Elizabethan England was an active commercial and trading nation. Although most of these towns were small, they were becoming important centers for the buying and selling of goods. Trade fairs were a major part of the economy, drawing merchants from around the country and even from overseas. England's GEOGRAPHY made it ideally suited to overseas TRADE, since no part of the country was more than about 70 miles from the sea. With several navigable rivers connecting the interior to the coast, many goods could be transported quickly and inexpensively by boat to ports along the coast. Most of these ports traded with particular regions of Europe. For example, goods from Newcastle went mainly to German and Dutch ports, as well as to those on the Baltic Sea. Other port cities traded primarily with France, Spain, or Portugal. London was the only port from which merchants could trade simultaneously with many different countries. In fact, by the 1580s, overseas trade through London brought in about 90 percent of all taxes raised from imported goods.

For many years the English controlled the wool trade in Europe from the Dutch city of Antwerp. There, an English trading company called the Fellowship of the Merchant Adventurers sold wool to merchants who marketed it throughout Europe. In exchange, European merchants brought their goods—spices, wines, other textiles, and manufactured goods—to Antwerp for English merchants to sell in England. By the 1580s, however, the political situation in Europe had changed, Antwerp declined in importance, and the Merchant Adventurers left the city.

As England sought new markets, individual merchants stepped up their efforts to establish trade in the faraway Turkish empire, where trade was dominated by nations in the Mediterranean region. England had also begun to establish colonies in the Americas and to compete aggressively for trade in India and the Far East. By the time of Shakespeare's death in 1616, England had laid the foundations of a commercial empire that would eventually stretch around the globe. (*See also* **Coins and Currency; Exploration; Markets and Fairs; Poverty and Wealth.**)

COUNTERFEITING AND CLIPPING

While it may have been easy to make counterfeit coins, they were difficult to use. Counterfeit coins were easy to spot and the penalties for making them were harsh. Regarded as traitors to the crown, counterfeiters were punished by hanging, drawing, and quartering. Young offenders might be given milder sentences. Counterfeiting was also called clipping, perhaps because one of the ways to make counterfeit coins was to "clip" tiny bits of metal from genuine coins. When enough bits of metal had been accumulated, they could be melted down and used to make other coins.

BATTLES

See *Warfare.*

BEAUMONT, FRANCIS

See *Playwrights and Poets.*

BIBLE

There is little doubt that the Bible, with its characters, stories, ideas, phrases, and rhythms, influenced William Shakespeare. Although none of the plots of his plays is directly based on the Bible, all of them contain references to biblical figures and stories. According to one study, Shakespeare's plays include quotations or references from more than 40 books of the Bible. For example, in the comedy *As You Like It,* one character compares a group of couples about to be married to the pairs of animals rescued by Noah from the Great Flood: "There is sure another flood toward, and these couples are coming to the ark" (V.iv.35–36).

The rhythms of Shakespeare's language are frequently similar to the flow and sound of the language in the English translations of the Bible that were available at that time. During the late 1500s, the two most popular versions of the Bible in England were the Geneva Bible and the Bishop's Bible. Shakespeare was probably most familiar with the Geneva Bible, which was first translated into English in 1560. Eight years later, the first edition of the Bishop's Bible appeared in English. Scholars continue to debate whether Shakespeare read the Bible extensively or gained his knowledge primarily from hearing it read. (*See also* **Shakespeare's Sources.**)

BLACKFRIARS

* *Dominican* belonging to an order of brothers and priests founded by Saint Dominic

* *elite* best of its kind
* *Jacobean* referring to the reign of James I, king of England from 1603 to 1625

In 1576 Richard Farrant, deputy master of a prominent troupe of boy actors called the Children of the Chapel, rented several rooms in an old convent for use as a theater. The Blackfriars, named for the Dominican* friars who formerly inhabited it, was the first indoor playhouse in London. Farrant died in 1580, however, and the Blackfriars returned to private use until 1600. In that year the actor Richard Burbage reopened the theater, having inherited it from his father, who bought the property in 1596. The Children of the Chapel returned to the Blackfriars and remained there until 1608, when the troupe lost its right to perform. Forced to seek new tenants and investors, Burbage persuaded several of his fellow actors in the KING'S MEN, including William Shakespeare, to share the theater's lease and profits with him. From 1609 until the closing of all London theaters in 1642, the King's Men made their winter home at the Blackfriars.

Blackfriars catered to audiences who were better educated and of higher social rank than those who attended the so-called public or outdoor theaters. This distinction was also reflected in the admission prices, which were as much as five times the prices in the public theaters. The elite* audience, the intimacy of the indoor setting, and the candlelit stage led to important changes in Jacobean* drama.

The seating arrangement at Blackfriars reversed the priorities of the outdoor theaters. At an open-air stage, a one-penny admission bought standing room near the stage, while the wealthiest patrons were secluded at a distance from the stage. Blackfriars put the expensive seats closest to the stage. The cheapest tickets, although several times more costly than those at the amphitheaters, gained spectators a bench in the gallery, located far from the stage.

The stage itself was only half the size of an outdoor stage. For this reason battles, duels, and other complicated scenes were difficult, even dangerous, to attempt. On the indoor stage, language and wordplay gradually replaced physical action as the focus of drama. (*See also* **Children's Companies; Elizabethan Theaters; Globe Theater.**)

BODLEIAN LIBRARY

See *Museums and Archives.*

BOOKS

See *Printing and Publishing.*

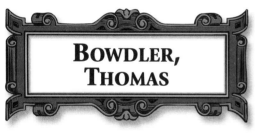

**BOWDLER,
THOMAS**

**1754–1825
Clergyman and editor**

* *expurgate* to remove morally harmful or objectionable material from a literary work

Thomas Bowdler is known for *The Family Shakespeare,* an expurgated* edition of the Bard's works. Bowdler added nothing to the original text; he simply removed words and phrases he thought unsuitable for reading aloud in front of women and children. His work gave rise to the term *bowdlerize,* coined in 1936, which refers to a work that has been "sanitized" for the general public.

The Family Shakespeare first appeared as a four-volume edition in 1807. In it Bowdler made substantial changes, such as removing large portions of *Romeo and Juliet* and *King Lear.* In a few cases, when he was unable to make the desired changes because the offending words or phrases were too deeply rooted in the text, he posted a warning to readers at the beginning of the work. This was the case for such works as *Measure for Measure* and *Othello.* Bowdler is said to have admired Shakespeare and felt that without the expurgated passages, the Bard's genius would "undoubtedly shine with more unclouded lustre."

It should be noted, however, that some historians believe it was Thomas's sister, Harriet, who actually prepared the first ten-volume edition in 1818. In the early 1800s it was considered "unseemly" for a woman's name to appear in print. For that reason, Harriet published the 1818 edition anonymously and attributed subsequent editions to her brother. Harriet Bowdler's "improvements" included the addition of four years to Juliet's age, making her 17 years old and her intense love for

Romeo more understandable and acceptable to Victorian England. (*See also* **Shakespeare's Works, Adaptations of; Shakespeare's Works, Influential Editions.**)

See *Museums and Archives.*

BRUTUS

ca. 85 B.C.–42 B.C.
Conspirator

Brutus is the main character of *Julius Caesar*. He is based on the historical figure Marcus Brutus, a Roman nobleman who conspired to assassinate the Roman ruler Julius Caesar in 44 B.C. Shakespeare relied heavily on the account of Brutus written by the Roman historian Plutarch.

The historical events the playwright dramatized in *Julius Caesar* are based on the political struggle that shook Rome in the final years of the Roman Republic. Caesar had become a dictator who was extremely popular with the citizenry. However, conservative Roman senators and other nobles feared that he intended to name himself emperor and to weaken their power. Brutus and another nobleman, Cassius, led a group of conspirators who assassinated Caesar on the floor of the Senate. This violent act sparked a civil war in which armies commanded by Brutus and Cassius were opposed by the forces of Caesar's nephew Octavian and Caesar's friend Mark Antony. Brutus and Cassius were defeated at the Battle of Philippi, and Brutus committed suicide.

Shakespeare portrays Brutus as a serious man who believes his intentions are noble. However, in relying strictly on reason to justify the assassination, Brutus overlooks the moral implications of his act and fails to recognize his own hidden desire for power. He tragically underestimates the strong feelings the murder will stir in Caesar's supporters and overestimates his own abilities as a political and military leader. The actions of Brutus and his co-conspirators help to bring about the downfall of the republic he had hoped to save. (*See also* **Antony and Cleopatra; Ides of March; Plutarch's Lives; Shakespeare's Sources.**)

CALIBAN

Caliban is a half-human creature who inhabits the island that serves as the setting for Shakespeare's play *The Tempest*. The son of a demon and an African witch, he shares his island home with PROSPERO, an exiled duke who is also a magician, and with Prospero's daughter MIRANDA. When Prospero and Miranda first arrived on the island, Caliban helped them to survive, but he later angered them by attempting to rape Miranda. The sorcerer has therefore enslaved Caliban through magic

A 1904 production of *The Tempest*, directed by Herbert Beerbohm Tree, presented Caliban as a hairy, beastlike creature resembling a werewolf.

spells. Resentful of Prospero's arrogant mastery, Caliban conspires with two shipwrecked servants to kill him, but the magician foils his plan.

Prospero, Miranda, and the other humans who find themselves shipwrecked on the island clearly see Caliban as less than human, a brute little better than a beast who must be controlled. Caliban's behavior early in the play seems to confirm their view. He appears coarse, lazy, dim-witted, and dangerous. In later scenes, however, he shows both intelligence and emotion. While some of the other characters in the play speak only in prose, Caliban speaks in verse, indicating a refined nature. In fact, he utters one of the most beautiful and poetic speeches in the play, describing the "sounds and sweet airs"(III.ii.136) that float through the air on Prospero's island. Audiences are also naturally inclined to sympathize with Caliban's resentment toward Prospero, who has taken away his home and his freedom when it was Caliban who first showed him how to survive in an unfamiliar environment.

Some critics have related Caliban to the native peoples of the Americas, accounts of whom had recently begun to reach Europeans of Shakespeare's time. Most Europeans believed that the people they called Indians were uncivilized, and they hoped to learn whether such humans were unrestrained savages or noble beings uncorrupted by society. Caliban can also be seen as a symbol of humanity's baser instincts. Identifying Caliban to the other characters in the final scene, Prospero says, "this thing of darkness I / Acknowledge mine" (V.i.275–76), hinting that the "darkness" he acknowledges comes from his own nature. According to this interpretation, Caliban's decision at the end of the play to submit to Prospero's mastery and "seek for grace" can be viewed as suggesting the possibility of redemption for flawed human beings. (*See also* **Exploration; Morality and Ethics; Race and Ethnicity.**)

CASTLES

Hundreds of massive stone castles dotted the English countryside during the Middle Ages. They served as homes and defensive fortifications for powerful lords and their families. During the Wars of the Roses—the English civil wars of the 1400s—these castles were the sites of fierce battles for the throne of England. When the wars ended, most of the castles were abandoned or fell into disrepair. Several remained intact, however, serving as reminders of England's tumultuous past. Shakespeare dramatized events from the Wars of the Roses in *Henry VI, Parts 1, 2, and 3,* and in *Richard III,* using actual castles as settings for these plays. Castles also figure prominently in several of Shakespeare's other history plays, including *Richard II* and *Henry IV, Parts 1 and 2,* as well as in the tragedies *Macbeth* and *Hamlet.*

DEPOSING KINGS. The events in *Richard II* and *Henry IV* occur at the beginning of the conflict that will lead to the Wars of the Roses. In *Richard II,* the traitor Henry Bolingbroke sentences King Richard's friends Bushy and Greene to death outside Bristol Castle, located in western

England. Later, Bolingbroke captures Richard at Flint Castle, an English fortification built in northern Wales in the 1200s. In the play's final scene, Richard is murdered in Pomfret Castle—the site of numerous political executions—and Bolingbroke becomes King Henry IV.

Shakespeare wrote *Henry IV* in two parts, as two separate plays; in both of them Warkworth Castle serves as the headquarters of the Percy family, a rebel group fighting to overthrow King Henry IV. Warkworth Castle was built during the 1100s in the county of Northumberland, where its ruins can still be seen.

REBEL STRONGHOLDS. The events portrayed in *Henry VI* and *Richard III* take place at the height of the Wars of the Roses. In *Henry VI*, written in three parts, the king of England is once again challenged by nobles who seek to overthrow him. In *Henry VI, Part 2*, the king and queen flee a rebellion in London and take refuge in Kenilworth Castle—a fortification located near Shakespeare's childhood home. In *Henry VI, Part 3*, Sandal Castle in Yorkshire serves as the stronghold of the duke of York, who claims to be the rightful heir to the throne. Middleham Castle, also in *Henry VI, Part 3*, is the home of another rebellious noble, the earl of Warwick. Middleham Castle turns up again in *Richard III*, the last of

The castles owned by kings and lords in the Middle Ages served as both splendid homes and fortified strongholds. Many of Shakespeare's histories and tragedies feature scenes set in castle locations.

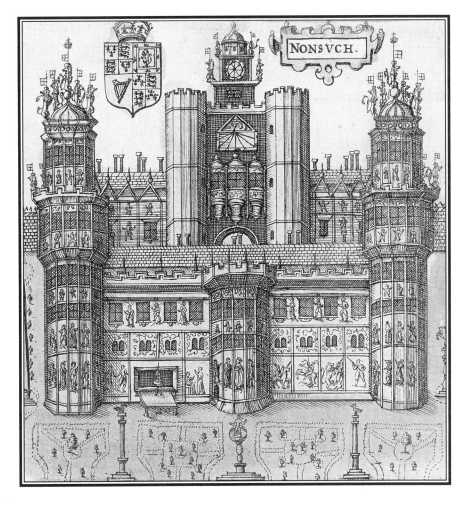

NONSVCH.

THE BLOODY TOWER

Begun after 1066 by William the Conqueror, the Tower of London has served as a royal residence, prison, place of execution, arsenal, royal mint, menagerie, and office of public records. During the early 1500s, King Henry VIII had several people beheaded there, including his second wife, Anne Boleyn. Queen Mary even briefly imprisoned the young Princess Elizabeth in the Tower. More recently, several spies were executed there by firing squad during World War I. In Shakespeare's *Richard III*, the Tower serves as the prison and later the execution chamber of King Richard's two nephews.

Shakespeare's plays about the English civil wars. In this play, Middleham is where three nobles are executed. Pomfret Castle appears in *Richard III* as the setting for another execution. Describing the dreadful history of this castle, one character exclaims, "O Pomfret, Pomfret! O thou bloody prison!"(III.iii.9).

SCENES OF TRAGEDY. *Macbeth* is a play about blind ambition and the murder of a king. Macbeth, a Scottish general, and his wife, Lady Macbeth, reside in Inverness Castle, where they hatch a plot to kill King Duncan and become rulers of Scotland. It is here, in the castle, that Duncan's murder occurs. Later in the play, Macbeth is in residence at Dunsinane Castle. The three witches, who had predicted at the beginning of the play that Macbeth would become king, assure him that he will remain safe "until Great Birnam wood to high Dunsinane hill / Shall come against him" (IV.i.92). In the final act, the noble who leads the English forces against Macbeth orders his troops to carry tree branches from the woods as camouflage for their attack on the castle. So Birnam Wood does in fact come to Dunsinane, and Macbeth meets a bloody end.

Shakespeare's use of a castle setting for an entire play is unique to *Hamlet*. Most of the play's action is set within Elsinore Castle on the northern coast of Denmark. Elsinore is also one of the few castles mentioned in Shakespeare's plays that are still in use. This fortress, whose actual name is Kronborg Castle, was built between 1574 and 1585, and has been in use continuously since that time. (*See also* **Court Life; History in Shakespeare's Plays: England; Plays: The Histories; Tower of London.**)

CENSORSHIP, LICENSING, AND COPYRIGHTS

* *sedition* resistance to or rebellion against lawful authority
* *profanity* vulgar or antireligious language

State and church officials played significant roles in determining the content, licensing, and publication of plays in Shakespeare's England. A royal official, known as the MASTER OF THE REVELS, read every play before it was staged to determine whether it contained any unacceptable material, such as sedition* or profanity*. Plays that were approved by the master of the revels received a license permitting them to be performed in public. Fewer rules existed for controlling the content of printed materials. Most dramatists did not publish their works, however, because play scripts normally belonged to the ACTING COMPANIES that performed them.

In Elizabethan England, playwrights and actors were forbidden to question England's religious or political leaders. At the same time, even mild profanity was outlawed. For example, passages in which Shakespeare used the word "God" had to be rewritten with words such as "Heavens" and "Jove" as substitutes. The master of the revels often removed or rewrote sections of plays that he considered objectionable, and some plays were prohibited entirely. One such work was *Isle of Dogs*, a political satire* written by Thomas Nash and BEN JONSON in 1597. The censor felt that this comedy would incite rebellion against the crown,

* *satire* literary work ridiculing human wickedness and foolishness

THE DEADLY CENSOR

Content was not the only thing that could prevent a play from being performed. Plays could not be staged during outbreaks of plague because of the danger that disease would spread among the audience. The definition of an outbreak varied. Before 1604, an outbreak was declared when the number of victims killed by plague reached 50 per week. Afterward the total was reduced to 30 per week, making it even more likely that the theaters would be closed. Closures lasted weeks or even months, and many acting companies were ruined during extended outbreaks of plague.

* *monopoly* exclusive right to engage in a particular type of business

and as a result Jonson and two actors were jailed. The play so angered the authorities that they closed all of London's theaters for the summer.

Not all censorship was official. Playwrights were aware of the laws regulating their works and normally censored their own material before it reached the master of the revels. Portions of *Hamlet* that appear in modern versions of the play were probably omitted in Shakespeare's time to avoid trouble with the censors—such as the speech in Act I Scene 4 that describes Danes as drunkards, which might have offended Queen Anne, the Danish-born wife of JAMES I. In addition, powerful nobles and foreign officials could force playwrights to change material. For example, one noble family objected to Shakespeare's portrayal of Sir John Oldcastle—one of the family's ancestors—as a drunken, thieving character in *Henry IV, Part 1*. Forced to change the identity of Oldcastle, Shakespeare renamed his character FALSTAFF, but he used his subtle wit to outsmart the censors, leaving in a reference to the fat knight as the "old lad of the castle" (I.ii.41).

Unlike plays, most printed material did not require a license. For a time authorized owners of presses were free to publish what they chose. In the 1530s and 1540s, however, the crown began to control publishing by granting licenses to certain publishers, giving each of them a monopoly* on specific types of books, such as religious writings. In 1586 the crown outlawed the establishment of presses in locations other than LONDON and the university towns of Cambridge and Oxford. Interestingly, none of these laws greatly affected playwrights because they earned their living by selling their work to acting companies, not to publishers.

Another reason that playwrights had little interest in publishing was that the printer, not the author, owned the rights to published material. Until the enactment of the Copyright Act of 1710, legal copyright for authors did not exist in England. Because publishers could change a work without consulting the author, many poor and badly mangled versions of plays were published. (*See also* **Acting Companies, Elizabethan; Printing and Publishing.**)

CEREMONIES AND RITUALS

* *christening* ceremony at which a child is named and baptized

* *baptize* to admit a person into the Christian faith by means of sprinkling with or submersion in holy water

Elizabethans marked important occasions in their lives with formal ceremonies and traditional procedures, or rituals. Significant milestones, such as birth, marriage, or death, were the most common reason for these observances. In addition to marking an event as noteworthy, ceremonies and rituals enabled people to express their shared beliefs and values. Each detail of a ceremonial service had a symbolic meaning. For example, a white cloth placed on a baby's head during its christening* represented purity and freedom from sin.

In Shakespeare's time, births were fearful occasions because many women died during childbirth and many infants also perished. After giving birth, the mother was believed to be in danger from FAIRIES and other supernatural creatures until she was able to attend church. It was also commonly believed that if a baby died before being baptized*, he or she would go to hell. Therefore, the baby's baptism and christening were

Ceremonies and Rituals

At christening ceremonies, which are still held, a newborn baby is named and baptized. By sprinkling the infant with holy water, the priest officially admits the child into the Christian church.

See color plate 6, vol. 1.

* *wake* watch kept over the deceased before the body is buried

almost as important as its birth. Great care was taken to choose a proper name, preferably a family name or one from the Bible. Biblical names were associated with certain virtues, such as wisdom or bravery. Elizabethans believed that the virtue linked to a name was transferred to the baby.

Marriage ceremonies occurred in two stages. The first part was the "handfasting" or betrothal, roughly equivalent to a modern engagement. The couple clasped hands, kissed, and promised either immediate marriage (by saying "I do") or marriage in the future (by saying "I will"). Sometimes rings in the form of two hands holding a heart were exchanged. Other times, a coin was split and each lover kept half of it until the wedding day.

Weddings took place in public places during the day. The bride's head was typically crowned with a wreath of flowers or wheat, symbolizing fertility. Wedding dresses—usually reddish-brown—were decorated with colorful ribbons called love knots. Bachelors snatched the ribbons off the dress and pinned them to their hats. The groom's clothing was decorated with branches of rosemary, which symbolized manliness. After the couple married, the wedding guests went to the groom's home, where they ate, drank, danced, and celebrated for hours, days, or weeks, depending on the wealth of the families involved. On the wedding night, the guests escorted the couple to bed and then served them spiced wine. After the newlyweds drank, the guests toasted "prosperity to the marriage" as a sign that the marriage ceremony had been properly performed.

Funerals involved as much symbolism as any other ritual in Elizabethan England. People left detailed notes describing how they wished to be buried, including how they were to be dressed and who could handle the body. Professional mourners were often hired to make the funeral procession more impressive. Coffins, draped in black, were decorated with evergreen branches to remind the participants that the soul never dies. Following the procession, a wake* was held at the deceased person's home, where cold meats and other foods were served. Wakes, like weddings, were enormous feasts that could last several days or more. In *Hamlet*, the prince remarks sourly that his mother's second marriage occurred so soon after his father's death that "the funeral bak'd meats / Did coldly furnish forth the marriage tables" (I.ii.180–81) (*See also* **Death and Funerals; Magic and Folklore; Marriage and Family; Witches and Evil Spirits.**)

CHAMBERLAIN'S MEN

See *King's Men.*

CHARACTERS IN
SHAKESPEARE'S
PLAYS

A person's character is often defined by how he or she behaves in different circumstances. Most people have a complex mix of good and bad traits, formed from a wide range of influences—many of which they themselves do not always recognize. Like real people, the major personalities in Shakespeare's plays have great psychological depth, so much so that critics have sometimes applied the tools of psychoanalysis to understand them better.

Some Shakespearean characters are so vivid that they have been regarded as having a life of their own. In an "Essay on the Dramatic Character of Falstaff" (1777), Maurice Morgann treated the fat knight as if he were a real person. Morgann introduced the school of "character criticism," which served as a popular approach to Shakespeare's plays for more than a century, reaching its climax in 1904, when the scholar A. C. Bradley published a brilliant analysis of Shakespeare's tragic heroes. Bradley's book, *Shakespearean Tragedy,* was so persuasive that many people considered it the definitive authority on these protagonists*. More recently, however, scholars have come to see dramatic characters as complex combinations of the playwright's words, actors' portrayals, directors' contributions, and audiences' responses to particular performances.

SHAKESPEARE'S CREATIONS. As they exist on the page, Shakespeare's characters are products of the author's mind. Unlike real people, they do not have a life or history of their own. Their existence is in what the playwright causes them to say and do, and everything they say and do serves a dramatic purpose.

Even when Shakespeare includes characters named for real historical figures, he changes them to suit the needs of his plot and the tastes of his audience. They cannot, therefore, be seen as true pictures of historical figures. For this reason, examining details of the lives of real people will not necessarily enhance one's understanding of the playwright's characters. Research by historians suggests, for example, that the real King Richard III was not the absolute villain encountered in Shakespeare's play. It is not even clear that the man was physically deformed. The playwright's purpose in making the king so villainous probably had something to do with the fact that England's ruling Tudor family had captured the throne from Richard. To remain in favor with those in power, Shakespeare may have felt that he had to portray Richard in the most negative light possible.

Another influence on the character of Richard and other Shakespearean villains is the VICE figure in medieval* morality plays. The Vice, who always accompanied the Devil in these entertainments, was the embodiment of evil, and he scornfully mocked all that was virtuous and good. In spite of this, he was a strangely attractive figure—lively, witty,

* *protagonist* central character in a dramatic or literary work

* *medieval* referring to the Middle Ages, a period roughly between A.D. 500 and 1500

and energetic—who frequently provided comedy. The Vice is an example of a stock character—a personality type with a few obvious traits who appears again and again in different plays. Shakespeare frequently borrowed such figures from his sources but then made them more complex, adding layers of different traits to the identifying characteristics of the original model. Through this technique, he transformed stock figures into some of the greatest and most complex personalities in all of world drama.

See color plate 10, vol. 2.

In an early play, *The Comedy of Errors*—written before his method had fully matured—Shakespeare adapted an ancient Roman comedy, *The Menaechmi*, by Plautus. The original play is full of stock characters, such as the nagging wife, the lecherous husband, the scheming servant, and the heartless mistress. Shakespeare not only added more characters to Plautus's script but also made the existing ones more complicated and human. For example, in his play the nagging wife, Adriana, truly loves and worries about her husband while he in turn spends time with another woman only when his wife drives him from the house. Characters in *Othello* contain elements of the Roman stock types: the beautiful woman (DESDEMONA), the lovesick young man (Roderigo), the scheming servant (IAGO), and the foreign soldier (Othello). Shakespeare included aspects of the Vice in Iago, but his greatest change was in the personality of Othello. Shakespeare's source for the play presented this character as a violent ruffian, but Shakespeare's Moor is noble, mysterious, unsure of himself, and (later) violently jealous yet capable of loving tenderness.

The playwright's primary tool is LANGUAGE. This is especially true in Shakespeare's later plays, as he gradually refined his poetic technique. His characters do not simply express standard, high-flown sentiments that might be delivered by anyone in a similar situation. Instead, their words are tailored so that everything they say helps the audience relate to individual personalities. Moreover the flow of IMAGERY in their dialogue makes these characters so multifaceted that no single performance could possibly reveal everything there is to know about them.

In creating the characters for his plays, Shakespeare often changed or enhanced the features they had in the source material. For example, the three witches in *Macbeth*—portrayed by Shakespeare as evil spirits—were presented in his source as "fairies" with the ability to predict the future.

DUELING CRITICS

Around 1930 a reaction began to set in against character criticism, the school of critical thought that approached Shakespeare's plays primarily through the analysis of his characters. A new school of thought, called historical criticism, attacked character criticism as an erroneous idea that mistook art for life. Historical critics argued that Shakespeare's characters were products of his own imagination and that he himself was the product of a particular time and place. For this reason, understanding the psychological influences on a character was not always enough to explain his or her behavior. Sometimes it was more important to understand the historical factors that influenced Shakespeare when he created the character.

ACTOR AND DIRECTOR INTERPRETATIONS. Aside from the playwright's actual words, the primary factor in the creation of a character is an actor's portrayal. For many playgoers the actor's interpretation of a role is the most interesting aspect of a Shakespeare performance. Many viewers wish to see how performers, especially famous ones, tackle particular parts. Some, such as Hamlet, are seen as tests for actors. The prince of Denmark is so complex that it is possible to produce many different interpretations of his nature and motivation. An actor who plays Hamlet successfully, especially if he presents the character in a new and exciting way, achieves a certain professional status by proving that he can handle the demands of such a challenging role.

Many actors are able to create unique interpretations of roles by combining parts of their own personalities with Shakespeare's characters. Sarah Siddons, famous for her portrayal of Lady Macbeth in the 1700s, is the first performer who is known to have prepared herself carefully for each part as modern so-called method actors do. By finding traits and emotions within herself that corresponded to those of Shakespeare's character, she produced a performance of notable intensity and power.

An actor's interpretation of a role can change the way the character is viewed. For example, Shylock in *The Merchant of Venice* was played for more than 100 years as a comic villain in a red wig and beard. In the mid-1700s the actor Charles Macklin reinterpreted the Jewish moneylender as a cunning and ferocious villain. Half a century later another great actor, Edmund Kean, presented Shylock as a quiet, tragic figure. Each of these performances caused a sensation when it was first introduced (and boosted the actor's reputation at the same time). What is most astonishing is that these conflicting interpretations are all consistent with the lines Shakespeare provided for the character.

It is likely that Shakespeare wrote certain parts with specific members of his acting company in mind. Richard Burbage, the troupe's leading player, was one of the period's greatest tragedians, and it is fairly clear that the challenging roles of Hamlet, Othello, Richard III, and King Lear were created with his talents and capabilities in mind. Two different comic actors in the company played the parts of FOOLS, and it appears that Shakespeare tailored these roles in his plays to the particular strengths of these men. Until the end of the 1590s, the clown roles were performed by Will Kempe, who introduced such buffoons as Dogberry in *Much Ado About Nothing* and Bottom in *A Midsummer Night's Dream*. When Kempe was replaced by Robert Armin, whose style of performance was somewhat more serious—even melancholy—Shakespeare's clowns changed. The roles created for Armin included such witty and sarcastic commentators as Feste in *Twelfth Night* and the Fool in *King Lear*.

Like actors, directors have had a profound effect on the way characters are portrayed. One way a director alters the presentation of a character is by deciding on a particular style or setting for the production. A famous production of *A Midsummer Night's Dream* in the 1970s, directed by Peter Brook, set the play in a kind of ring. Bottom was presented as a circus clown, and great emphasis was placed on the acrobatic skills of the

actors. In this instance the director's choice naturally affected the way the actors approached their parts as well as the way in which the audience viewed the play.

AUDIENCE PARTICIPATION. Probably the most subtle influence on the portrayal of a particular character is that of the audience itself. This influence lies partly in the fact that different groups of theatergoers have different standards for what they consider realistic and acceptable in a character. For example, few modern audiences would accept a rendering of Shylock that made him an object of ridicule or in any way connected his Jewishness with his villainy. Another role that can pose problems for actors and directors is KATHARINA in *The Taming of the Shrew.* In her final speech she not only submits willingly to her husband's authority and criticizes any woman who does otherwise; she actually offers to put her hand under her husband's boot for him to tread on if he wishes. Because this "taming" may be viewed negatively by modern audiences, the director and the actress playing Katharina may attempt to reinterpret the role in a way that is more acceptable to today's viewers.

Shakespeare's characters are highly complex, and it is perfectly reasonable to study them in the traditional way, as real people with histories and motivations all their own. Readers should remember, however, that Shakespeare created his plays and characters to be performed. It is only on the stage, where the actor, the director, and the audience all help to shape them, that Shakespeare's characters truly come alive. (*See also* **Actors, Shakespearean; Directors and Shakespeare; King's Men; Pageants and Morality Plays; Poetic Technique.**)

CHILDREN'S COMPANIES

Children's companies were groups of boy actors who performed in Elizabethan theaters. During the later years of Queen Elizabeth's reign, these troupes dominated the performance of drama. Although the actors were children, they performed plays written for adults and featuring adult characters.

Usually 8 to 12 boys made up a company. They worked under the direction of a choirmaster who designed pageants, wrote plays, taught the craft of acting to the boys, and arranged for court and public performances. Although the boys received no wages, they seem to have lived comfortably. When their voices changed as they matured, they were often placed at university or provided for in other ways. Early in Elizabeth's reign, the main function of the children's companies was to provide entertainment at court on holidays. Later the performers were organized into professional troupes who performed outside the court as well.

Several of these companies enjoyed great success, particularly the Children of the Chapel, who performed at BLACKFRIARS, and the Children of Paul's. For a time they even rivaled adult acting companies. Queen Elizabeth and her courtiers found the sophisticated, polished productions of the boys more enjoyable than those of the coarser adult companies. For

several years at the close of the 1500s, the children's companies and the adult troupes competed for audiences, but in 1590 the boy companies were closed down because they could no longer compete with their older counterparts. Some of the children's companies were revived over the following decades, especially as choirs, but eventually adults were providing nearly all the entertainment for both the court and the public.

CHURCH, THE

The Church of England was often referred to in Shakespeare's time as the established church of the new religion, Anglicanism. These names reflected the manner in which the church's founding had occurred. Disagreements over the nature of the church and its authority resulted in executions and assassination plots and eventually led to civil war.

THE PROTESTANT REFORMATION. The Church of England was established by King Henry VIII in 1534, when he severed ties with the Roman Catholic pope Clement VII, who refused to grant Henry an annulment* of his marriage to Katherine of Aragon. The king had begun to question the legality of his marriage to Katherine, especially since she had failed to produce a son. Henry's break with Rome occurred while some religious leaders were attempting to reform the Catholic Church. Known as the Protestant Reformation, this movement eventually led to the founding of separate Christian communities. In England, Henry's rejection of the pope's authority helped transform the nation from a Catholic kingdom to one that became predominantly Protestant.

Under the influence of such leaders as Martin Luther and John Calvin, Protestants maintained that the BIBLE, not the pope, was the highest authority over Christians. They also rejected the Catholic doctrine that good works enable people to gain entry into heaven; they argued that faith alone was required to achieve salvation*.

THE NEW CHURCH LEADERS. After Henry VIII established the Church of England, he named himself its supreme leader. He then shut down the country's monasteries and convents, seizing their property and wealth. Much of the rest of England's Catholic structure, however, remained in place. After the monarch, the archbishop of Canterbury and the archbishop of York presided. Bishops, who supervised territories called dioceses, were the next highest church officials. Like the archbishops, they sat in the House of Lords in PARLIAMENT and participated in making the laws of the land.

Bishops were also responsible for the priests who ministered to members of the local parish churches. Bishops' assistants, called archdeacons, visited each parish at least once a year to hold ecclesiastical* court, where they tried those who were accused of such offenses as sexual misconduct. Parish officials also included people who were not members of the clergy, such as churchwardens (who helped make decisions concerning the parish), parish clerks (who kept records of births,

* *annulment* formal declaration that a marriage is legally invalid

* *salvation* deliverance from the consequences of sin

* *ecclesiastical* relating to an established church

St. Paul's Cathedral was the center of social life in Elizabethan London. Under the Elizabethan Settlement of 1559, all English subjects were required to attend Anglican Church services at least once a month.

* *Communion* Christian ritual in which bread and wine are consumed in memory of Christ's death

baptisms, marriages, and deaths), sextons (who maintained the church grounds and cemetery), and beadles (who kept order during church services).

ELIZABETH'S COMPROMISE. When ELIZABETH I ascended the throne in 1558, she entered a heated struggle between those who wished to preserve the Catholic character of the Anglican Church and those who wanted to purge it of all Catholic influence. In 1559 she forged a compromise called the Elizabethan settlement, which accepted most Protestant beliefs while retaining many important Catholic rituals, such as baptism and Communion*.

COMPROMISE AND DISSENT. Elizabeth passed an act making herself the head of the Church of England. This act required all church and government officials to swear allegiance to the queen and her church and to renounce loyalty to any other leader. Church and state were officially united, and disloyalty to the Church of England was considered to be treason.

Catholics who refused to convert, called recusants, remained a small but stubborn minority. New laws were passed that banned Catholic worship and forced every English subject to attend an Anglican service at least once a month or face fines and imprisonment. In response the pope promised to pardon any Catholic who was willing to assassinate Elizabeth. At the other extreme were radical Protestants, known as Puritans, who believed that the Elizabethan settlement retained too many

features of Catholicism. Some Puritans disputed the authority of the queen and sought to replace bishops with nonclergy officials. Despite these conflicts, Elizabeth maintained her policy of compromise on religious issues for the rest of her long reign.

The next monarch, JAMES I, was less successful in curbing religious dissent. The nation was shocked when a group of Catholics tried to assassinate him in the GUNPOWDER PLOT of 1605. King James was also threatened by Puritans, some of whom disputed his authority as the head of both church and state. His failure to address Puritan dissent successfully led to the outbreak of civil war in 1642. Seven years later, the Anglican Church lost its leader when the victorious Puritans executed James's son and successor, Charles I. (*See also* **Government and Politics; Religion.**)

CITIES, TOWNS, AND VILLAGES

Although England was still overwhelmingly rural during Shakespeare's time, cities and towns were growing rapidly in size, population, and complexity. They were also becoming important centers of trade, education, and social life. People viewed cities and towns as an expression of humankind's best ambitions and achievements, as well as the sources of its worst problems.

LONDON. England's only city in the 16th and 17th centuries was LONDON. In the 1520s, approximately 50,000 people lived there, but by 1600 more than 200,000 called it home. London became the national center of finance, government, administration, law, religion, learning, and theater. London also set the tone for fashion and style. People from outlying towns and rural areas flocked to London in search of wealth, excitement, and opportunity.

* *metropolitan* referring to a city and its surrounding area, including suburbs

See color plate 12, vol. 1.

Officially, London's city limits were set by ancient defensive walls on three sides and by the Thames River on the fourth side. The area within these boundaries, known as the City, occupied only a few square miles, but the metropolitan* area was much larger. Access to the City was gained through gates in the walls. Several of these gates were substantial structures that resembled arches, while others were little more than doors allowing only foot traffic to pass. By Shakespeare's time the walls were no longer used to defend the City from attack, but the tradition of closing the main gates at night continued. The other entrance to the City was across the river. Only one bridge, the famed London Bridge, connected the City to the bustling suburbs of Southwark and Bankside across the Thames to the south.

Within the walls of the City stood notable buildings, such as the Tower of London (an ancient fortress), the Inns of Court (the residence of lawyers), the guildhalls (offices of tradesmen and merchants), St. Paul's Cathedral, and several government buildings. St. Paul's evolved from serving simply as the home of the Church of England into the City's social center. There Londoners exchanged news and gossip, conducted business, looked for work, and began an evening's revelry. City officials complained

Cities, Towns, and Villages

Shakespeare's birthplace, Stratford-upon-Avon, was one of the many towns in Elizabethan England that were closely tied to the surrounding farmlands. Stratford held a market for local farmers every Thursday, bringing many visitors from the countryside to the town.

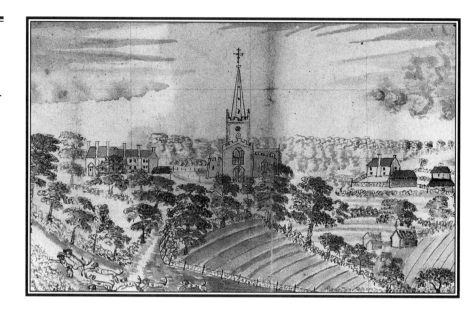

* *guild* association of craft and trade workers that set standards for and represented the interests of its members

that such activities were inappropriate for a place of worship, so they sometimes tried to restrict or remove them to another location. But custom overrode the law, and St. Paul's remained a popular meeting place.

The commercial trade of London was managed by 12 great guilds*, and the regulations they imposed gave their members a measure of unity and common purpose. This led them to concentrate their business operations in a particular area. The City's business districts were roughly arranged according to the types of merchandise or service available in each. Fresh fish, for example, were usually sold on Bridge Street, where a gate allowed ready access to the Thames. Other locales, such as Shoe Lane, also had names that announced their wares to potential customers. The groupings were not absolute, however, and less specialized markets developed on the wider streets and on London Bridge.

Merchants and tradesmen formed a newly prosperous urban class. The concentration of people in London and the need for new services also created opportunities for the development of a thriving middle class, not previously seen in smaller towns or villages. Merchants could own or rent the buildings in which their shops were located. Business was conducted on the ground floor while merchants and their families lived upstairs. If a building was large, the family that occupied it might also offer rooms to boarders. This combination of trade and home life produced the crowding and noise that made London so remarkable. Some buildings rose as high as five or six stories, but most reached only two or three. The narrow, crooked streets, a legacy of medieval* foot-paths, seemed even narrower because many upper stories overhung the street. This practice provided more room for housing, but it cast permanent shadows over the streets. Space was precious in the crowded city, so rooms were often divided into smaller spaces. Shanties* were even built between the buttresses* of St. Paul's Cathedral.

Most streets could accommodate only foot traffic. The coach, a recent innovation at the time, was restricted to wider streets and main

* *medieval* referring to the Middle Ages, a period roughly between A.D. 500 and 1500

* *shanty* small, poorly built shelter
* *buttress* stone or wood structure that supports the outer wall of a building

roads. Water travel was often easier than trying to maneuver through the teeming, muddy lanes of the City. Boat drivers, known as watermen, served as the taxi drivers of the day, moving passengers around town on the Thames. Unlike the coaches, which served only the wealthy, water taxis catered to all levels of society.

Outside the walls of the City lay the suburbs, where more room was available for development. Some suburbs contained aristocratic mansions and rural retreats. In Shakespeare's time the site of what is now Hyde Park was a royal hunting preserve noted for its herds of deer. Whitehall Palace, the chief royal residence, stood west of the City walls. Other suburbs were less elegant. South of the Thames, in Bankside and Southwark, undesirable businesses were found. Slaughterhouses and tanneries, banished from the City for health reasons, were welcome in these suburbs. Suburbanites could use thatch for roofs (forbidden in the City for reasons of fire safety), establish public theaters, operate brothels, and stage bearbaitings* and cockfights. Since they were beyond the reach of city officials, the suburbs became havens for criminals, the unemployed, the sick, and other social outcasts. Many Londoners viewed the suburbs with fear and contempt, considering them places of crime, violence, and disease. For this reason, Elizabethan literature frequently used the word *suburb* with derision, implying not only distance from the center of town but also shabbiness and squalor.

In general, London's City was not a crowded, filthy, or disease-ridden place during the time of Shakespeare. Elizabethans were very conscious of personal cleanliness, the City was still a relatively green place with numerous parks, and violence was rare. Elizabethan residents of London seem to have been healthier than previous generations of Londoners. According to historical records, they were taller and weighed more. Even though there were threats from foreign nations, England was at peace at home, and this tranquility allowed the nation and its chief city to grow and prosper.

LIFE IN THE TOWNS. As the population increased and trade expanded, towns across England grew. Towns usually developed along rivers or at the intersections of heavily traveled roads. Most towns included a parish church, a marketplace, a manor house, a municipal hall, a tavern, a schoolhouse, and a mill, which was used for grinding wheat. There were three types of towns. Regional capitals, such as York, Bristol, and Norwich, eventually became major cities. Next were the towns that became county government and market centers. Leicester, Manchester, Worchester, and Reading were examples of these regional centers. They might have been home to as many as 600 families. Finally, there were smaller towns, which were not administrative centers and which usually housed no more than 200 families. STRATFORD-UPON-AVON, Stamford, and Bridgewater were examples of these smaller towns. They retained a rural look and character, with trees, large gardens, orchards, barns, and stables within their borders.

Towns remained connected with the surrounding countryside. Many townspeople still owned lands and homes in the country, and even more were immigrants from rural areas. Towns of any size exerted a powerful influence on the surrounding region. They served as markets for agricultural

* *bearbaiting* Elizabethan spectator sport in which dogs were encouraged to attack a chained bear

THE PLAGUE: LONDON IN CRISIS

In the mid-1300s, London lost almost a third of its population to a severe outbreak of disease known as the Black Death, or plague. Serious outbreaks of the plague occurred several times during Shakespeare's lifetime, and London was never totally free from the disease, especially in the summer. Two main types of plague struck the City. The pneumonic form affected the lungs and swiftly killed all its victims. The more common bubonic form produced swelling in the lymph glands. Patients sometimes recovered from bubonic plague. When it struck, victims were quarantined, and public places, such as theaters, were closed to prevent the disease from spreading.

goods grown by farmers in the countryside. They also became convenient locations for small industries and schools. Large towns created enormous demands for fuel, water, and building materials, which were provided by suppliers in the countryside. Specialized production in certain regions—coal in the north, steel in Sheffield, woven goods in Norfolk—also worked to merge the rural economy with that of the nearby towns and cities.

The essential link between town and country was the roads. It is often assumed that the roads of this period were in terrible condition, but in fact roads generally held up well—although conditions did vary widely, since road maintenance was a local responsibility. Many parts of an excellent road system devised by the Romans still existed. The roads had been built primarily for people traveling on foot, for driving livestock to market, and for carts and wagons. Heavy loads—coal, timber, and ore—were usually shipped by barge or boat on a network of natural waterways.

The roads were reasonably safe. Weather and muddy conditions were the primary concerns of travelers. For most of the year, travel between town and country was easy, constant, and uninterrupted.

THE VILLAGE. The vast majority of people lived in small villages, groups of households clustered around a parish church or manor house. Most of the items people needed were made nearby, and a typical village included a blacksmith, a bakery, and a brewery. Life in the villages followed time-honored customs and was slower-paced than the bustle of the cities and towns. People rose early to work in the fields and went to sleep when the sun set. Farming was the chief occupation of villagers, and most were tenant farmers who rented their lands from the lord of a manor. AGRICULTURE was undergoing a series of transitions, including a change from raising grain to pasturing animals, such as sheep. Other changes included specialized farming—the raising of one kind of crop rather than a variety of crops. These changes sometimes put farmers out of work. Many of those who became unemployed joined the multitudes migrating to the towns and cities in search of a better life. (*See also* **Country Life; Guilds; Transportation and Travel**.)

CLASS

See *Social Classes.*

CLOTHING

In the Elizabethan era, clothing was a sign of status. Members of the upper classes dressed in costly and elaborate garments, displaying their wealth with rich fabrics and excessive decoration. Members of the lower classes were expected to dress more plainly, but many attempted to copy the clothing of the rich, often spending more than they

An Elizabethan lady of fashion made her waist appear smaller by wearing a tight corset and holding her skirts out from her body with an elaborate undergarment called a farthingale. A woman of lower social class might pad her skirts with a stuffed tube of fabric called a bum roll.

* *medieval* referring to the Middle Ages, a period roughly between A.D. 500 and 1500
* *genitals* external reproductive organs

* *bran* edible outer coating of cereal grain

could afford to appear stylish. The government repeatedly passed laws attempting to prevent people from dressing "above their station," but these laws were widely ignored. Many religious leaders of the time criticized their fellow Elizabethans, particularly those of low social rank, for their absurdly showy dress.

CLOTHING FOR MEN. Since the late medieval* period, men's clothing in England had consisted of three basic garments. The doublet was a short, close-fitting jacket, usually worn over an undershirt. A slightly longer outer jacket called a jerkin was generally worn over the doublet, and tight-fitting trousers called hose completed the outfit. These various garments were held together with points—ties fastened onto eyelets.

Until about 1500, these three garments were all fairly simple. During the reign of HENRY VIII, the influence of German fashion caused men's clothing to become more elaborate. Sleeves grew wider and puffier and were often slashed, meaning that small slits were cut in the fabric to expose the layer below. Jerkins developed longer skirts and heavily padded shoulders, and the doublet and jerkin were both heavily pleated. While a medieval jerkin had required only two yards of fabric to make, a pleated jerkin with skirt might require seven or eight yards. The doublet and jerkin opened in the front to display a codpiece, a decorated pouch that encased the man's genitals*. Codpieces were often so large that they could be used to carry money or store pieces of food.

As men's garments became more elaborate, they began to split into interchangeable parts attached with points. Sleeves were detachable, so that a single pair could be worn with many different doublets. The skirt of the jerkin also became detachable, and men's hose became more complex. Instead of one garment, they consisted of a pair of short trunks, called upper stocks or breeches, and a pair of nether stocks worn on the lower part of the leg. Sometimes an additional pair of hose called canions, which resembled modern cycling shorts, was worn between the breeches and stockings. These numerous pieces made getting dressed a very time-consuming process. Having clothing composed of separate parts made it possible for wearers to combine colors and fabrics, and it was not unusual to see an Elizabethan dressed in many different and unmatched materials.

The Spanish style, introduced in the 1550s, modified the slashed and broad-shouldered look with a tightened waist and a stiff torso. The waistline was lowered to make it appear narrower, and the doublet was stiffened with layers of quilting or buckram—sheets of linen dipped in glue. Breeches and sleeves were heavily padded to create a puffy appearance. This padding, known as bombast, was usually cotton but might be made of wool, horsehair, or even bran*. Bombast-stuffed trunks became so large that they were known as "Spanish kettledrums." The Houses of Parliament actually had to construct special seats to accommodate these huge breeches.

Completing the look was a high, stiff collar, known as a ruff, that held the chin aloft at a haughty angle. Starch, introduced from Holland in 1564, was used to create stiff ruffles in a series of figure eights around

Clothing

ELIZABETHAN ACCESSORIES

Elizabethan aristocrats wore numerous accessories to match the splendor of their garments. Gentlemen wore shoes with pointed toes, carried fancy handkerchiefs, and covered themselves in jewels. Hats ranged from flat velvet caps to tall, stiff cylinders. Ladies wore soft, high-heeled shoes, belts known as girdles, and hats that might be similar to men's or simple squares of cloth or lace. They also wore large amounts of jewelry and carried such items as a mask, mirror, and fan, often attached to the girdle for easy carrying. They wore elaborate hairstyles and made up their faces with lead-based cosmetics, which were not known at the time to be poisonous.

the neck. The ruff might extend out more than a foot, and it often had to be wired into place. Another new development was knitted silk hose or stockings, which had a smooth, skin-tight fit, unlike the earlier hose, which had tended to bag around the knees and ankles. Codpieces became less prominent and disappeared altogether by 1600.

CLOTHING FOR WOMEN. Women's fashions, like men's, were fairly simple until about 1500. A simple undergarment called a shift or chemise was topped with a snug-fitting kirtle, or underdress, and an outer gown that fit tightly to the waist and fell in loose folds below. The German styles of the early 1500s influenced women's clothing less than men's, but gowns did become heavier and more layered, using much more material. Skirts became fuller, and sleeves grew so ample they sometimes reached the ground. The outer gown often opened in front to reveal the kirtle, and the bodice was cut low to expose the chemise.

While gowns became larger and fuller, headgear grew smaller. Large pointed or padded headpieces changed over time to a simple hood worn well back on the head, allowing a lady of fashion to show off her hair. Meanwhile women's clothing, like men's, began to split into separate pieces. The kirtle separated into a skirt and a bodice. The bodice, like the doublet, developed detachable sleeves, and the front part of the bodice eventually became a separate stomacher, which was worn underneath the bodice, showing through the laces.

Spanish styles affected women's clothing as well as men's. Both sexes wore high ruffs, padded shoulders, and tight corsets to make the waist narrower. As the century progressed, the stomacher became a more rigid garment worn outside the bodice to produce a narrow, pointed waist. Women's skirts also grew immensely wide, held out with large fabric-draped hoops called farthingales. Spanish farthingales gave a bell-like shape to the skirts, while French farthingales, or "catherine wheels," were drum-shaped. Those who could not afford a farthingale might pad their skirts with a bum roll, a sausage-shaped tube of padding worn around the hips. The kirtle—which in the mid-1500s referred to a skirt rather than an entire dress—was hung over the farthingale.

Atop the kirtle went a heavy gown, usually open below the waist to expose the underdress, with attached sleeves. The bodice of the gown was often cut low, requiring the high ruff to be open in the front and set off with "butterfly wings" of stiff gauze behind the head. The low neckline might be filled in with a piece of sheer material called a partlet. An Elizabethan gown could require between 17 and 30 yards of fabric and might cost as much as 13 pounds—at a time when it was possible to survive on 3 or 4 pounds a year.

SUMPTUARY LAWS. The elaborate fashions described above were worn mostly by the ARISTOCRACY. By wearing extremely fancy outfits, they proclaimed to the world that they were not required to work for a living and had servants to help them dress. Likewise, the plainer clothing of the middle classes and peasants advertised their social status. The ruff, for instance, could only be worn by gentry*. Different colors were also

* *gentry* people of high birth or social status

associated with different classes. Blue was often worn by the servant class, while only royalty was permitted to wear deep red.

However, as England grew more prosperous, those who could afford fine clothing—and some who could not—began to copy the dress of the nobility. It was no longer possible to identify a person's SOCIAL CLASS by his or her dress. Sumptuary laws, which placed restrictions on the clothing that could be worn by people of a particular class, were designed to address this problem. They also served the purpose of protecting the English economy. Those who spent more than they could afford for clothing might run through all their money and become bankrupt. Also, many fancy fabrics and styles were imported from abroad, and as more people chose to wear them the English clothing industry suffered.

See color plate 1, vol. 3.

The English government had attempted many times to regulate clothing, but the strictest sumptuary laws ever passed were those enacted by Queen Elizabeth's privy council* in October 1559. These laws stated that only noblemen of the rank of earl or higher could wear "cloth of gold, silver or tinsel," silk, or sable*. Other furs, woolen cloth not made in England, and velvet of crimson, scarlet, and blue were limited to those of the rank of knight or higher, as was the use of silk in hats, bonnets, nightcaps, belts, hose, or shoes. Embroidery of any sort could be worn by the nobility or by a gentleman with an income of 200 pounds a year or more.

* **Privy Council** body of advisers serving an English monarch

* **sable** mammal of the weasel family found chiefly in northern Asia and prized for its luxurious black fur

To enforce these regulations, the council ordered all the lords and masters within the City of London to examine the clothing of their servants and apprentices and to take away any unlawful clothing. An exception was made for those too poor to replace the forbidden garments; they were permitted to keep the clothes until they wore out. Sumptuary laws passed in 1597 dealt with the problems of servants wearing their masters' cast-off clothing. Despite this strict legislation, however, the middle and lower classes continued to violate the codes of dress. Soon after Elizabeth's death, Parliament repealed all of the sumptuary laws. (*See also* **Coins and Currency; Costumes; Craftworkers; Government and Politics.**)

COINS AND CURRENCY

* **mint** to make coins by shaping and stamping metal; also the place where coins are made

In Elizabethan England, money consisted of coins, which came in a wide variety of sizes and denominations. Paper money was nonexistent. The pound (£) was the standard unit of exchange, although no coin called a pound actually existed during Shakespeare's time. Instead, the pound was a measure of weight that was used to represent a sum of money—20 shillings or 240 pence. Coins were minted* in silver and gold, the latter being the more valuable.

Sovereigns were impressive gold pieces, worth a little over a pound (which would have been about $400 worth of purchasing power today), or a pound and a half for an extra large sovereign. Other gold coins included royals (worth about 10 to 14 shillings), angels (worth about 7 to 10 shillings), and nobles (similar in value to angels). Angels and nobles

Coins and Currency

are the gold coins most often mentioned in Shakespeare's works. In *King John*, for example, the King describes his plan to seize money from the monasteries as setting "imprisoned angels . . . at liberty."

Silver coins included crowns (worth one-quarter pound, or five shillings), half-crowns, shillings, sixpences (half a shilling), and an astounding number of smaller coins, the smallest of which was a farthing (a fourth of a penny). A farthing (the size of a shirt button) was actually too small to be minted. To buy an item that cost a farthing, one paid with a penny and received a three-farthing piece in change.

Any attempt to translate Elizabethan wages and prices into modern equivalents would be complicated by factors such as inflation and the variable prices charged for goods and services. However, in broad terms, a live chicken cost a penny, as did a loaf of bread or a pint of ale. A pig was priced at a shilling, and a cow cost a pound. An unskilled laborer earned five or six pence per day, or about seven pounds per year.

An actor earned roughly ten shillings per week. This does not, however, translate into an annual income of £25, since stage work was seasonal. Admission to the theater cost a penny for standing room in an outdoor amphitheater, while a seat in the gallery cost another penny. A printed copy of a play sold for sixpence. Playwrights usually received £5 or £6 for a script; some, such as Shakespeare, also earned a percentage of the profits from performances. Records show that Shakespeare, who had become a wealthy man, paid £60 in silver for the home in STRATFORD-UPON-AVON to which he retired. (*See also* **Banking and Commerce.**)

Paper money did not exist in Shakespeare's day. Coins, the only form of currency, were minted by stamping gold or silver disks of various sizes and weights with the monarch's face.

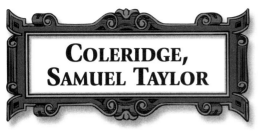

COLERIDGE, SAMUEL TAYLOR

1772–1834
Poet and literary critic

* *ambiguous* unclear; able to be interpreted in more than one way
* *Romantic* referring to a school of thought, prominent in the 1800s, that emphasized the importance of emotion in art
* *protagonist* central character in a dramatic or literary work

* *classical* in the tradition of ancient Greece and Rome

Although best known as the poet who wrote "Kubla Khan" and "Rime of the Ancient Mariner," Samuel Taylor Coleridge was also one of the most significant literary critics of his time. Coleridge's interpretations of Shakespeare's plays marked a turning point in the field of Shakespearean criticism. While previous critics had tended to interpret Shakespeare's more complex and ambiguous* plays as artistically flawed, Coleridge and other Romantic* critics saw these plays as "problems" for the audience to unravel. Coleridge emphasized Shakespeare's superior skill in blending different parts together to form a whole.

Many of Coleridge's ideas were inspired by the work of the German critic and philosopher August Wilhelm von Schlegel, which he had studied in Germany. Schlegel, like many critics of his time, focused on the characters in Shakespeare's plays. He noted that the playwright's protagonists* often have subtle faults and motives that they do not recognize in themselves. He also observed that the plots of some plays do not point clearly to a single interpretation but can be viewed in many different ways. Schlegel attacked the view that such complications indicate a lack of unity. Instead, he suggested that the unity of the plays stems from their ability to combine and reconcile seemingly contradictory elements.

Coleridge built on Schlegel's ideas with the concept of "organic regularity." Plays in the classical* tradition had what he called "mechanical regularity." They conformed to Aristotle's idea that the location, time, and action of a play should be continuous. Many critics had found fault with Shakespeare for violating Aristotle's rules. *The Winter's Tale,* for example, contains a 16-year gap in its story line. Coleridge believed that Shakespeare's plays held together despite their disjointed action because they were guided by an internal structure that he described as "organic," or natural. To him, the plays did not seem like artificial constructions, but like natural objects that grow according to their "essential principle."

Coleridge's criticism was also significant because it explored Shakespeare's use of POETIC TECHNIQUE as well as the plays' DRAMATIC TECHNIQUES. He argued that the plays appeal to the imagination, which he defined as the ability to break down barriers of time and space and create a balance between opposing forces. Even "unrealistic" acts within the plays, such as the enchantments cast by fairies in *A Midsummer Night's Dream,* can be perceived as essentially believable in the realm of the imagination.

Very little of Coleridge's Shakespearean criticism was published while he was alive. The first collection of his ideas about Shakespeare was Thomas Ashe's 1883 volume, *Coleridge's Lectures and Notes on Shakespeare and Other English Poets.* This publication based most of its content on listeners' notes from a series of lectures Coleridge gave between 1808 and 1819. A later volume, published by Coleridge's nephew, was based on fragments of Coleridge's lecture notes and on comments he had scribbled in the margins of books. Since 1930, the definitive edition of Coleridge's views on Shakespeare has been *Coleridge's Shakespearean Criticism,* by T. M. Raysor, which contained Coleridge's own words from his original lectures. A more recent edition, *Coleridge's Criticism of Shakespeare* (edited by R. A. Foakes), was published in 1989. (*See also* **Literature Inspired by Shakespeare; Shakespeare's Works, Changing Views.**)

COLONIALISM

See *Exploration; Tempest, The.*

COMEDIES, THE

See *Humor in Shakespeare's Plays; Plays: The Comedies.*

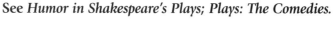

COMEDY OF ERRORS, THE

One of Shakespeare's earliest plays, *The Comedy of Errors* is possibly his first comedy. The plot centers on the confusion and chaos that result when a pair of long-separated twin brothers, both named Antipholus, find themselves in the same city—together with their servants, who are also twin brothers and who are both named Dromio. *The Comedy of Errors* is largely a farce—a silly, slapstick comedy featuring exaggerated characters and far-fetched situations. Even so, it displays Shakespeare's early control over the comedic form and his developing interest in the inner lives of his characters.

PLOT SUMMARY. The play is set in the city of Ephesus, which forbids entrance to people from the nearby city of Syracuse. Act I begins with a story told by Aegeon, a Syracusan merchant who has been captured in Ephesus while seeking his long-lost son. He explains to the duke of Ephesus that he and his wife once had identical twin sons and purchased another pair of identical twin boys as slaves for their sons. Unfortunately, during a stormy sea voyage with his family, Aegeon was separated from his wife, one of his sons, and one of the slaves. He raised the other two boys in Syracuse, but he has not seen either of them for several years. Moved by this sad tale, the duke gives Aegeon one day to raise the large sum of money he will require to buy his freedom.

See color plate 10, vol. 2.

The next scene presents Antipholus of Syracuse—the son raised by Aegeon—in the streets of Ephesus, looking for his lost twin. He orders his servant Dromio to return to their inn and guard their money. Soon Dromio enters the scene—not Antipholus's slave, but his twin, Dromio of Ephesus. Dromio believes that Antipholus of Syracuse is his own master and tries to persuade him to come home to dinner. Antipholus asks about his money, but Dromio claims that he never received it; he then flees an angry Antipholus's blows. Antipholus ponders this behavior, recalling that Ephesus has a reputation as a city of thieves and witches.

Act II opens in the house of the other son, Antipholus of Ephesus. His wife Adriana and her sister Luciana are at home when Dromio of Ephesus enters and describes his alarming encounter with Antipholus. Suspecting her husband is with another woman, Adriana orders Dromio to bring Antipholus home. Meanwhile, Dromio of Syracuse returns to Antipholus of Syracuse, who scolds him for claiming ignorance about the money. The puzzled Dromio denies any knowledge of the incident. Adriana and Luciana then appear, thinking they have found Adriana's husband. Antipholus of Syracuse is naturally surprised, but he decides to go home with them in order to learn more.

In Act III, Antipholus of Ephesus arrives at his home with his servant Dromio and two friends, a merchant and a goldsmith. Since the twins from Syracuse have already entered the house, the Ephesians are turned away from the gate as impostors. Furious, Antipholus of Ephesus storms off, vowing to visit a well-known courtesan* and to give her a gold necklace that Angelo the goldsmith will soon have ready.

Inside the house, Antipholus of Syracuse has fallen in love with Adriana's sister Luciana, who is understandably shocked by the behavior of the man she believes to be her sister's husband. Dromio of Syracuse, meanwhile, is alarmed to learn that an ugly kitchen maid named Nell thinks he is her husband. The two Syracusans decide to leave, convinced that they are surrounded by witches. Before they depart, Angelo arrives and delivers the gold necklace to the wrong Antipholus.

The confusion mounts throughout Act IV. A merchant comes to Angelo and demands the money he is owed. Angelo promises to bring it as soon as Antipholus pays for the necklace. Antipholus of Ephesus appears on the scene with Dromio of Ephesus, sending the servant to buy a rope, with which he intends to beat his wife for locking him out of his house. Dromio departs, and Antipholus approaches Angelo, complaining that he has not received the necklace. An argument results, and the merchant has Antipholus arrested.

At this point Dromio of Syracuse enters, mistakes Antipholus of Ephesus for his master, and reports that he has found a ship that will take them away. Baffled and angry, Antipholus orders Dromio to return home and get money for bail. Dromio, although confused, returns to the house and receives money from Adriana and Luciana. He then returns to the town square and sees Antipholus of Syracuse, who is wearing the necklace given to him by Angelo. Dromio reports that he has

* *courtesan* prostitute associated with wealthy men or men in attendance at a royal court

A Royal Shakespeare Company production of *The Comedy of Errors* in 1983 exaggerated the play's absurd nature by dressing the actors in clown costumes.

* *priory* religious house

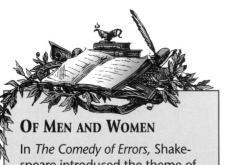

OF MEN AND WOMEN

In *The Comedy of Errors,* Shakespeare introduced the theme of romance that was missing from his classical Roman source. In traditional Roman culture, marriage was not seen as a romantic attachment and the faithlessness of husbands was often tolerated. Thus Adriana's anger and jealousy were seen as merely signs of her bad temper. But in Shakespeare's version, her anger comes from her independent spirit and her jealousy from her genuine love for her husband. By inventing Adriana's sister as a love interest for Antipholus of Syracuse, Shakespeare also added a poetic note that is absent in the Roman play.

obtained the bail money, but Antipholus has no idea what his servant means. Into this confusion walks the courtesan, who asks for the necklace she has been promised. Thoroughly annoyed, Antipholus of Syracuse curses the courtesan, whom he has never seen before. She decides to visit Adriana and tell her that her husband has gone mad.

Meanwhile, Antipholus of Ephesus remains under arrest. Dromio of Ephesus returns with the requested rope, but his master angrily demands the bail money that Dromio of Syracuse was sent for. While Dromio protests, Adriana arrives with Luciana, the courtesan, and a doctor named Pinch. Adriana hires Pinch to heal her husband's madness, so the doctor takes the furious Antipholus and Dromio away to their home. After the men leave, Antipholus and Dromio of Syracuse enter. The women run away, assuming that the men have broken free of Pinch and have returned to punish them.

Act V opens with Angelo and the merchant on the street next to a priory*. Antipholus and Dromio of Syracuse arrive, and Angelo sees the necklace around Antipholus's neck. Angelo accuses Antipholus of lying about not receiving the necklace. They have drawn their swords to fight when Adriana appears, together with Luciana and the courtesan. She pleads with the men to help her bring her husband home to be treated for his madness. The Syracusans seek refuge inside the priory.

As the others stand disappointed outside the priory, the duke of Ephesus passes by with Aegeon, who has been sentenced to death for his presence in Ephesus. Antipholus and Dromio of Ephesus soon happen upon the crowd as well, having escaped the treatments of Pinch. Accusations fly as the Ephesians, the women, the goldsmith, and the merchant bombard the duke with appeals for justice. Aegeon pleads with Antipholus of Ephesus to pay his ransom, but Antipholus crushes the old man by insisting that they have never met.

Bewildered by the contradictory claims, the duke asks the Abbess—the woman who runs the priory—for an explanation. The Abbess emerges from the priory with Antipholus and Dromio of Syracuse, suddenly bringing the two sets of twins together. As the assembled crowd absorbs this shock, the Abbess herself recognizes Aegeon as her husband and reveals that she is Aemilia, the wife he lost at sea so many years ago. The duke promptly grants Aegeon his freedom and the group enters the priory to celebrate this joyous reunion.

SOURCES AND HISTORY. Shakespeare's play is based largely on *The Menaechmi,* a play by the ancient Roman author Plautus. This source, written in Latin, is more simply constructed than *The Comedy of Errors;* it contains only one set of twins, the two Antipholuses. Shakespeare may have taken the idea of two sets of twins from *Amphitryon,* another play by Plautus. Shakespeare also added the opening story of Aegeon, which he probably borrowed from more recent plays of the Middle Ages and the Renaissance.

The Comedy of Errors was first performed on December 28, 1594, at Gray's Inn in London, to an audience of law students and their companions. Ten years later, the play was received at the royal court. In the 1700s and 1800s, it became a staple of British theater, and directors frequently

took liberties with the script. In the 1900s, the play was sometimes staged as an opera or musical. A 1976 film version directed by Trevor Nunn starred Judi Dench as Adriana, and several productions have aired on television.

COMMENTARY. *The Comedy of Errors* is often considered an "apprentice work," lacking the greatness of Shakespeare's later efforts. The characters and dialogue are unsophisticated, and the plot does not stray far from the dramatic conventions* of Shakespeare's time. Still, most critics acknowledge that Shakespeare moved beyond the previous limits of the genre* in several ways. By adding the second set of twins, the story of Aegeon, and the love affair between Antipholus of Syracuse and Luciana, Shakespeare not only gave the play a higher degree of comic possibility, but also added elements of tragedy and romance. While most of the action involves the broad comedy of mistaken identities and crude beatings, many of the longer speeches give insight into the characters' turbulent emotions—particularly their sense that their identities remain incomplete without the lost members of their families. The play also addresses the characters' roles within society as they relate to their spouses, their ruler, and the law. Even within the confines of a simple dramatic form, the young Shakespeare had begun to develop the themes that he would later explore in his greatest works. (*See also* **Humor in Shakespeare's Plays; Plays: The Comedies; Shakespeare's Works, Adaptations of.**)

* *convention* established practice
* *genre* literary form

CORDELIA

Cordelia is the youngest daughter of King Lear. Although her role and influence in the play are profound, she appears only briefly on the stage. In the play's first scene, her father banishes her from his kingdom for refusing to declare her absolute devotion to him. Some critics see her actions in this scene as stubborn, cold, and proud. When she reappears in later scenes, however, Cordelia proves her sincere loyalty and love for her father, sacrificing herself to support him after he is rejected by her treacherous sisters, Regan and Goneril.

In the love-contest that opens the play, Cordelia declares that she cannot honestly promise all her love to her father, because she knows that she will marry someday and pledge her love to her husband. Mistakenly regarding Cordelia's disobedience as a lack of affection, Lear disinherits her. She then leaves Britain to marry the king of France, who recognizes her true virtues. After Regan and Goneril banish Lear to wander in the wilderness, Cordelia returns with an army, intent on reclaiming the crown for her father. Reunited, Cordelia and Lear are defeated in battle and imprisoned by Edmund, the ambitious scoundrel who has been scheming to capture the throne. Cordelia and Lear are sentenced to death. Edmund is defeated by the faithful Edgar, who had accompanied Lear into the wilderness, but not before Cordelia is killed by an assassin. Lear avenges his daughter's death by slaying her executioner, and in the final scene, grieving over her body, he dies of a broken heart.

Coriolanus

The death of the innocent Cordelia is one of the most tragic moments in Shakespearean drama. This 19th-century engraving shows King Lear grieving over his daughter's lifeless body.

Some critics view Cordelia as rigid and unfeeling when she refuses to do her father's bidding at the beginning of the play. Others regard her honesty as a sign of her strength of character. However the reader chooses to interpret Cordelia, her steadfast loyalty is a major element of the play. (*See also* **Bowdler, Thomas; King Lear; Plays: The Tragedies; Shakespeare's Works, Adaptations of.**)

CORIOLANUS

* *patrician* member of the upper class who traced his ancestry to a senatorial family in the earliest days of the Roman Republic
* *plebeian* member of the general body of Roman citizens, as distinct from the upper class
* *tribune* ancient Roman political leader who represented the interests of the common people

The central character of *Coriolanus* is a patrician* Roman general, Caius Martius, whose excessive pride, explosive temper, and contempt for the plebeians* causes his destruction. As the tragedy begins, Martius angers the plebeians by refusing to distribute free grain during a famine. After defeating the Volscians—Rome's enemies—near their capital Corioli, Martius earns the name Coriolanus. His victory helps regain the people's favor, and with some hesitation they support his election to consul—the highest office in Rome. Before the vote is final, however, the tribunes* convince the plebeians to withdraw their approval by reminding them that Coriolanus has always been an enemy of the common people. Coriolanus becomes angry and declares that the plebeians are unfit to choose Rome's leaders. He is later forced to apologize, but when a tribune calls him a traitor, he becomes enraged and again insults the plebeians. After the tribunes exile him, he joins the Volscians and attacks Rome. The tribunes and patricians plead with him to spare the city, but he refuses until his mother appeals to him to make peace. Unable to deny her, Coriolanus negotiates a treaty that saves his native city. In revenge for what he sees as a betrayal, Tullus Aufidius, the leader of the Volscians, incites a mob of his followers to kill Coriolanus.

68

In this 1972 production by the Royal Shakespeare Company, Coriolanus (Nicol Williamson) confers with his friend Menenius (Mark Dignam) and the members of the Roman Senate.

See color plate 5, vol. 3.

The two main themes of the play are the destructive consequences of Coriolanus's pride in his noble birth and military skill and his contempt for the common people. Coriolanus is a brave warrior, but his arrogance and quick temper make him easy to manipulate. The tribunes purposely infuriate him in order to turn the plebeians against him and increase their own political power. Coriolanus's anger and scorn lead to his exile and eventually to his death.

Scholars believe that Shakespeare wrote *Coriolanus* around 1609. The play is based on a tale in PLUTARCH'S LIVES, a collection of biographies about ancient leaders. Additional elements of the play were inspired by events during Shakespeare's time. In 1607, English landowners converted huge areas of farmland into pastureland for sheep, resulting in a food shortage that led to riots by the poor. This situation parallels the famine that causes the plebeians to riot at the beginning of the play.

Until relatively recently, *Coriolanus* was not particularly popular. The first known production of the play was staged in 1681 and even that was not the original play but an adaptation. The play's tale of conflict between rich and poor made it popular during the early 1900s, when communist* countries, such as Russia, competed for power with capitalist* countries such as the United States. (*See also* **History in Shakespeare's Plays: Ancient Greece and Rome; Marxist Interpretations; Shakespeare's Works, Adaptations of; Social Classes.**)

* *communist* referring to an economic system in which the state owns all property and all goods are shared equally among the people
* *capitalist* referring to an economic system in which individuals own property

COSTUMES

The Elizabethan word for costumes was *apparel,* and it occurs often in theatrical documents. Apparel—the clothes actors wore on stage—was rich, showy, and expensive, a vital feature of staging when the set contained little but bare boards. People paid to see display; actors were the fashion models of the 1500s.

Costumes

An Elizabethan ACTING COMPANY invested substantial funds in its apparel. An inventory in actor Edward Alleyn's handwriting lists the costumes belonging to the Admiral's Men—83 items in all, including "Clokes," "Gownes," "Jerkings and doublets" (two types of jackets), "frenchose" and "venetians" (two types of hose, or tight-fitting trousers), and "antik sutes" (gaudy or showy outfits). An actor's share in the company's apparel was valued at about £200 in an age when an ordinary working man might earn £5 a year. English sumptuary laws, which determined what clothing was permissible for a person of a given rank to wear, aided the companies in obtaining costumes. A Swiss traveler noted in 1599 that

> it is the English usage for eminent lords or knights at their decease to bequeath and leave almost the best of their clothes to their serving men, which it is unseemly for the latter to wear, so that they offer them for sale for a small sum to the actors.

As POLONIUS says in *Hamlet*, "the apparel oft proclaims the man" (I.iii.72), and the primary function of Elizabethan costume was to identify a character's social rank and occupation. The quality and price of the garments was an indicator of rank, at least in theory; many Elizabethans, including Puritans*, complained that people often dressed above their station. Scholars know from woodcuts and other illustrations what certain stage types looked like. An academic, such as Christopher MARLOWE's Doctor Faustus, wore a long gown and a cap and held a book. A gentleman wore a ruff*, a lady an expensive farthingale*, and a soldier carried a sword. The play *The Roaring Girl*, based on the life of a London woman named Mary Frith (also known as Moll Cutpurse) who habitually dressed in men's clothing, showed the heroine's masculine character by having her smoke a pipe on stage.

The use of costume as a symbolic indicator of type extended to color. Purple costumes were for the rich and powerful, tan or navy blue for servants. Queens and courtesans* wore aquamarine, a bluish green. Color might signify a character's emotional state as well as social rank. The color black went with death and white with innocence; the lovelorn often appeared in willow green, a grayish-green shade. One intriguing use of color in the Elizabethan theater is a garment listed in theater manager Philip HENSLOWE's records: "a robe for to goo invisibell," perhaps black.

Elizabethan actors did not seek historical accuracy in costume. In *Julius Caesar,* for example, the character of Casca says that Caesar "plucked me ope his doublet" (I.ii.265), an Elizabethan garment rather than an ancient Roman one. A drawing created by Henry Peacham in 1595 is the best source of information for modern scholars about Elizabethan costume styles. It appears to be the artist's impression of a performance of *Titus Andronicus.* The costumes shown are a combination of the styles of the play's ancient Roman setting and those of the Elizabethan era, with a few Oriental touches added to the costumes of such characters as Tamora, Queen of the Goths. Based on this drawing, it appears that the Elizabethans were unconcerned about mixing contemporary, historical, and exotic styles. A few plays, however—such as John Webster's *The White*

* *Puritan* English Protestant who advocated strict moral discipline and a simplification of the ceremonies and beliefs of the Anglican Church

* *ruff* high, stiff collar worn by Elizabethan nobility
* *farthingale* large fabric-draped hoop worn by Elizabethan ladies to hold their skirts out from the body

* *courtesan* prostitute associated with wealthy men or men in attendance at a royal court

Devil (1612)—displayed a trend toward greater historical realism, which would eventually come to dominate stage costuming.

In the 1700s, the great Shakespearean actor David Garrick took costume blends to a higher level of sophistication. To make his characters appear more realistic to the public, he acted in "modern dress," adapting it to suit the character he was playing. His Romeo was simply a young Englishman of the times, while his Hamlet wore a French suit of the latest fashion. Creases became important costume features. When Garrick's Hamlet faced his father's ghost, he turned his back on the audience to display a diagonal crease from shoulder to hip, a fashion statement that delighted his fans. Costume was making great strides from the primitive showiness of Shakespeare's day.

The greatest advance toward historical accuracy came in the 1800s. The posters for Charles Kemble's 1823 production of *King John* declared that the play had been produced "With the attention to Costume Never equalled on the English Stage. Every character will appear in the precise HABIT OF THE PERIOD." The considerable effort and expense undertaken by costume designer J. R. Planché created a sensation, and the movement soon spread to other Shakespeare plays. All later producers had to acknowledge the role of "archaeology," as it became known, in stage presentations. The words *authentic* and *correct* became vital to the stage's sense of itself. It was also during this period—1883, to be exact—that the word *costume* was first used to refer specifically to theatrical garb.

This great tide of historical accuracy in stage productions gradually ebbed during the 1900s. Since World War II, four main styles of Shakespearean costuming have emerged. The first is the historical style, which aims to represent the particular period in which the play is set—such as

In Shakespeare's day actors typically dressed in Elizabethan clothing, with touches added to indicate their character types. A few plays called for specific, extravagant costume pieces, such as the donkey's head worn by Bottom in *A Midsummer Night's Dream.*

ancient Rome, the Middle Ages, or the Renaissance. This type of period authenticity has been largely channeled into film productions. A second approach is to use modern dress—for example, giving *The Two Gentlemen of Verona* a poolside setting. A third style is period analogue, which changes the historical period of the play and uses costumes and sets that reflect the new time period. Setting *Much Ado About Nothing* in the aftermath of the Spanish-American War (around 1898) or *Love's Labor's Lost* just before World War I (in 1914) is an example of this approach.

The dominant costume style today, however, appears to be a blend of costume periods, often called eclectic. Individual actors dress in different styles, allowing their characters to "inhabit" different time periods. Through such costuming choices, directors can make wide-ranging references, which tend to be held together by a dreamlike logic. In a production of *Antony and Cleopatra,* for example, Octavius might wear a long black Victorian* frock-coat while the other characters dress in a vaguely Roman style. By clothing this character in a different style, the director can indicate that Octavius dwells in a different universe.

At the same time, the extravagance of Shakespeare's day is still alive. Modern acting companies, such as the ROYAL SHAKESPEARE COMPANY, maintain expensive costume departments with large warehouses of costly silk and leather garments. Over time, the theater has kept in touch with the importance of costuming in creating an effect. The overall development of Shakespearean costumes shows a movement from the eclectic style of Shakespeare's day to a more historically accurate style and back again. (*See also* **Actors, Shakespearean; Art Inspired by Shakespeare; Clothing; Playwrights and Poets.**)

* *Victorian* referring to the reign of Victoria, queen of England from 1837 to 1901

COUNTRY LIFE

* *medieval* referring to the Middle Ages, a period roughly between A.D. 500 and 1500

England was still an overwhelmingly rural nation during Shakespeare's lifetime, with about eight of every ten people living in the countryside. Country life had changed little since medieval* times and was still influenced by the agricultural cycles of planting and harvesting. Far-reaching changes that would transform rural life in fundamental ways were occurring throughout the nation.

VILLAGE LIFE IN THE PAST. Almost all country people—men, women, and children—worked as farmers. For centuries, AGRICULTURE had been dominated by tenant farming, in which farmers paid rent by working a certain number of days each year for a nobleman. In exchange, the tenants received permission to cultivate a piece of the nobleman's land for their own use. On these small, scattered pieces of land, tenants were able to raise just enough cabbages, radishes, carrots, and pumpkins to feed their families. For better or worse, this agricultural system began to change when noblemen found ways of obtaining greater profits from their land.

CHANGES ARRIVE. For a time in Elizabethan England, people were paying a high price for wool. Realizing they could earn immense sums of

Grain was Elizabethan England's chief crop. All types of grain were ground into flour for making bread, but wheat flour was especially prized for the flavorful breads it produced.

WOMEN'S WORK

Elizabethan women who lived in the country faced the never-ending task of "keeping house." In addition to caring for their children, they gathered firewood, baked bread, milked cows, churned butter, tended to chickens, washed clothes, spun yarn, made candles, and prepared meals. Most items used in a household were homemade, and few were available for purchase. Many women also labored in the fields during planting and harvesting seasons.

money, many landowners decided to convert their farmland into pasture for raising sheep. First, however, they had to remove the tenants who occupied parts of the land. Landowners did this by raising rents, which drove many tenants off lands that they and their ancestors had farmed for centuries. As a result, the number of unemployed people roaming England's countryside soared. Many of the jobless migrated to towns and cities to search for work.

The loss of farmland to sheep breeding caused a decrease in the supply of food. At the same time, growing populations in towns and cities caused an increase in the demand for agricultural products. As a result, food prices rose. Realizing this, some landowners who had converted their cropland into grazing land for sheep decided to grow wheat, barley, oats, and other crops again. They did not wish to return to the inefficient method of cultivating many small strips of land, however, so they combined their fields and farmed large tracts of land. This new, more efficient farming method required fewer laborers and thus caused even more unemployment.

SURVIVAL OF VILLAGE LIFE. Despite these upheavals, many people remained in the countryside and managed to find work. But even for those with jobs, life was hard. Most laborers woke at dawn and walked to work in the nearby fields. There they plowed the earth, planted seeds, and gathered the harvest. They rested for a short while in the afternoon and ate a simple meal of bread and cheese before they returned to work until dusk. When they went home, they ate and sometimes sang songs and told stories before going to bed. Although landowners lived better lives, all but the wealthiest personally oversaw the work in the fields and kept careful track of what laborers planted and harvested.

Most farmers had little or no education. Some sent their children to petty schools, which usually gathered in a home or church. These schools, which educated children until the age of about seven, taught basic reading and writing. In contrast, wealthy landowners often hired

See
color plate 11,
vol. 1.

* *poaching* trespassing for the purposes of
stealing fish or game (wild animals hunted
for food)

private tutors to teach their children mathematics, geography, history, map drawing, penmanship, and Latin (the language of scholars, lawyers, and the clergy).

Most of the necessities of life were made right in the village. A typical village included a bakery, a brewery, a tannery, and a blacksmith. Traveling laborers, such as tinkers who fixed broken pots and pans, were often the only source of news from the outside world. Once or twice a year, villagers traveled to nearby towns to buy and sell goods at the town market or to purchase something from a specialty craftsperson, such as a shoemaker.

Country life, however, was not all labor and monotony. Great feasts occurred in the wintertime. Livestock, such as pigs and cows, were too expensive to feed during the winter months, so villagers slaughtered most animals around November (known as the Blood Month). Afterward, because there was no refrigeration, they dined on meat for several days. Wealthy noblemen raised and hunted deer in parks used only by the upper classes. The lower classes were forbidden to hunt in these parks and were sometimes hanged if caught poaching*. Falconry and hawking were also popular pastimes among the wealthy. Falcons and hawks were trained to swoop down and kill other birds, such as quails and pheasants. (*See also* **Cities, Towns, and Villages; Games, Pastimes, and Sports.**)

COURT LIFE

* *courtier* person in attendance at a royal
court

In Shakespeare's day, *court* referred to the residence of England's king or queen as well as to the monarch's formal assembly of family members, advisers, high government officials, servants, and other attendants. The most powerful courtiers* belonged to the Privy Council—a small group of trusted advisers. In addition to being the center of political power, courts were also places of lavish entertainment, extravagant apparel, and fabulous feasts.

THE COURT OF ELIZABETH I. During most of Shakespeare's life, England was ruled by Queen ELIZABETH I. Crowned in 1558 (six years before Shakespeare was born), Elizabeth ruled until 1603 (13 years before Shakespeare died). Her father, King HENRY VIII, and his father, Henry VII, had already greatly increased the prestige of the English court by inviting famous European writers and artists to work at court, adding refinement to court life.

Elizabeth followed in the footsteps of her ancestors. She was an enthusiastic supporter of the arts, including literature and theater. In addition, she was highly intelligent, exceptionally well educated, and very strong willed, a combination that enabled her to dominate her court and transform it into a major cultural center. The most famous artists of the day painted her portrait; the leading poets praised her beauty and wisdom; and the best-known musicians entertained her with songs composed in her honor. Elizabeth also invited Shakespeare and his acting company, the Chamberlain's Men, to perform at her court a total of 32 times, almost as many times as all the other acting companies combined.

In addition to being a cultural center, Elizabeth's court was elegant and lively. Courtiers competed with one another to wear the most beautiful and elaborate clothing and jewelry. No detail was overlooked. Some men even dyed their beards purple or orange to match their outfits. Elizabeth herself was always gorgeously dressed and adorned with priceless jewels. She was said to own 500 jewel-studded dresses. One visitor to Elizabeth's court from abroad wrote about his visit that "It was more to have seen Elizabeth than to have seen England!"

Elizabeth's daily court amusements were quite lavish. They included banquets, dances, festivals, games, tournaments, and spectacles, such as fireworks and staged sea battles. When Elizabeth traveled with her court through the country, she often stayed at the homes of noblemen, whom she expected to provide her with similar entertainment. The queen also expected the noblemen to present her with expensive gifts. One gift she received was a necklace strung with gold roses, each of which was studded with a diamond. Because of these expenses, the cost of a visit from the queen was immense.

THE COURT OF JAMES I. King JAMES I succeeded Elizabeth and was the reigning monarch when Shakespeare died in 1616. Like Elizabeth, James sought to make his court a place of beauty and entertainment. In fact, James deliberately tried to make his court the envy of all the other European monarchs. He spent huge sums of money on court amusements, which were lavish in the extreme. His favorite entertainments were MASQUES, which mixed music, dance, and poetry and included performances by members of the court. At the climax of a masque performed in 1609, James's wife entered the room draped in jewels and costumed as Queen Cleopatra.

Although James lacked Elizabeth's great intelligence and learning, he loved the theater and, like Elizabeth, supported it with his money and praise. He became the patron* of Shakespeare's acting company, which he renamed the KING'S MEN, and he invited the group to perform frequently at his court. In the 13 years that Shakespeare lived under James's rule, his plays were performed 177 times at court, an average of once a month.

MAINTAINING THE COURT. The main residence of England's court was Windsor Castle, located about 20 miles west of London. The court moved frequently, however. In fact, every month or so the court was entirely packed up and transported from one castle to another. Hundreds of carts were heaped with furniture, supplies, and belongings and drawn over bumpy roads to the next residence. The move was carefully planned in advance so that meals and beds would be ready for the huge royal party at stops along the way. The frequent moves were necessary to allow for thorough cleaning of the last place of residence. There was no plumbing or sanitary waste disposal in Shakespeare's time, even in royal castles, so waste and debris accumulated rapidly. Outbreaks of plague* were another reason for frequent relocations of the court.

Although English society and culture became increasingly conservative during the reigns of Elizabeth and James, life at court became

THE REVELS OF THE KING

A letter written by a member of King James's court provides an eyewitness view of the excesses of court life. The letter describes an amateur performance at court that turned into a drunken brawl. The lead female performer tripped and fell into the king's lap, covering him with the cream, jelly, cakes, and other treats she had been carrying. When the king rose to dance, he also stumbled and fell and had to be carried off to his bed, still smeared with food. "The show went forward," the letter continues, "and most of the presenters went backward, or fell down, wine did so occupy their upper chambers."

* *patron* supporter or financial sponsor of an artist or writer

* *plague* highly contagious and often fatal disease; also called the Black Death

increasingly showy. The extravagance of court life and the competition for power and prestige among the courtiers provided Shakespeare with a rich source of material for plots and characters in his plays. The support provided by Elizabeth and James was also a primary reason for Shakespeare's financial success as a playwright. (*See also* **Acting Companies, Elizabethan; Castles; Government and Politics; Royalty and Nobility.**)

CRAFTWORKERS

Craftworkers made up a vibrant part of the ebb and flow of Elizabethan society—its commerce and manufacturing, its capacity to provide for the needs and luxuries of everyday life. Throughout England the clamor of these skilled laborers could be heard—from the ringing of the blacksmith's hammer as it struck the anvil, to the whirring of the spinner's wheel, to the shuffling of the bookbinder's press. Pungent chemical smells emerged from the leather worker's shop, and the scents of beeswax and animal fat wafted out of the candle maker's store. Each day apprentices spilled from the shops into the streets, young men and women taking a short break from the trades they were learning under the strict rule of master craftworkers.

The business of the craft trades operated under the firm regulations of the craft guilds, organizations that controlled nearly every aspect of manufacturing. Through the guilds craftworkers provided England with nearly all of its finished goods, offering consumers a wide selection of everything from weapons and furniture to glassware and waistcoats.

WORKERS AND THE GUILD SYSTEM

* **medieval** referring to the Middle Ages, a period roughly between A.D. 500 and 1500

English guilds, first established in medieval* times, began as associations of craftsmen who did related work. Similar to modern labor unions, guilds set standards for their professions and protected the interests of their members. Over the centuries the guilds achieved significant political influence in cities and towns throughout England. By Shakespeare's time they were well-established institutions and were granted royal charters that gave them the right to operate and defined their areas of influence. From time to time the guilds reorganized themselves by splitting or merging, and on occasion they redefined or rearranged the crafts that fell within their control.

THE RULE OF THE GUILDS. The London guilds were formally known as livery companies, a designation that referred to the elegant apparel (called livery) that their members wore on special occasions, such as when they marched in parades and processions and made dignified appearances at ceremonies and other gatherings.

In Shakespeare's day London had 12 "great" guilds, that is, guilds that boasted the most members, money, and influence. The goldsmiths (makers or sellers of gold items), grocers (sellers of foodstuffs), and salters (producers and sellers of salt) were a few of these. The mercers sold cloth and textiles, as did the drapers. The fishmongers sold seafood, and the ironmongers sold metal goods. The haberdashers sold a wide variety of men's hats, accessories, and small personal items, such as combs, buttons, and pens. The dyers brought color to England's textile industries, and the vintners kept the country supplied with ale, beer, wine, and liquor. In addition to the 12 major guilds, there were about 60 smaller ones for such professions as chandlers (makers of candles), glaziers (manufacturers of glassware), stationers (printers and publishers), musicians, and barbers.

Guilds existed in various combinations in different parts of England, but establishing a craft business in any town would have been difficult without the approval of the local guild. The guilds had legal authority to control everything from prices to working hours, and they could fine, shut down, or chase away uncooperative craftworkers. If a farrier, for example, wanted to sell horseshoes for less than the minimum price set by the guild, he had to locate his workshop outside the city limits, where the organization had no authority. Nevertheless, some industries that relied on poor workers, such as spinners and knitters, operated outside the guild system. Those who worked in these businesses usually did so in their homes and sold their products to middlemen.

One of the biggest challenges for the Elizabethan guilds was to absorb the numerous craftworkers who emigrated from the European continent. These newcomers were mainly Protestants fleeing religious persecution. Many possessed more skills at their crafts than English workers, and they brought new techniques and designs to such industries as glassblowing, cloth making, dyeing, weaving, and metalworking. English workers often resented the competition, but the hard work of these

See color plate 5, vol. 1.

One familiar type of craftworker in Elizabethan England was the smith, who made items from metal. Smiths were named for the materials they used—for example, goldsmiths, silversmiths, or blacksmiths (those who worked with iron).

immigrants and the high-quality products they produced raised English crafts to new heights and increased the kingdom's ability to trade profitably with the rest of the world.

FROM APPRENTICE TO MASTER. There were three basic categories of craftworkers: apprentice, journeyman, and master. A master craftsman might hire several journeymen, who already had some experience, and several apprentices, who had much to learn.

The apprentice system operated throughout England. Apprentices were typically young boys who were considered too poor to study at school or serve at a noble court. When they were about age 14, their families or the government committed them to the care of a master, usually for a period of seven years. The apprentice received no wages but often lived and ate in the master's house. The master was expected to give the student a civic and moral education as well as teach him a trade. Apprentices could benefit from a kindly master, but many had to endure harsh conditions and strict punishments from more difficult ones.

The pressures of learning a trade were relieved in the streets, marketplaces, theaters, and fields, where apprentices gathered to enjoy their few free hours. In their uniforms—blue shirt and coat, white pants, and round woolen caps—apprentices sang songs, held footraces, and engaged in chaotic brawls using fists and clubs.

After a period of apprenticeship, young craftworkers could apply to the guild to become journeymen. In addition to the required fee, apprentices were usually expected to submit a sample of their work, called a proof piece. As journeymen, craftworkers could hire themselves out for wages. If they became skillful enough, they could present another work—a masterpiece—to the guild in the hope of becoming masters. Masters could own businesses and take on journeymen and apprentices. In some cases workers simply took over the businesses when their masters retired or died.

WOMEN IN THE WORKPLACE. Roles for women outside the home in Elizabethan England were generally limited, but exceptions were common. Women composed a significant segment of the workforce in the textile industries, for example, turning wool, cotton, flax, and hemp into fabric and garments. Young women also became apprentices. About 10 percent of children apprenticed by their parents were girls, and among poor children apprenticed by local governments about 25 to 30 percent were girls.

In some cases women learned their husbands' trades and were allowed to inherit businesses if they were widowed. Records show that women worked as blacksmiths, leather tanners, and tailors, among other occupations. A few women even had their own apprentices and were permitted to join the guilds. As early as the 1400s, female laundry workers in London organized their own guild.

A STEP UP ON THE SOCIAL LADDER. The craft trades offered a way for young people of low social rank, especially young men, to rise in status.

By becoming a master and shop owner, a craftworker could amass enough wealth to become a landowner and enjoy a measure of respect and influence in his town. A successful master might also become an official in a guild or on the town council. In some cases even wealthy families apprenticed younger sons—who would not be eligible to inherit the family fortune—to masters of prestigious trades, such as goldsmithing.

Poor people from rural areas, however, were prohibited from becoming apprentices. This ban reflected the guilds' belief that they included only the better classes of people. As it happened, craftworkers themselves were often held in low regard by landowners from more distinguished families. Craftworkers, particularly master shopkeepers and traders, were often portrayed as narrow-minded people, concerned only with running their businesses and making a profit. The upper classes often ridiculed the clumsy attempts of craftworkers to achieve higher status and ridiculed their ignorance of social graces. One popular stereotype suggested that tradesmen neglected their wives, who could therefore be easily seduced by aristocratic young men.

CRAFTS IN ELIZABETHAN ENGLAND

The names and numbers of the guilds only hint at the variety of occupations in Elizabethan England. A list drawn up in London in 1422 included 111 separate trades, many of which grew as commerce and technology flourished under the reign of Queen ELIZABETH I (1558–1603).

THE CLEANING CREW. Sopers were craftworkers who produced soap for bathing, laundering, and other needs. Records show that organized production of soap began in London by 1524. The trade boomed in the 1600s in the city of Bristol, where sopers imported olive oil from Spain to make castile soap, named after a Spanish province. Laundry soap consisted of ash from burned wood mixed with tallow, a type of animal fat. English sopers also produced varieties of soap in the form of small balls and solid blocks.

The London women who formed the launderers' guild used several methods for cleaning clothes. The garments were brushed and beaten to shake out dust, dirt, and lice or washed in pots of hot water. To remove stains laundresses applied a special soap made of egg whites, several minerals, and bile from the organs of bulls. Heavily soiled fabrics were bleached in a process called bluing, a day-long procedure in which stained fabrics were soaked in sheep excrement and rubbed with an herbal paste.

LEATHER MAKERS. Tanners prepared animal hides for manufacture into leather goods. This ancient craft changed little over the centuries. Raw hides were first cured to keep them from rotting. To cure the hides, tanners laid them out in piles of salt for several days or soaked them in salt water for a shorter period. Tanners then trimmed, sorted, and washed the hides before applying lime and other natural chemicals to loosen and remove the animal hairs.

LUXURY IMPORTS

As England's economy thrived under the reign of Queen Elizabeth, its foreign trade increased dramatically. Merchants began to import many finished goods from Europe and beyond, producing competition for English craftworkers. Fine clothing was an especially popular import. Some people in the English craft industries found themselves becoming retailers, selling finished foreign goods instead of producing their own. This trend continued as prosperous Elizabethans had extra money to spend on luxury items from abroad.

The next step was to soak the hides in vats of tannic acids from certain types of wood and tree bark. After a series of soakings, the leather would remain well preserved. The tanner then added natural oils to restore the leather's suppleness, drying and moisturizing the leather to achieve a balance of strength and flexibility. Finally, the leather was buffed to a smooth finish and dyed with pigments. The prepared leather was then sold to other craftworkers, such as saddlers, glove makers, shoemakers, and others who made finished equipment and clothes.

LIGHTING THE WAY. Chandlers produced candles for use in homes, workshops, churches, and elsewhere. Like tanning, candle making was an ancient craft. Chandlers made expensive wax candles by pouring melted beeswax over a hanging wick. Molds could also be used to shape the candle around the wick. Another popular method of candle making was the use of tallow, or melted animal fat, which produced candles that were less expensive but emitted more smoke while burning. Chandlers made these candles by repeatedly dipping the wick in hot tallow, allowing each layer to cool and harden between dippings.

PAPER AND PRINTING. The technology of the printing press arrived in England by the 1470s, leading to a boom in paper production and to the printing of thousands of books, pamphlets, and posters. Paper was made by shredding and crushing old linen rags and hemp ropes in water to create a pulp of fibers. A large, flat wire screen was dipped into the pulp, which was spread on the screen, pressed, and dried.

Early printers were often first trained as goldsmiths or silversmiths, who used small stamps to press letters into their metalwork. These stamps were readily adapted to ink printing. Eventually, apprentices trained directly as printers. Master printers had a relatively high status, for they were much in demand. They associated frequently but cautiously with nobles, clergymen, and government officials who had the wealth and authority to sponsor or censor printed materials, including the plays of William Shakespeare. (*See also* **Guilds; Social Classes; Trade; Work.**)

CRIME AND PUNISHMENT

Many of the same crimes that disrupt modern societies—such as theft, arson, and murder—existed during Shakespeare's time. However, the Elizabethan criminal justice system differed greatly from most present-day judicial systems. Penalties were far more severe than they are today because most Elizabethans believed that England was a lawless and dangerous place.

TREASON. Elizabethan law established three main categories of crimes—treason, felonies, and misdemeanors. Treason was considered by far the worst offense of the three. Two distinct types of treason existed under English law—high treason and petty treason. High treason referred to offenses that seriously threatened the monarchy, such as plots against the ruler's life

Minor offenses were often punished by confining the perpetrator in the stocks, which usually held the prisoner's legs as he sat on a bench.

* *counterfeit* to make a fake copy, especially of money

* *draw* to remove a person's internal organs

* *quarter* to divide a person's body into four parts

or authority. Crimes that undermined the sovereign's ability to rule, such as counterfeiting*, were also considered acts of high treason. Petty treason, by contrast, did not involve a threat to the sovereign, but to any other person to whom one was legally obliged to show obedience. For example, a wife was required to obey her husband, and a servant was required to obey his or her master.

The penalty for high treason was death, often in a particularly gruesome manner. Hanging, drawing*, and quartering* were the usual sentences imposed, but not all those convicted of high treason suffered such a fate. Important persons might be imprisoned under fairly comfortable circumstances before being hanged. Those found guilty of committing a less serious form of high treason—for example following a traitorous leader—might receive a lesser sentence or be pardoned altogether. In the final scene of *Richard III*, for example, after Henry of Richmond and his army have defeated King Richard, Richmond proclaims that he will pardon any soldiers who fought for Richard if they will return and submit to his authority. Although petty treason did not threaten the sovereign, it was still considered a serious crime. A wife found guilty of murdering her husband, for example, could be burned at the stake.

FELONIES. A wide range of crimes were considered felonies, including violent acts (murder or assault) and property crimes (robbery or horse theft). Several odd or unusual actions were also classified as felonies. These included hunting at night with a painted face and practicing witchcraft. The penalty for most felonies, even crimes against property, was death. Authorities believed that harsh punishments deterred potential outlaws from committing such crimes in the first place. There is little evidence, however, that the threat of capital punishment did much to discourage crime. In any

event, most of those convicted of felonies had their sentences reduced to lesser punishments. By today's standards, even these penalties were extreme. They included cutting off fingers and hands, although many times a less vital item, such as an ear, was removed.

The executions of convicted felons were conducted publicly. A hanging often drew large and enthusiastic crowds who watched the event from bleachers. People would take the day off from work to attend a hanging, and vendors would sell everything from refreshments to illustrated poems describing the condemned person's life. Ironically, hangings also drew criminals, such as pickpockets, who preyed on the crowd that gathered to watch another pickpocket meet his death. The bodies of executed criminals were frequently displayed in a public place afterward as a warning to others.

MISDEMEANORS. Lesser crimes, or misdemeanors, included petty theft and vagabondage*. Petty thieves sometimes had the letter *T* burned onto their faces or thumbs. This enabled others to identify them as people who should not be trusted. Before sentencing, judges often checked a criminal's thumbs to see if he or she had been convicted of the same crime earlier. Vagabondage was not always considered a crime, but those who seemed able-bodied and capable of working were likely to be prosecuted. Rather than waste time and money on prosecuting and punishing vagabonds, local officials often simply chased them out of town.

Convicted of a misdemeanor, a perpetrator might be restrained in the stocks or the pillory. The stocks held an offender's feet while he or she sat on a rail or bench. The pillory confined the person's hands and head. Unable to defend themselves against the violence of passers-by, some pilloried prisoners were seriously hurt and even killed. In *King Lear*, the disguised earl of Kent is put into the stocks as punishment for attacking a servant—a penalty the duke of Gloucester protests as unfitting for a king's servant, since it is usually inflicted on lowly folks for "pilferings and common trespasses."

Whipping was another common punishment for minor offenses. The whip used to lash offenders was usually designed to cut the skin but not do serious damage. One of the reasons physical punishment was so popular in Shakespeare's day was that few jails existed to hold criminals. Housing prisoners cost money that the crown was reluctant to spend. Law enforcers found it easier and cheaper to whip a thief or cut off the hand of a felon than to build prisons.

CRIMINAL JUSTICE. Various types of courts existed in Shakespeare's England, each of which had its own area of responsibility. These included both state and Church courts, the latter dealing mainly with crimes of sexual misbehavior. The Star Chamber was a state court that dealt with crimes that threatened public order, such as treason, riots, or official misconduct by government ministers. Most cases, however, were tried by assizes (court sessions held twice a year) or general quarter sessions (held four times a year). The assizes usually occurred when high-ranking law officials called judicial commissioners traveled to the various counties in

* *vagabondage* wandering from place to place and begging

THE RACK

Perhaps the most feared instrument of torture used during Elizabethan times was the rack. Authorities used this device to stretch a prisoner's body until his or her joints pulled apart. In 1593, Thomas Kyd, a playwright, was placed on the rack after being caught with writings that denied Church teachings. Kyd claimed that the papers belonged to the playwright Christopher Marlowe, who was killed in a fight only a few weeks later. It is unknown whether Marlowe's death was connected to Kyd's confession. Also unknown is whether Kyd's death the following year was the result of injuries inflicted on him by the rack.

the realm. They typically handled more serious crimes. General quarter sessions were presided over by lesser law officials, called justices of the peace. In both courts a grand jury considered charges against a number of prisoners during a session (about 20 to 100 at the assizes, fewer at the quarter sessions). Those indicted* by the grand jury were tried by a separate jury of 12 men. The jury usually heard several cases and then decided all of them afterwards.

* *indict* to charge a person with a crime

Convicted criminals could request—and even pay for—a pardon, and in some cases the judge delayed execution of the sentence, giving the prisoner time to make an application. One special way of avoiding conviction was called *benefit of clergy.* The prisoner read aloud, in Latin, a passage from the Bible. If the representative of the local bishop felt that the convict read the passage well enough, he authorized the prisoner's release. This law originated during medieval* times, when only the clergy knew how to read. During the Middle Ages, the ability to read proved that one was an ordained minister and therefore exempt from prosecution. BEN JONSON—Shakespeare's friend and a fellow playwright—successfully pleaded benefit of clergy after killing an actor during a fight. Authorities later changed the law so that a person could use benefit of clergy only once and could not use it at all in serious cases such as murder. (*See also* **Law; Tower of London.**)

* *medieval* referring to the Middle Ages, a period roughly between A.D. 500 and 1500

CRITICS AND SCHOLARS

See *Shakespeare's Reputation; Shakespeare's Works, Changing Views.*

CURTAIN THEATER

See *Elizabethan Theaters.*

CYMBELINE

* *deity* god or goddess

Although classified in the FIRST FOLIO as a tragedy, *Cymbeline* is actually a romance that blends elements of comedy and tragedy. It was Shakespeare's second experiment in the new form of tragicomic drama—*Pericles* being the first—and the playwright used many of the traditional elements of romance, including love, adventure, villains, and deities*. Some critics argue that Shakespeare failed to weave together the separate threads of the story, resulting in a somewhat disjointed play.

As the action begins, King Cymbeline of Britain is furious with his daughter Imogen for marrying Posthumus Leonatus, an impoverished nobleman. The queen is also angry, because she wanted Imogen to marry Cloten, her son from a previous marriage. In response the king and queen banish Posthumus to Rome. There Posthumus rashly agrees to a wager with a villain, Iachimo, who boasts that he can seduce Imogen. To

In this Royal Shakespeare Company production of *Cymbeline* (1988), the villain Iachimo (Donald Sumpter) steals a bracelet from the arm of the sleeping Imogen (Harriet Walter). He plans to convince Imogen's husband, Posthumus, that she has been unfaithful.

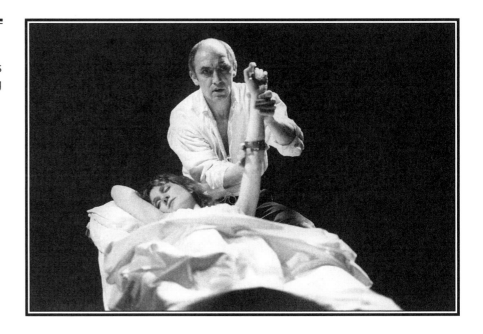

tribute money or other valuables paid by one nation to another as a sign of respect and submission

win the bet, Iachimo sneaks into Imogen's bedroom, steals a bracelet given to her by Posthumus, and takes note of the furnishings in the room. When he returns to Rome, he convinces Posthumus that he has succeeded in persuading Imogen to commit adultery. Enraged, Posthumus sends a letter to his servant Pisanio, ordering him to kill Imogen. Pisanio does not believe that Imogen has betrayed his master, and he persuades her to disguise herself as a boy and take refuge with the Roman ambassador Lucius until Posthumus regains his senses. On the way, however, Imogen loses her way in the countryside.

After wandering for two days, she finds a cave occupied by Belarius, a general who had been exiled several years earlier by Cymbeline. Belarius lives there with Imogen's brothers, whom he kidnapped as infants in revenge against the king. In the meantime, Lucius has gathered an army to attack Cymbeline, who has refused to pay the tribute* he owes to Rome. Belarius, the king's sons, and Posthumus return to Britain to defend their country against Roman invaders. By this point Posthumus, regretting his decision to have Imogen killed, wishes to die. He dresses as a Roman peasant so that he will be captured and executed. During his imprisonment, however, Posthumus has a vision of the Roman god Jupiter, who says that Imogen will once again embrace him. In the final scene Posthumus and Imogen are reunited. Cymbeline makes peace with Belarius and rejoices that his long lost sons are still alive. The king also agrees to pay Britain's tribute to Rome, restoring peace to both nations.

Drama historians believe that Shakespeare wrote *Cymbeline* between 1609 and 1610 to be performed at BLACKFRIARS theater. The play is based on several sources, including a history of legendary British kings and a romantic drama called *The Rare Triumphs of Love and Fortune. Cymbeline* is one of Shakespeare's least popular plays. Critics complain that its characters are inconsistent, sometimes showing comic traits and at other times tragic ones. Shakespeare, who had skillfully woven various narratives together in other plays, seems to have been less successful in *Cymbeline.* Instead, he appears to have relied on a complex final scene in which all the conflicts and dilemmas are conveniently resolved. Some scholars have argued that Shakespeare was still learning to work in a genre* that was new to him and that in his later romances, such as *The Winter's Tale* and *The Tempest,* he managed to avoid the inconsistencies that mar *Cymbeline.* (*See also* **History in Shakespeare's Plays: England.**)

* *genre* literary form

DANCE

* *yeoman* farmer who owns the land he cultivates

Dancing was widely popular in Elizabethan England. In palaces, monarchs and nobles stepped and pivoted in intricate patterns as they performed the most recent court dances. In villages, peasants and yeomen* leaped and whirled in the air as they danced in the traditional country manner. Dancing was a group activity, and performances by individuals were rare. For Elizabethans, the sight of many people moving together in harmony was associated with the ordered movements of the universe, in which stars, planets, and moons revolved in an eternal heavenly dance.

Queen ELIZABETH I was known as an avid dancer, both in formal gatherings at court and on the spur of the moment. The dances performed at her court were heavily influenced by French and other European fashions. One of the more popular court dances was the French *bransle,* in which a chain of dancers held hands and walked, skipped, or glided sideways to the beat of the music. The *bransle,* a difficult word for the English tongue, became known as the brawl. Court dances could be solemn and stately, or they could be lively and energetic. The pavane, a slow, processional dance, was often followed by the *cinquepace,* a vigorous and bouncy dance, in which performers took four hopping steps then jumped high into the air. Elizabeth was said to have practiced this physically demanding dance for her exercise.

Dancing was a major part of the annual celebrations that took place on May Day. The group of costumed dancers, shown here, illustrate the month of May in Edmund Spenser's *The Shepheardes Calendar* (1579).

Dancing was as popular in the country as it was at the royal court. The morris, performed exclusively by men, blended dance and pantomime. Dancers wore bells on their legs, and some of them disguised themselves as deer, wearing antlers on their heads and galloping in the streets as other dancers pantomimed hunting and shooting them with arrows. Another popular dance was the maypole, or round, dance. This dance was performed around a tall pole decorated with flowers and colorful ribbons, which the participants wove into patterns as they danced in circles. The maypole dance was usually performed on May Day, a pre-Christian celebration intended to ensure a bountiful harvest.

Dance also had an important place in Elizabethan drama. Shakespeare's comedies often ended with a dance. He used dance as a signal to his audience that harmony and order had been restored. In his comedies life is often thrown into disorder. For example, in *The Merry Wives of Windsor,* a jealous husband (Mr. Ford) wrongfully suspects his wife of committing adultery with a fat, greedy, and lecherous knight (Sir John Falstaff). After Mrs. Ford's innocence is established and Falstaff has been exposed as a schemer, everyone reunites in a dance. (*See also* **Falstaff, Sir John; Music Inspired by Shakespeare.**)

DARK LADY

* *sonnet* poem of 14 lines with a fixed pattern of meter and rhyme
* *plague* highly contagious and often fatal disease; also called the Black Death

The Dark Lady is a mysterious, unnamed character of dark complexion and questionable morals who figures in more than two dozen of William Shakespeare's sonnets*. Shakespeare appears to have written most of his verse in the early 1590s, when London's theaters were closed due to an outbreak of plague*. Of the 154 sonnets Shakespeare wrote in his lifetime, 27 seem to focus on the Dark Lady.

It is unclear whether the sonnets are autobiographical or simply exercises in literary imagination. The emotional depth expressed in many of them, however, has led most scholars to believe that they were inspired by events in Shakespeare's life. The sonnets addressed to the Dark Lady express an intense passion for, and anguish about, the nameless woman. In several poems Shakespeare praises her haunting beauty. In Sonnet 132, he writes:

> And truly not the morning sun of heaven
> Better becomes the grey cheeks of th' east,
> Nor that full star that ushers in the even
> Doth half that glory to the sober west,
> As those two [mourning] eyes become thy face.
> (5–9)

Yet in the preceding sonnet, the poet has rebuked the lady, writing "In nothing art thou black save in thy deeds" (13).

The Dark Lady may have been a composite of several women, brought to life by the poet's imagination. Some scholars see the infidelities and betrayals of the Dark Lady as Shakespeare's argument that friendship between men is superior to romantic love between men and women.

See also **Sonnets, The.**

* *abbess* female head of an abbey or convent
* *courtesan* prostitute associated with wealthy men or men in attendance at a royal court
* *vintner* person who makes or sells wine

Attempts to identify the Dark Lady with certainty have failed, but there has been much speculation. Some scholars have suggested that she was Lucy Morgan, a dark-skinned abbess* of Clerkenwell, who was a well-known courtesan*. Others believe that the Dark Lady was Mary Fitton, a lady-in-waiting at Queen Elizabeth's court. Still others opt for Emilia Bassano, the daughter of a court musician from Venice. Another possibility is Mrs. John Davenant, the wife of a vintner*, whose son William claimed to be Shakespeare's illegitimate son. (*See also* **Sonnets, The.**)

DEATH AND FUNERALS

Death was a constant presence in the everyday lives of Elizabethans. Most people died at home rather than in hospitals. Each evening church bells tolled to announce the deaths that had occurred that day (six rings for a woman and nine rings for a man). Funeral processions—an almost daily sight—were another reminder of death. In addition to providing an opportunity to mourn, funerals enabled well-to-do Elizabethans to display the wealth and status of their families.

Children were the most vulnerable to DISEASE, and records indicate that about 25 percent of them died before their tenth birthday. Women were also in great danger during childbirth because doctors possessed little knowledge about how to deal with complicated deliveries. In fact, many women gave birth in lying-in rooms, which were furnished as fitting places either to celebrate a successful birth or to mourn the death of a mother or child. In addition to the dangers of disease and childbirth, many Elizabethans lost their lives to famine, accidents, and violence.

Elizabethans developed methods of comforting the terminally ill. For example, it was customary for a dying person to bestow gifts on loved ones or impart family secrets from the deathbed. This practice enabled the dying person to reward those who had served faithfully. It also ensured that family and friends would gather to pay their respects and grieve together.

* *bereaved* person or people suffering the death of a loved one

* *wake* watch kept over the deceased before the body is buried

* *psalm* sacred song or poem

Elizabethans also developed elaborate rituals that helped ease the suffering of the bereaved*. Grieving spouses or parents reclined on mourning beds (couches draped in black velvet), where they were comforted by relatives and friends. Widowers sometimes wore lockets or rings containing a strand of their dead spouse's hair. Wakes* were typically held at the home of the deceased, where the rooms were draped in black and mirrors were covered or turned to the wall. In some parts of England, mourners sang to the dead person about the journey to the afterworld.

Funerals were crucial to Elizabethans. A large funeral procession, in which mourners accompanied the corpse to the graveyard, signified the importance of the deceased. An impressive funeral procession included musicians who marched and chanted psalms* to the music of bells and cymbals. Following them were relatives and servants dressed in black robes and holding branches of rosemary and evergreen (symbols of immortality). The casket was draped in black, with branches of rosemary

and evergreen tied to the sides. Poor people were sometimes hired as mourners to make a funeral procession appear more impressive.

Funeral processions varied, depending on who had died and the cause of death. The procession for an unmarried girl was led by the deceased's friends, who dressed in white and carried a garland of flowers with a white glove in the center (a symbol of virginity). Those killed by contagious diseases, such as plague*, were buried quickly and often at night. As one might expect, many people could not afford elaborate funeral processions. Coffins were only for the wealthy, and the poor were usually wrapped in shrouds for burial.

Although funeral processions were sometimes elaborate, burial was simple. A minister usually read a passage from the Bible and then gravediggers lowered the corpse into the ground without ceremony. Feasts were held to commemorate the deceased. Wealthy Elizabethans often commissioned artists to ornamental impressive gravestones and monuments in their honor. In this manner they hoped to be remembered by future generations.

* *plague* highly contagious and often fatal disease; also called the Black Death

See color plate 8, vol. 1.

DESDEMONA

* *Moorish* referring to invaders from North Africa who conquered Spain during the Middle Ages

* *medieval* referring to the Middle Ages, the period roughly between A.D. 500 and 1500

* *infidelity* sexual unfaithfulness

* *martyr* one who suffers and dies rather than renounce his or her beliefs

Desdemona is a tragic and heroic figure in Shakespeare's play Othello. After marrying Othello, a Moorish* general in the service of the Italian city of Venice, Desdemona is unjustly accused of adultery and murdered by her jealous husband. Too late, Othello discovers Desdemona's innocence and realizes that he had been fooled into doubting his wife's faithfulness by the lies of IAGO, an officer in his army and a supposed friend. Because of the virtues Desdemona demonstrates throughout her ordeal, she is considered to be one of the greatest heroines in Shakespeare's works.

An angelic female personality such as Desdemona was familiar to Shakespeare's audience from medieval* morality plays—dramas in which characters representing good struggle against characters representing evil. Among the many virtues that Desdemona exemplifies in *Othello* are strength, loyalty, and love. She displays her moral strength and courage by marrying Othello despite the racial prejudices of Venetian society and the opposition of her father, who believes her relationship with the Moor is "against all rules of nature" (I.iii.101). Although her husband is eventually driven to treat her brutally, Desdemona remains faithful and loving to him, saying "Unkindness may do much, / And his unkindness may defeat [destroy] my life, / But never taint my love" (IV.ii.159–61).

Desdemona's character emphasizes one of the main themes of *Othello*, which is that appearances are deceiving. Even when she learns that her husband suspects her of infidelity*, she remains loyal and loving. In spite of Desdemona's many good qualities, some critics writing during the 1700s and 1800s argued that her suffering in the play is deserved. They point out that she defied her father by marrying Othello against his wishes. This argument, however, is a minority viewpoint, and most critics regard Desdemona as a martyr*. (*See also* **Othello**.)

DIPLOMACY AND FOREIGN RELATIONS

Diplomacy—the art of peacefully settling disputes—was essential to the survival of England during the reign of ELIZABETH I (1558–1603). During this period the nation's Protestants and Catholics were often on the brink of war against each other. In addition to this internal threat, the country was in frequent danger of invasion from France and Spain. England was a tempting target for these two wealthy powers because it was weak, divided, and without a standing army or navy. Under the circumstances the use of diplomacy was vitally important.

DIPLOMACY AT HOME. England's religious strife had begun in 1534, when King Henry VIII renounced the authority of the Roman Catholic Church over England and established the Church of England. Later Henry's daughter Mary I tried to restore Catholicism as the state religion. Her brutal oppression of Protestants, including numerous executions, earned her the name "Bloody Mary."

When Elizabeth inherited the throne of England, she used her considerable skill at diplomacy to restore peace among the warring religious groups. Her first major act as England's monarch was the passage of the Elizabethan settlement, a collection of laws regulating religion. Although these laws made Elizabeth the leader of the Church of England, they also restored some Catholic traditions, such as Communion* and the sign of the cross. This compromise helped keep most Protestants and Catholics loyal to the queen.

Elizabeth also had to compromise with Parliament, England's legislative body representing the people. Although the monarch ruled the nation, only Parliament had the power to pass laws and levy taxes. For

* *Communion* Christian ritual in which bread and wine are consumed in memory of Christ's death

One of Queen Elizabeth's greatest assets was her skill in diplomacy. Many of the foreign ambassadors hoped to persuade her to marry a foreign lord. Although Elizabeth never married, and perhaps never intended to wed, she frequently encouraged such suits.

Diplomacy and Foreign Relations

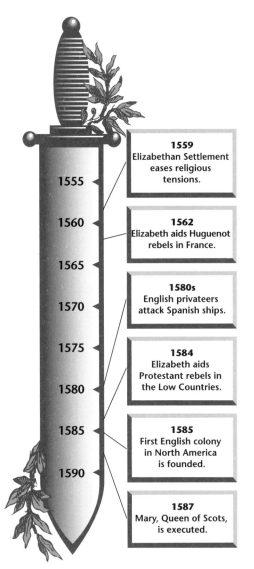

1559
Elizabethan Settlement eases religious tensions.

1562
Elizabeth aids Huguenot rebels in France.

1580s
English privateers attack Spanish ships.

1584
Elizabeth aids Protestant rebels in the Low Countries.

1585
First English colony in North America is founded.

1587
Mary, Queen of Scots, is executed.

1555
1560
1565
1570
1575
1580
1585
1590

this reason, Elizabeth had to ask Parliament for money when she wished to build an English naval force. The queen and Parliament often disagreed about how best to run the country. One of the main sources of dispute was what should be done with Elizabeth's cousin Mary, Queen of Scots.

Mary had inherited the throne of Scotland in 1542. A devout Catholic, she opposed the spread of the Protestant faith in Scotland. Her rule ended in 1567, when she was forced to flee to England after marrying the man suspected of assassinating her first husband. Mary was an unwelcome guest, however, because everyone knew that she would inherit England's throne if Elizabeth died. As a result, Elizabeth kept Mary locked away in various castles for many years. Parliament repeatedly insisted that Mary be executed. The queen resisted until it was discovered that Mary and others had plotted to assassinate her. Finally, Elizabeth signed a warrant in 1587 to have her cousin beheaded.

DIPLOMACY ABROAD. The art of diplomacy was even more important abroad than at home, where Elizabeth had the advantage of being the reigning monarch. Elizabeth's intelligence and resourcefulness served her well in negotiations with foreign powers. She spoke several languages, including Greek, Latin, French, and Italian. This was important because it enabled her to speak directly to the person with whom she was negotiating rather than through a translator.

In addition to her cleverness and cunning, Elizabeth's status as an unwed queen was an advantage in foreign negotiations. During her lifetime most peace treaties between nations were sealed with royal marriages. She permitted suitors from France, Denmark, and other kingdoms to court her, using the prospect of marriage to keep these nations friendly toward England. For example, in 1572 Elizabeth pretended to consider marriage to the French duke d'Alençon. This enabled her to enlist France's help in protecting England from Spain.

The queen did not conduct all diplomatic missions personally, however. England had ambassadors at the royal courts of several kingdoms, including France, the Netherlands, and Venice. Other nations also sent their ambassadors to England. Even enemies, such as Spain, had diplomats in Elizabeth's court during the early days of her rule.

OTHER FOREIGN RELATIONS. Diplomatic negotiations were not the only methods Elizabeth employed to strengthen England while avoiding war. The queen was also skilled at playing off her enemies against one another and at encouraging rival groups within enemy nations to start rebellions. One of Elizabeth's principal strategies was to encourage French and Spanish Protestants to rebel against their Roman Catholic monarchs.

In 1562 a civil war erupted in France between the nation's Catholics and Protestants (known as Huguenots). Seizing the opportunity to divide France, Elizabeth aided the leader of the Huguenot forces, Henry of Navarre, with money and other assistance. Her help enabled Henry to overcome his Catholic rivals and become King Henry IV of France.

Although Henry converted to Catholicism when he ascended the throne, he maintained good relations with Elizabeth and joined her in an alliance against Spain, their common enemy.

During Elizabeth's reign, Spain was England's most formidable enemy. Spain had expanded its power on the continent into the Low Countries, which included the present-day nations of Belgium, Luxembourg, and the Netherlands. Foreign rule, however, was opposed by many in the region, especially Protestants, who resented being ruled by Catholic Spain. Elizabeth encouraged the Protestants to rebel against their Spanish rulers, and she permitted Englishmen to travel to the region to join the fight.

* *galleon* Spanish merchant ship

Elizabeth also took steps to counter Spain's expanding power overseas. English ships raided galleons* carrying gold and silver from South America to the treasury of Spain. The Spanish called these raiders pirates, but the English referred to them as privateers, sailors licensed by the queen to attack enemy ships. Privateers also raided Spanish settlements in the New World*, stealing whatever valuables they could.

* *New World* landmass of North and South America

In response to these and other provocations, King Philip II of Spain launched an attack on England, using the SPANISH ARMADA, a naval force of 130 ships. England's smaller, faster ships repelled the invasion. Although the defeat of the Spanish Armada was a triumph for England, the country still lagged behind Spain in EXPLORATION.

Elizabeth wanted to imitate Spain's success in gaining access to overseas goods and markets through exploration. In 1577 the queen ordered the English privateer Francis Drake to sail to the Pacific Ocean. Drake reached the Pacific and also succeeded in circumnavigating the globe— the second time in history this feat had been accomplished (the first to do so was the Portuguese explorer Ferdinand Magellan). In 1585 Walter Raleigh landed on Roanoke Island (off the coast of present-day North Carolina) and established the first English settlement in North America. Meanwhile, other English adventurers established trade relations with Persia, Turkey, and Venice. These explorations established contacts for future English trade ventures, such as the East India Company, which greatly enriched the nation. They also laid the groundwork for an overseas expansion that eventually would make England one of the largest empires in history. (*See also* **Government and Politics; Religion; Spies; Warfare.**)

DIRECTORS AND SHAKESPEARE

* *block* to assign actors specific places onstage to stand when delivering their lines

In today's theaters, television studios, and film sets, directors exert enormous influence over Shakespearean productions. They determine how the text of a play is transformed into a vibrant performance. Their decisions affect many aspects of the production: interpretation of the script, casting, acting style, scenery, costumes, blocking*, and stage effects. Despite their immense importance, however, directors as we know them today did not exist during Shakespeare's lifetime. Instead, staging decisions were probably made by lead actors and by other members of

convention established practice

acting companies. Plays—whether comedy, history, or tragedy—were presented in accordance with the conventions* of the age.

Like most customs, theatrical conventions have changed over time. Acting styles, stage effects, audience expectations, and laws regulating theaters have all evolved, and these in turn have affected the ways in which plays are produced. Unhampered by the constraints of an earlier time, new methods of staging have come into being, so that ultimately each performance has become a unique interpretation, almost as much a creation of the person who directs it as of the playwright.

THEATER IN SHAKESPEARE'S TIME

To keep up with the constant demand for new plays, most Elizabethan acting companies performed six days a week, often staging a different play every day and adding a new one every two weeks or so. This hectic schedule left little time for directorial decision making, or even rehearsals; thus, actors relied heavily on conventions.

CASTING. Casting in Elizabethan theatrical companies was simple; lead actors, such as Richard Burbage and Edward Alleyn, received the starring roles in plays that were written with them in mind. Similarly, Shakespeare and his fellow dramatists often created lesser roles with specific actors in view, making casting decisions easier.

Less experienced actors were usually typecast. That is, they played the parts for which they were best suited. Because Elizabethan custom prevented women from performing in public theaters, adult companies also included one or more boys, who played the female roles.

VISUAL EFFECTS. A stage assistant called a tire-master was in charge of apparel, or COSTUMES. Apparel was an important part of Elizabethan theatrical productions, because modes of dress helped the audience identify the social rank and occupations of various characters. Elizabethan audiences expected to be entertained when they went to the theater, and rich garments provided color and dazzle at a time when actors were performing on stages that normally consisted of little but bare boards.

REHEARSALS AND STAGE DIRECTIONS. Because there was little time for rehearsals, actors probably relied primarily on their experience to guide their actions onstage. Although the lead actor undoubtedly would have had a major influence on the manner in which a play was staged, all the players were considered "fellows" and worked as a team to make each show a success.

Actors often used formal gestures that the audience immediately recognized. They also used visual clues—such as a disheveled appearance to signal insanity—to communicate certain information quickly and effectively to the audience.

Establishing cues and entrances was the responsibility of stage assistants called book-keepers (because they created and maintained the

EXPERIMENTAL SHAKESPEARE

London-born director Peter Brook has established a home base in a shabby, rundown theater in Paris, France. Eliminating all barriers between the actors and the audience, Brook spreads consistent, even lighting throughout the theater and uses no special effects.

One of his most notable productions was a version of *A Midsummer Night's Dream* that he directed in 1970. Contained in a "white box," suggestive of a gymnasium or rehearsal room, the actors did much of their work on trapezes.

* **prompt book** annotated copy of a play, which contains instructions for entrances, exits, music, and other cues

prompt book*). Shakespeare himself provided guidance to actors in the form of written stage directions, and in all likelihood he also communicated many of his thoughts orally. As he gained experience as a playwright, his textual stage directions became lengthier and more detailed. The elaborate directions in such later plays as *The Tempest* and *Henry VIII* appear to reflect an increase in authorial input, as though the playwright was quietly insisting that he wanted each scene performed a certain way.

The lead actors, called sharers because they owned a share in the acting company, probably guided many of the decisions about how the scripts were enacted. As the most accomplished performers in the company, they knew what worked onstage and how best to evoke a desired response from the audience. In addition to receiving the starring role of each play, lead actors were expected to stand at center stage—the best spot—when delivering most of their lines.

AGE OF ADAPTATIONS

The theatrical conventions of Elizabethan England continued uninterrupted until 1642, when the government closed the theaters. By the time of the Restoration* and the reopening of the theaters in 1660, however, the English stage had changed in several significant ways.

* **Restoration** referring to the period in English history, beginning in 1660, when Charles II was restored to the throne

MAJOR AND MINOR CHANGES. One of the most notable changes came about as actresses began to replace boys in women's roles. Another important shift occurred with the granting of a monopoly to two acting companies, the King's Company and the Duke's Company. The Duke's Company, run by William Davenant, boasted the greatest Shakespearean actor of the day, Thomas Betterton. Betterton continued the acting traditions and character interpretations that had been established by Richard Burbage. Although descriptions of his acting style are few, it is likely that Betterton's acting was characterized by the grandiose* manner that was popular at the time.

* **grandiose** characterized by an exaggerated manner

REWRITING THE BARD. Despite having the most popular English actor in his company, William Davenant believed that Shakespeare's plays needed something more to draw audiences. In adapting Shakepeare's *Macbeth*, Davenant added music, songs, and dancing witches. He also modified the story so that Lady Macbeth, rather than Macbeth himself, meets the three witches. The title page of his 1674 adaptation of *Macbeth* reads, "*Macbeth, A Tragedy*: With all the Alterations, Amendments, Additions, and New Songs. As it is now Acted at the Dukes Theatre." Altering Shakespeare's works represented a new trend that kept the original texts off the stage for many years.

THE ACTOR-MANAGER

An important forerunner of the modern director was the actor-manager, a leading man who also oversaw the artistic and business operations of a company. Among the first and most famous of these creative hybrids was David Garrick.

DIRECTING BY EXAMPLE. Following the death of Thomas Betterton in 1710, Garrick became the most acclaimed actor in England. As a wealthy co-owner of his theater, Garrick directed productions as he pleased. Fed up with the formal acting style of the past, Garrick introduced a more natural approach, and he directed the other actors in his company to follow his example. Although revolutionary at the time, Garrick's naturalism would be considered stiff and formal by today's standards. Nevertheless, he influenced many of the great actors who followed him, including John Philip Kemble (1757–1823), Sarah Siddons (1755–1831), and Edmund Kean (1787–1833).

LASTING IMPACT. David Garrick's most lasting influence on the art of directing Shakespeare's plays resulted from his sizable talent as a self-promoter. He worked with several artists and engravers to create images of his performances. A painting of Garrick playing Richard III, for example, captures the actor rearing back after being startled by the ghosts of the victims who have come to foretell his imminent defeat in battle. This and several other images from Garrick's productions became famous, and many of his successors used them to imitate his acting style, costumes, and set designs.

THE AGE OF SPECTACLE

Until the 1800s many Shakespearean actor-managers were still using the conventions of Elizabethan productions. As in the past, theaters were intimate spaces where the actors performed only a few feet from their audience. Scenery was simple. In fact Garrick often used the same scenery for different plays. Costumes received little attention. Most productions used apparel from several time periods in the performance of a play.

All this changed during the 1800s. Shakespeare had become a classic, a writer of enduring excellence whose plays demanded special attention and respectful treatment. Producers (most of them actor-managers) wanted to ensure that the scenery, costumes, and other aspects of their productions were in keeping with the period and setting that a given text implied.

SPECTACLE AND HISTORY. A law passed in 1843 permitted new theaters to establish their own acting companies. With increased competition for audiences, actor-managers had to find new ways to fill the seats in their theaters.

Charles Kean, a famous English actor of the 1800s, is perhaps best remembered for the lavish sets of his Shakespearean productions. He blended historical accuracy with a love of spectacle. As manager of the Princess's Theater, he directed many of Shakespeare's plays with a special emphasis on the authenticity of the costumes and sets. His production of *A Midsummer Night's Dream* included re-creations of the ancient Roman cities of Pompeii and Herculaneum. He even employed scholars to advise the builders of his elaborate scenery.

DISTINCTIVE ROLES

Taking their cues from the movie industry, theater companies also began to distinguish between a producer and a director. Beginning in the United States and spreading to England in the 1950s, the producer came to be the person responsible for mounting a play or film, primarily from the legal and financial angles. The producer delegates to the director the business of bringing the work into being. In simple terms the director is given a budget and told to put on the show.

IRVING AND TREE. Another actor-manager, Henry Irving, followed in Kean's footsteps by creating lavish productions that amazed and delighted his audiences. Like Kean he valued historical accuracy. For his production of *Coriolanus,* Irving had sets built to resemble Etruscan* public buildings and private homes.

Perhaps the only producer to rival Irving in extravagance was Herbert Beerbohm Tree. The Shakespearean productions directed by Tree were so elaborate that they lasted more than three hours and required long intermissions while the scenes were changed. Tree's continuing hit from 1898 to 1913 was *Julius Caesar,* which he regularly staged to include a forum scene of 100 supers* (250 on the occasion of a royal celebration).

CHANGES IN EUROPE. The German duke of Saxe-Meiningen was a talented amateur, with the wealth and power to create his own company. In 1881 he brought his Meiningen Players to London in a production of *Julius Caesar* that created quite a stir. Not only had numerous actors been hired for the crowd scenes, they were also exceedingly well rehearsed—not at all like the unruly mob of supers that London audiences were used to. The duke began the modern trend of strong offstage direction. Unfortunately, however, his actors were criticized for being mediocre, their talents bound in the straitjacket of ensemble* drill. Russian dramatist Alexander Ostrovsky thought that Caesar's entrance was stunning, but he noted that the moment the character opened his mouth, he seemed "more like some third-rate provincial schoolmaster than mighty Caesar." It seemed that first-rate acting could not flourish under tyrannical producers.

LESS IS MORE

By the beginning of the 1900s, some producers were beginning to refocus their attention on Shakespeare's texts, which had been obscured by the lavish sets and costumes of the 1800s. Because of time-consuming scene changes, Shakespeare's texts had often been abridged* to keep the plays from running too long. In addition, the fledgling film industry of the early 20th century would soon prove to many that the stage could not compete with movies for special effects. But not all producers wished to return to the past. Although they revived some old traditions, they rejected others and created new ones of their own.

BACK TO BASICS. The time was ripe for new ideas, and Harley Granville-Barker supplied them. An actor, playwright, and theater manager, Granville-Barker approached *The Winter's Tale* in 1912 in what is generally accepted as the first Shakespearean production of modern times. It focused on Shakespeare's text, not on the staging. "On or about December 1910," said novelist Virginia Woolf, "human nature changed." She was referring to the kind of realism that Granville-Barker was bringing to the stage. Out went productions that were upholstered and pictorial, dominated by massive sets and obsessed with historical detail. The new trend

* *Etruscan* characteristic of Etruria, an ancient civilization in central Italy that reached its peak in the early 500s B.C.

* *super* supernumerary, a performer hired to play a nonspeaking role

* *ensemble* referring to a group working together to produce a single effect

* *abridge* to shorten or condense a work, while attempting to retain its original meaning

Directors and Shakeapeare

See color plate 8, vol. 3.

was toward swiftness, uncluttered stages, and rapid scene changes. Granville-Barker used nonrealistic backgrounds, and costumes in a medley of styles. Most important, he used Shakespeare's full text, interrupted by only a single intermission.

Although Granville-Barker was an actor of distinction as well as a playwright and scholar, he stood outside the staging. The role of the actor-manager was disappearing. The future of Shakespearean productions lay with an increasingly dominant figure, a director whose name in the credits would appear above even the names of the leading actors.

Signs of the coming era were obvious in the 1930s, when Tyrone Guthrie (the English director who helped start the Stratford Festival in Ontario and later founded the Tyrone Guthrie Theater in Minneapolis) and Russian-born Theodore Komisarjevsky created their provocative, sparkling, and original productions of Shakespeare's plays. Guthrie staged a modern-dress version of *Hamlet*, with Alec Guinness, in 1938; Komisarjevsky directed *The Merry Wives of Windsor* as a musical farce* with Falstaff costumed as the Austrian emperor Franz Josef.

UNTRADITIONAL DIRECTORS. Today's directors reject the idea that there is a "correct" way to direct a Shakespeare play. They search for a new interpretation that extends the life of a Shakespearean work, making it more meaningful to modern audiences. For example, British director Jonathan Miller interpreted *The Tempest* as a neocolonial fable. He based many of his ideas on Ottave Mannoni's *Prospero and Caliban*, a work of social anthropology* about the people of Madagascar. Mannoni saw Caliban and Ariel as different forms of black response to white rulers. So Miller cast two black actors as Caliban and Ariel. He depicted the island as a state on the verge of independence, with Prospero as a colonial governor preparing to leave. This vision transformed the text into something both contemporary and convincing.

In 1965 British director Peter Hall created a *Hamlet* that defined its generation. His prince (played by David Warner) was a graduate student, dressed in an academic robe and a long scarf, torn away from Wittenberg University and resisting the authoritarian* system in which he is forced to live. A staging of the play in 1991 by the American Repertory Theater in Cambridge, Massachusetts, saw the action quite sympathetically from the viewpoint of Claudius and Gertrude. Here was a second marriage, with the son retained from the first making trouble for his mother and stepfather. Many members of the audience recognized the situation, having been through similar experiences themselves.

The Shakespearean director of today has become a figure of immense prestige. In 1999 the great Japanese director Yukio Ninagawa brought an English-language *King Lear*, starring Nigel Hawthorne, to London. The investment was £1.3 million (around $2 million). Only a world-class director could command that much money. In the economics of global Shakespeare, the director has become a very important figure indeed. (*See also* **Acting Companies, Elizabethan; Acting Companies, Modern; Actors, Shakespearean.**)

DISEASE

phlegm thick, slimy mucus found in the respiratory tract

D uring the Elizabethan era, knowledge about how to prevent and cure disease was limited. Doctors believed that most illness resulted from an imbalance of four vital bodily fluids—blood, phlegm*, black bile, and yellow bile—known as humors. The real cause of many ailments, however, was poor SANITATION. In cities and towns throughout England, residents dumped their garbage into the streets and nearby ditches. These dumps were breeding places for disease and for disease-spreading rats. Occasionally, these rats became infested with fleas, which carried one of the world's deadliest diseases—plague.

Plague came in two forms: pneumonic and bubonic. Pneumonic plague infected the lungs and was almost always fatal. Bubonic plague was more common; it was characterized by swollen, purple blotches under the skin and killed more than half of its victims. In the mid-1300s, a devastating outbreak of bubonic plague—also known as the Black Death—killed about one-third of the population of Europe.

Five epidemics of plague struck England in the 1500s. The less severe epidemics struck during Shakespeare's lifetime, and LONDON was never completely free of the disease. In 1603, for example, plague killed more than 30,000 Londoners. When plague deaths reached more than 30 per week, authorities closed public theaters to slow the spread of the illness from person to person.

Another common and deadly ailment in Elizabethan England was smallpox. This highly contagious virus killed about 30 percent of those infected and left survivors with terrible scars. Physicians usually recommended surrounding a smallpox victim with red curtains, which were thought to absorb disease. During an epidemic in 1562, Queen ELIZABETH I almost died of smallpox.

Many people believed that God had sent the plague and other diseases to punish sinners. For this reason prayer was often part of the treatment. Other remedies included holding a plucked chicken against the swollen blotches to draw out the disease, placing peeled onions around the house to absorb contagion in the air, and wearing amulets* to ward off evil. The most common treatment for all ailments, however, was bloodletting (drawing blood from the veins). Often done with the aid of leeches*, bloodletting was thought to restore the proper balance of the humors and drain disease from the body. Unfortunately, this practice sometimes killed the patient, who was already weakened by illness. (*See also* **Medicine.**)

amulet small object or ornament worn as a magic charm to ward off evil

leech bloodsucking worm formerly used by physicians to bleed their patients

Perhaps the most dreaded disease in Shakespeare's England was the plague. An outbreak of plague in 1603 killed 30,000 people in London, causing many of the city's residents to flee to the countryside in hope of escaping the disease.

Disguises

DISGUISES

See
color plate 4,
vol. 2.

* *doublet* short, close-fitting jacket, usually
worn over an undershirt
* *jerkin* long jacket, usually worn over a
doublet
* *hose* tight-fitting trousers

Disguises play an important role in several of Shakespeare's works. Two of the most common forms of disguise in the plays are women dressing as men and nobles masquerading as commoners. Regardless of the type of disguise assumed, however, characters hide their identities for two main reasons: to escape harm and to gain information or power that would normally be unavailable to them.

DRESSED FOR SUCCESS. Elizabethan men and women wore very different apparel; thus a person wearing doublet*, jerkin*, and hose* was assumed to be a man. Several of Shakespeare's best-known heroines disguise themselves as men by donning these masculine garments.

Female characters impersonating men play an essential part in *As You Like It, The Merchant of Venice, The Two Gentlemen of Verona*, and *Twelfth Night*. In *As You Like It*, ROSALIND flees to the Forest of Arden with her friend Celia. In response to Celia's fears that they will be targeted by assailants because they are unescorted women, Rosalind disguises herself as a man, saying, "Were it not better, / Because I am more than common tall, / That I did [dress myself in] all points like a man?" (I.iii.114–16).

Once in the forest, however, Rosalind finds a new purpose for her male apparel—testing the devotion of Orlando, her lover. Masquerading as a boy named Ganymede, she persuades Orlando to court her as if she were Rosalind, thus enabling her to judge his sincerity. Her disguise frees her from the rules of courtship, which prohibit women from taking an active role in romance. Similar situations motivate other female Shakespearean characters to put on male clothing. In *The Two Gentlemen of Verona*, for example, Julia masquerades as a man in order to spy on her beloved, who is serving at the royal court. And in *Twelfth Night*, Viola

Several Shakespearean comedies feature women disguised as men. In this scene from *The Merchant of Venice* (Royal Shakespeare Company, 1981), Portia (Sinead Cusack) disguised as a lawyer tries to prevent Shylock (David Suchet) from taking revenge on Antonio.

dresses as a man to protect herself from danger after being shipwrecked and stranded in a strange land.

In *The Merchant of Venice,* sexual disguise enables Portia to masquerade as a lawyer, an occupation restricted to men, in order to save the life of her husband's best friend. Wearing men's garments, she presents herself in court as a young lawyer named Balthazar. Her clever ruse and ingenious defense saves Antonio from Shylock, the moneylender who demands a pound of flesh as payment for an outstanding debt. Like Rosalind, Portia also uses her concealed identity to test her beloved's devotion. While disguised as Balthazar, she asks her husband to part with a ring he had earlier promised he would keep forever.

Another reason that Shakespeare wrote about women impersonating men was to heighten the humor of certain scenes. Because Elizabethan law prohibited women from appearing on stage, boys played all female roles. This led to amusing complications when boys presented as women disguised themselves as boys. (In *As You Like It* a boy would have played a woman dressed as a boy who pretends to be a woman!)

NOBLES INCOGNITO. In several Shakespearean plays, noblemen conceal their identity in order to gather information. In *Henry V,* for example, the king travels through his army's camp pretending to be a soldier and learns what ordinary men think about his leadership of the war they are fighting. One man, Michael Williams, reveals what very few subjects would knowingly say to their king. He asserts that if soldiers die in a just war they will have to answer to God for their own sins.

> But if the cause be not good, the king himself hath a heavy reckoning to make, when all those legs, and arms, and heads chopp'd off in a battle, shall join together at the latter day and cry all, "We died at such a place"—some swearing, some crying for a surgeon, some upon their wives left poor behind them, some upon the debts they owe, some upon their children [unprovided for].
>
> (IV.i.134–41)

In *Measure for Measure,* Duke Vincentio disguises himself as a friar in order to spy on Angelo, the stern deputy he has left in charge of Vienna. Unbeknown to Angelo, the duke witnesses his deputy's abuse of power. The duke's disguise also enables him to save chaste Isabella from Angelo's threat of blackmail and Claudio from being executed for a relatively minor offense.

Like King Henry, however, the duke learns that some of his subjects lack respect for him. The disguised ruler hears himself called a drunk, a lecher, and "a very superficial . . . fellow" (III.ii.140–41). (*See also* **Clothing.**)

DOCTORS

See *Medicine.*

DOMESTIC TRAGEDY

* **classical** in the tradition of ancient Greece and Rome
* **protagonist** central character in a dramatic or literary work

omestic tragedy is a form of drama that deals with the misfortunes of ordinary people. It first emerged during the Elizabethan era as a departure from classical* tragedy, which focused on the lives of kings, heroes, and other extraordinary people. As compared to classical tragedy, in which the protagonist's* fate may affect an entire kingdom, the unhappy ending of a domestic tragedy is more personal.

Domestic tragedies were very popular in the late Elizabethan era. There are more than 20 known domestic tragedies dating from this period, and probably at least 20 more existed that have since been lost. The first domestic tragedies were based on Elizabethan murder stories. *Arden of Feversham*, written around 1591, dramatized the story of a man who was murdered by his wife and her lover, while *A Yorkshire Tragedy*, written around 1606, portrayed a father who destroyed his family in a fit of insanity. Some critics have claimed that Shakespeare may have written one or both of these plays. Most believe, however, that Thomas Kyd wrote *Arden of Feversham*. The author of *A Yorkshire Tragedy* may have been Thomas Heywood, who wrote the 1607 domestic tragedy *A Woman Killed With Kindness*. Heywood is also believed to have written *A Warning for Fair Women*, a domestic tragedy dealing with the murder of a merchant by his wife.

While none of Shakespeare's plays are considered domestic tragedies, some of them have elements in common with domestic tragedy. For example, a few of the comedies, such as *The Merchant of Venice* and *Much Ado About Nothing*, focus on the lives of common people and have plots that show the potential for tragedy, even if they turn out happily in the end. There are also elements of domestic tragedy in the love-plots of *Romeo and Juliet* and *Othello*. (*See also* **Playwrights and Poets**.)

DRAMATIC TECHNIQUES

* **soliloquy** monologue in which a character reveals his or her private thoughts

ne of the reasons students find Shakespeare's plays so challenging is that his dramatic techniques cannot be reduced to a few simple rules or formulas. For almost every technique he uses in one play, it is possible to find him using the exact opposite in another. His settings include taverns and palaces, battlefields and magic forests, bedrooms and courts of law—often interspersed within the action of a single play. Events range from stately processions to intense soliloquies*, tender love scenes, drinking brawls, marching armies, masked balls, and plays within a play. Shakespeare's free-form drama uses an immense range of strategies to create comic effect, draw contrasts and comparisons, develop character, and intensify the themes that dominate a given plot. Somehow he manages to use these strategies without being used by them. He avoids allowing his devices to turn into rigid rules that would restrain his creativity.

OVERALL STRUCTURE. Most Renaissance plays were organized in accordance with the five-act structure developed by Seneca, an ancient Roman dramatist. Seneca divided his tragedies into distinct sections, each

framed by choruses. In Shakespeare's early productions, however, act divisions were not made explicit. In the public playhouses where Shakespeare's plays were produced at the beginning of his career, a play was normally performed without interruption from beginning to end. The most significant structural units, from the audience's perspective, were the scenes, marked by exits and entrances that indicated shifts in time or locale.

Late in his career, Shakespeare began writing plays for the more exclusive indoor theaters. These performance spaces were smaller and more intimate than the outdoor playhouses. In addition they had artificial lighting, which made evening performances possible. In what really amounted to private settings, it became customary to emphasize act divisions with musical interludes. This custom shifted the focus of performances from individual scenes to the traditional five-act structure. Interestingly, no printed collections of Shakespeare's plays were consistently divided into acts and scenes until 1709, when Nicholas ROWE published the first critical edition of the plays. Later editions copied Rowe's act and scene divisions.

Another variation in the overall structure of Shakespeare's dramatic works is his use of subplots, which usually provide alternative perspectives on the main plot. In *King Lear* the principal action, involving the king and his three daughters, is paralleled by a subplot involving the earl of Gloucester and his two sons. Shakespeare weaves these two strands together, having his characters interact in ways that highlight both the similarities and the differences between the two old men. Both suffer as a result of hasty judgments they make about their children, but the king and the duke respond in different ways. Lear is driven to madness and Gloucester to despair.

DIFFERENT TYPES OF SCENES. Although Shakespeare's plays conform more or less to the five-act model, he uses a great variety of scenes within this structure. The openings of his plays, for example, do not conform to any set pattern. The first scene frequently involves some sort of exposition, or explanation of the situation at the play's outset. This exposition, however, can be presented in several different ways. Some plays open with a prologue, a short address to the audience delivered by the Chorus, a character who functions more as a narrator standing outside the plot than as a character within it. In *Richard III*, by contrast, the first person to address the audience is the leading character. Other plays, such as *King Lear*, disclose the initial situation through a dialogue between two minor characters. The opening scene often sets the tone for the entire drama, as in *Macbeth*, where the appearance of the three witches is a signal that supernatural elements will play a significant role in the action to come.

The overall effect of Shakespeare's plays depends partly on the balance he manages between different scenes. Many of his plays alternate the action between two main settings, shifting back and forth as the events develop. In *Antony and Cleopatra*, for example, the action begins in the self-indulgent luxury of the Egyptian court, then switches to the

See color plate 12, vol. 2.

See
color plate 9,
vol. 2.

harsh formality of the Roman political scene. Placing the two environments side by side exaggerates the contrast between them. Similarly, in *Henry IV, Part 1*, the playwright sets the tensions and insecurities of King Henry's court against the rowdy scenes in the tavern. One episode turns the tavern into a parody of the court, with FALSTAFF and the prince performing mock impersonations of the king. In *Measure for Measure*, Shakespeare contrasts two settings to create an ironic effect. Characters tend to speak honestly in the prison but deceptively in the court of the supposedly honorable judge Angelo.

The length of Shakespeare's scenes is also significant. For example, many military encounters are presented as a sequence of short skirmishes, with the settings bouncing back and forth from one side of the battlefield to the other. These rapid shifts of perspective create a sense of urgency. Dramatic tension can also be heightened—or relieved—by the inclusion of humorous interludes within a tragic plot. Comic characters, such as the gravediggers in *Hamlet* and the drunken porter in *Macbeth*, provide a break in the grim tragedy of these plays. But they also prolong the suspense by delaying the catastrophic events that the audience knows are in store: OPHELIA's funeral and the discovery of King Duncan's murdered body. Speeches of the minor characters also accentuate the atmosphere of death in these plays.

INTERACTIONS BETWEEN CHARACTERS. One difference between Elizabethan drama and most modern drama is that characters in the plays of Shakespeare's era often reveal their private thoughts to the audience in soliloquies. The audience's first impression of the villainous Richard III, for example, comes from a solo appearance at the beginning of the play, where he tells the audience directly who he is and what he plans to do. In other plays, by contrast, Shakespeare introduces his protagonist* through the eyes of another character. *Antony and Cleopatra* opens, for example, with a conversation between two minor characters about how Antony's love for the Egyptian queen has changed his personality. This view of the two lovers inevitably shapes the audience's reaction to these characters.

One type of character that Shakespeare often uses to achieve a particular dramatic effect is the messenger. At the beginning of *Macbeth*, the soldiers who bring news from the battlefield to King Duncan serve several functions. First, they help establish an aura of bold and direct action that will continue throughout the play. Second, they provide background, helping the audience identify the king's allies and his enemies. Finally, and perhaps most importantly, they portray Macbeth as a brave, loyal, and fearless fighter. This characterization of the hero as an honorable warrior provides a vivid contrast to the bloody tyrant that he will become by the end of the play. In *Richard III* the messengers who arrive with bad news for the king (Act IV, Scene ii) help develop Richard's character in a different way. Instead of establishing the king's character, they show how his personality is changing. As the messengers tell of one disaster after another, the audience can see Richard's confidence and brutal control of his surroundings begin to collapse. These emissaries help create the

* *protagonist* central character in a dramatic or literary work

atmosphere of panic and disintegration that will characterize the play's concluding scenes.

STAGE DIRECTIONS. Some of the interactions between characters in Shakespeare's plays depend on the structural features of Elizabethan playhouses. For example, the stage itself was usually very deep, extending far out into the audience. This depth made it easy to create eavesdropping scenes, in which one character appears on the stage without being noticed and overhears the other characters' conversation. Shakespeare not only included many such scenes in his plays, but he created a twist on the theme in such plays as *Much Ado About Nothing,* where several characters arrange conversations specifically for the purpose of having another character overhear them.

Shakespeare also helped his characters interact by making effective use of different levels in the performance area. Outdoor playhouses included an upper gallery directly above the stage. The famous balcony scene in *Romeo and Juliet* put this feature to good use by placing the two young lovers on different levels, visually emphasizing the barriers between them. Another effective use of the upper level is Antony's death scene in *Antony and Cleopatra,* where Cleopatra hides in a monument and the dying Antony is lifted up to her waiting arms. An even higher level, a window known as the top, is mentioned in the stage directions of *The Tempest* and *Henry VI, Part 1.*

Shakespeare also had GODS, such as Jupiter in *Cymbeline,* and other figures descend from "heaven" by lowering actors on a rope from a section of the second gallery that was covered by a canopy. This part of the theater's superstructure could also conceal the machinery used to produce sound effects. Trapdoors in the stage below enabled Shakespeare to include underground levels as well, such as Ophelia's grave in *Hamlet* and MALVOLIO's prison in *Twelfth Night.*

Some of Shakespeare's special effects, however, could not be achieved with the resources he had available in the theater. Instead, he relied on his audience's willingness to suspend its disbelief—that is, to accept the world on the stage as real without questioning its unrealistic qualities. For example, when characters with magical powers (such as OBERON and PROSPERO) need to become invisible, they simply say that they are. Viewers accept that these characters are invisible to other characters, even though they are plainly visible to the audience.

At other times, by contrast, Shakespeare seems deliberately to remind the audience that the actions on the stage are part of a play, an artificial reality. For example, when Hamlet instructs a group of traveling players to "Suit the action to the word, the word to the action" (III.ii.17–18), his words remind the viewers that Hamlet himself is a character being played by an actor. Similar self-references appear in *Macbeth,* such as the king's personification of Life as "a poor player / That struts and frets his hour upon the stage, / And then is heard no more" (V.v.24–26). (*See also* **Directors and Shakespeare; Elizabethan Theaters; Playhouse Structure; Poetic Technique; Prose Technique; Quartos and Folios; Shakespeare's Sources.**)

SETTING THE SCENE

For many years scholars believed that Shakespeare's plays had originally been performed on a bare stage with little or no scenery. Current evidence indicates, however, that some Elizabethan productions used fairly elaborate scenery. Theater manager Philip Henslowe kept an itemized list of stage properties in his possession, which included such unusual items as a tomb, a mossy bank, a bay tree, a "Hell mouth," a "city of Rome," and a "cloth of the sun and moon." Most of Shakespeare's plays do not call for such elaborate sets, but many scenes require some sort of furniture, such as a bed, tables and chairs, or a throne on a raised platform.

Dreams

DREAMS

* *soothsayer* person who can predict the
future

A powerful dream sequence occurs
near the end of *Henry VIII*. In this engraving by poet William Blake, the dying Queen Katherine sees herself surrounded by dancing figures clad in
white, which she describes as "spirits
of peace."

Dreams play a major role in many of Shakespeare's works. In the
plays they serve two major functions: to provoke guilt for past
deeds and to foretell events to come. Many of Shakespeare's characters compare dreams with waking reality, often noting that things that
seem real may be as insubstantial as dreams

Prophetic dreams, which warn of future events, feature especially
prominently in *Julius Caesar*. Early in the play, Caesar receives numerous
warnings of his upcoming assassination. A soothsayer* urges him to "Be-
ware the IDES OF MARCH" (I.ii.23) (the day on which he will be murdered),
but Caesar dismisses the man as a "dreamer." He pays more attention to the
nightmare of his wife, Calpurnia, in which she sees his statue pouring blood
and the citizens of Rome bathing their hands in it. She takes this dream as
an omen of his death and begs him not to leave the house that day. One of
the conspirators plotting against Caesar persuades him to leave, however, by
telling him the dream was actually a "fair and fortunate" vision, signifying
that Caesar will be the source of the "nourishing blood" of Rome. Ironically,
both interpretations of the dream turn out to be correct: Caesar is indeed
murdered, but his death prompts the civil war that eventually ends with
the establishment of the Roman empire. Another prophetic dream occurs
immediately after Caesar's murder, when the poet Cinna dreams of feasting with the dead Caesar shortly before he himself is murdered.

The function of dreams for arousing guilt is seen most clearly in *Macbeth*. After murdering the king, Macbeth hears a voice cry, "Macbeth does
murder sleep" (II.ii.33), and in a later scene he talks with his wife about
the terrible dreams they have both had every night since the murder. Lady
Macbeth's dreams eventually haunt her so severely that she walks and
talks in her sleep, trying desperately to wash imaginary bloodstains from
her hands. Another dramatic example of a guilt dream occurs in *Richard
III* on the night before the battle in which King Richard will be killed. As
he sleeps, he is haunted by ghosts of all the people he has murdered to
gain power; they curse him and predict his defeat. The spirits then shower
blessings on Richard's rival, who will win the battle and become King
Henry VII. One of Shakespeare's most vivid speeches follows as Richard
awakens in terror, unable to run from the horrors within himself.

But if dreams frequently reflect events in the real world, reality itself
is often compared to a dream in Shakespeare's plays. In *Romeo and Juliet*,
Mercutio delivers a well-known speech about Queen Mab, the fairy who
supposedly brings dreams, explaining how she causes different people to
dream about the things that are closest to them. He then dismisses such
phenomena as "vain fantasy," suggesting that the real world has better
things to offer. In other plays characters such as PROSPERO in *The Tempest*
suggest that "real" life is no more solid than a dream; it melts away into
death, leaving "not a [wisp of cloud] behind" (IV.i.156).

Not surprisingly, the play that focuses most on dreams is *A Midsummer Night's Dream*. After spending a night in the enchanted forest, the
young lovers in this comedy remember the events that occurred there in a
confused way, as if they have been asleep. The duke of Athens dismisses
their memories as "more strange than true" (V.i.2), pointing out that "the
lunatic, the lover, and the poet" (V.i.7) are all capable of perceiving things

that are not real. Yet as the audience has seen, the forest's enchantments are real; they simply inhabit a reality different from that of Athens. In this context, the duke's remarks vividly illustrate the power of dreams in Shakespeare's plays. They show characters a deeper truth, more powerful than the solid facts of reality. Moreover, by comparing dreamers to poets, Shakespeare suggests that art may serve a similar purpose, making dreams as substantial as the actors who bring them to life on stage. (*See also* **Macbeth, Lady.**)

DUELS AND FEUDS

Elizabethans greatly valued personal honor, and insults or injuries to an individual or his family often caused long-running feuds. Injured parties sometimes sought revenge through duels, or armed man-to-man combat. Duels, usually fought with swords, were formal battles conducted according to a specific set of rules. Despite the opposition of Elizabethan authorities, private combats were recognized methods of settling disputes during the late 1500s and early 1600s.

THE RISE OF DUELING. During much of Shakespeare's lifetime, dueling was a rarity in England. For the most part, sword fights were confined to other European countries, especially France, Italy, and Spain. In the late 1500s, however, dueling became more popular in England, especially among courtiers*. Members of the royal court began wearing rapiers as part of their everyday dress. These thin swords, with three-foot blades, were excellent dueling weapons. Courtiers dueled more

* *courtier* person in attendance at a royal court

Many Elizabethans learned the principles of the honorable duello from a fencing manual by Vicentio Saviolo, in which this illustration appeared. Saviolo condemned the Elizabethan practice of fighting duels over trivial matters, which he saw as dishonorable.

often than ordinary people because in the rancorous world of the royal court, they were insulted more often. Insults challenged personal honor, and courtiers regarded honor as one of their most treasured possessions.

Support for dueling was not confined to courtiers, however. Many Elizabethans regarded it as a good way to settle feuds between rival families. They preferred to have two men settle a dispute through personal combat rather than allow a feud to spread among dozens of family members, costing lives and disturbing the social order. In addition, many people supported dueling as a method of achieving justice when the English courts failed to punish criminals. Although the law provided punishments for those who physically injured others or stole their property, it failed to protect personal honor. Elizabethans often cited this as a reason for supporting private combat.

OFFENSES AND RULES. Many offenses could lead to a duel, including disagreements over property, accusations of cowardice, and cheating at cards or dice. The worst offense to a man's personal honor, however, was to be accused of lying. This insult, which Elizabethans called "giving the lie," could be redressed only through armed man-to-man battle.

Duelists conducted private combat according to strict rules of etiquette. Because dueling was relatively new to most Elizabethans, several books were published to explain the rules of armed man-to-man combat. One of the first rules stated that the insulted party had the right to challenge his offender to a duel. The challenge was presented in a letter called a *cartel*. The writer was required to use the plainest possible language and to avoid any insults. In England the rules stated that it was the right of the man who had been challenged to pick the dueling weapons that would be used.

Once the rivals agreed to duel, each chose a second, a friend who was responsible for ensuring that the fight was conducted fairly. The combatants typically met in a remote area at dawn. In addition to his second, each man brought with him a servant and a scout, who kept a lookout for authorities and other intruders. After reciting a prayer, the contestants walked about 12 paces apart and faced each other. Each held a dagger for parrying* in one hand and a rapier for thrusting in the other. At the signal "On guard, gentlemen!" the rivals leaped toward each other, deflecting sword thrusts with the dagger while lunging with the rapier. Doctors sometimes attended duels and attempted to save the life of the defeated fighter. Nevertheless, sword fights often resulted in the death of one of the participants.

ATTEMPTING TO STOP THE BLOODSHED. Elizabethan authorities strongly opposed duels and feuds. They regarded acts of personal vengeance as a sign of disrespect for the law and for the monarchy as well as a threat to public order. Those found guilty of avenging a wrong by dueling often received punishments that were as harsh as those received by ordinary criminals. Queen ELIZABETH I forbade her courtiers to take the law into their own hands. During her reign she imprisoned several

* *parry* to deflect or evade a blow from a weapon

noblemen for ignoring her instructions to refrain from fighting each other. When King JAMES I ascended the throne, he also opposed duels. In 1613 he issued his *Proclamation Against Private Challenges and Combats,* which condemned private combat.

Despite King James's proclamation, Englishmen continued to use duels to settle feuds and other disagreements. In fact swordplay increased during the king's reign. Several theories have been advanced to explain this, including the increasing influence on England of France and Italy, where dueling was a widespread practice. The most likely explanation for the increased violence, however, was a rivalry between James's Scottish courtiers and the English courtiers who resented them. Some determined combatants went so far as to arrange their private battles in foreign lands to avoid English laws against duels.

Monarchs and other authorities were not the only critics of duels and feuds during the Elizabethan era. In his plays Shakespeare exposed the foolishness of private sword fights, especially through his use of comedy. He ridiculed the tendency of members of the royal court to duel over trivial matters. In *As You Like It* a fool named Touchstone remarks that he "did dislike the cut of a certain courtier's beard" (V.iv.69–70) and that the dispute was not settled until they discovered an excuse for disallowing any insults and then "measured swords and parted" (V.iv.87).

Shakespeare also condemned feuds in his plays through the tragic consequences of such quarrels. He begins *Romeo and Juliet* by telling the audience of an "ancient grudge" between the Capulet and Montague families, "Where civil blood makes civil hands unclean" (Prologue, 4). The feud ultimately results in the deaths of several family members, including the young lovers of the play's title. (*See also* **Morality and Ethics; Revenge and Forgiveness.**)

ECONOMY

See *Banking and Commerce; Trade.*

EDUCATION AND LITERACY

See color plate 10, vol. 1.

Shakespeare's audience was raised in a culture in which language played an important role. Most theatergoers, from the poor spectators standing on the ground to the wealthy nobles sitting in the box seats, were literate enough to appreciate the beautiful language in his plays. Aside from their shared basic literacy—the ability to read and write—however, the poor and the wealthy had very different educational backgrounds.

THE PETTY SCHOOL. In the late 1500s attendance at educational institutions was purely voluntary. At about age five or six, children went to a

THE LANGUAGE OF LEARNING

Oxford and Cambridge had special terms for various faculty members and students, some of which are still in use. A *proctor,* for example, was a disciplinary officer who patrolled the streets at night looking for rowdy undergraduates. A *commoner* was a student who paid for his "commons" (his food and other expenses). The term *bachelor* was used as it is today: a person who had received the first or lowest degree granted by the university (usually a Bachelor of Arts). A *scholar* received money to cover the costs of his education. Scholars wore distinctive academic robes and had special seats in the dining room and at chapel.

* *classical* referring to the tradition of ancient Greece and Rome

Grammar school students had to recite their lessons in Latin, which was considered the language of the educated. This woodcut of an Elizabethan classroom appeared in a 1573 Latin grammar text.

petty school, a type of elementary school that was run privately or as part of a parish. Its primary function was to teach reading, but students, both boys and girls, also learned to write and perform simple arithmetic.

Pupils in the petty schools first learned the alphabet from a hornbook, which was made from a single sheet of paper covered by a thin slice of transparent horn. The paper was mounted on a piece of wood with a handle. The alphabet was often printed on the paper, which might also contain a prayer or another passage from the Bible.

After they mastered the hornbook, children moved on to a primer. This small book contained a set of English prayers and a catechism—questions and answers about religious doctrine.

Petty schools were noisy, dirty, and often presided over by teachers with limited educational backgrounds. Students from poorer families were often taken out of school to work for their parents. Wealthy or highly intelligent boys continued their education at grammar schools.

THE GRAMMAR SCHOOL. At the age of seven, the more gifted or well-to-do boys attended a grammar school. Some of these schools, such as Winchester and Eton, were founded as far back as the 1400s. The grammar school was a demanding environment for young boys. Grammar school teachers were usually highly educated men who knew several languages, including Greek and Latin.

Elizabethans considered Latin an essential part of an educated person's background. Queen ELIZABETH I even delivered some of her public speeches in Latin, especially when she spoke at the universities. The study of Latin was so important that by the time boys reached advanced levels of study—at the age of 11 or 12—they were required to speak Latin in everyday conversations. Studying Latin also exposed the boys to classical* authors, such as the great Roman writers Cicero, Cato, Ovid, Seneca, and Virgil, whose work strongly influenced Shakespeare.

Boys attended grammar schools for five to ten years, and classes typically lasted from six in the morning until half past five in the evening. Shakespeare probably attended the King's New School in STRATFORD-UPON-AVON.

THE UNIVERSITIES. After grammar school many students (who were then 14 or 15 years old) attended one of the two universities outside London: Oxford or Cambridge. Only men were permitted to attend universities in the 1500s—a barrier to women that lasted well into the 1800s. Each of the two universities was made up of smaller "colleges." As in the grammar schools, classical studies were the most important subject in the universities. Many members of Shakespeare's audiences were university students or graduates, who recognized the many references to classical literature and mythology that appear in his plays.

EDUCATING YOUNG WOMEN. Girls had fewer educational opportunities than boys had in Elizabethan England. Only a few grammar schools accepted girls—and only those between the ages of seven and nine. Wealthy families sometimes hired private tutors to educate their daughters at home, but most parents believed that the best path for a girl was domestic training for becoming a wife and mother. Noble girls were often sent away to become ladies-in-waiting, preparing for what was considered a respected social position. Poorer girls became servants or worked in shops.

Elizabethan women read sermons, the Bible, and other religious materials. As a result many women began to participate in the growing number of new religious groups, such as the Quakers, that sprang up in the 1600s. Their early education at the petty schools, however limited, had opened the door to broader possibilities for English women.

For the first time in England's history, a large segment of its population had access to education and knowledge. It is not surprising, therefore, that literature and drama flourished in Shakespeare's time, due in large part to the educated and literate members of the Elizabethan audience. Like Shakespeare, they too had a deep love for, and understanding of, the power of language. (*See also* **Elizabethan Theaters; Schools and Universities.**)

EDUCATION OF SHAKESPEARE

See *Shakespeare, Life and Career.*

ELIZABETH I

1533–1603
Queen of England

* *annulment* formal declaration that a marriage is legally invalid

Elizabeth I, who ruled England throughout most of Shakespeare's life, is one of the most admired monarchs in history. Her 45-year reign was a time of prosperity, political intrigue, and a great flowering of the arts. "Good Queen Bess" is remembered both for her ability to survive the political and religious challenges that would have destroyed lesser rulers and for her support of the theater and other arts.

ELIZABETH'S RISE TO POWER. Elizabeth I was the only child of King HENRY VIII by his second wife, Anne Boleyn. When they first met, Anne was a lady-in-waiting to Henry's first queen, Katherine of Aragon. Queen Katherine had been unable to give Henry a male heir to the throne, so he was eager to end their marriage and try to have a son with Anne. England was then a Catholic country, and the Catholic Church prohibited divorce, so Henry attempted to persuade the pope to grant him an annulment*. After the pope refused the king's request, Henry decided to withdraw England from the Catholic Church. He declared himself the head of the new Church of England, annulled his own marriage to Katherine, and married Anne, who was already pregnant with Elizabeth.

Anne and the king had not hidden their affair from Queen Katherine, and this behavior made the new queen widely unpopular. The king soon lost interest in Anne, possibly because she too failed to give him a

Elizabeth I

son. In 1536, just three years after he married her, King Henry charged Queen Anne with adultery and had her executed. He took a third wife, who gave him the son he had wanted, and young Elizabeth's position at the royal court became very insecure. She came close to being executed at least once, and no one expected that she would ever gain the throne. When King Henry died, he passed the crown to his only son, Edward. If Edward died without children, the throne would go next to Princess Mary—the king's only child by Katherine of Aragon—and finally, if Mary also had no children, to Elizabeth. As it turned out, this was exactly what happened.

Elizabeth I assumed the throne in 1558 at the age of 25. Her 45-year reign helped bring stability and prosperity to a troubled realm.

ELIZABETH IN SHAKESPEARE

In spite of Queen Elizabeth's support of Shakespeare, there are surprisingly few references to her in his works. One passage in *A Midsummer Night's Dream*, which describes a maiden priestess who avoids being struck by Cupid's love arrows, is believed to refer to Elizabeth. In a scene in *Henry VIII*, a play that some scholars believe was cowritten by John Fletcher, a priest witnessing the birth of Elizabeth foretells that she will be the most virtuous ruler in history. Other possible references, much less flattering, are found in *King John* and *Richard II*, which dramatize unpleasant events similar to some that occurred during Elizabeth's reign.

* *Anglican* referring to the Church of England
* *excommunicate* to formally exclude from church membership
* *Privy Council* body of advisers serving an English monarch

ELIZABETH AND THE CHURCH. Elizabeth's half brother, King Edward VI, did not live past his 15th birthday. When Mary, a devout Catholic, took the throne in 1553, she was determined to return England to the Catholic Church. For five years she brutally persecuted Protestants, earning the nickname "Bloody Mary." When Elizabeth, a Protestant, succeeded Mary in 1558, she wanted to unite the warring Protestants and Catholics within the Church of England.

Elizabeth reformed the church according to a compromise that came to be known as the Elizabethan settlement. One of her first acts as queen was to pass the Act of Uniformity, which attempted to make the Church of England a "middle way" between Protestant and Catholic modes of worship. It outlawed the practice of Catholicism and required everyone to attend Sunday services in the Church of England or pay a fine. At the same time it revised the Protestant prayer book and certain rituals to make them more acceptable to Catholics. Most, but not all, of the trappings of Catholic worship were removed from Anglican* churches. The mostly Catholic Parliament passed the Act of Uniformity by the narrow margin of 21 to 18.

The Elizabethan settlement did not entirely eliminate religious tensions in England. Puritans—Protestants who wanted to "purify" the Church of England of Catholic influences—felt that the church under the settlement was still too close to Catholicism. Meanwhile Catholics, who wanted Elizabeth to return England to Catholicism, attacked her for making the Church of England too Protestant. Pope Pius V excommunicated* her, and his successor actually encouraged attempts on her life. Some Catholics plotted (unsuccessfully) with Queen Mary of Scotland to overthrow Elizabeth. Spain, a major Catholic power, became a powerful rival to England. In 1588 Spain sent an armada—a fleet of ships—to attack England. Miraculously, the English navy defeated the Spaniards, but tensions such as these made England's position as a Protestant power a very delicate one.

ELIZABETH'S COURT. Part of Elizabeth's success as a ruler was the result of her careful selection of skilled advisers to serve in her Privy Council*. Her chief adviser throughout much of the period was Sir William Cecil, appointed in 1558 and later named Lord Burghley. A cautious politician in matters of foreign policy, Burghley helped secure more than 40 years of peace and prosperity for England. At home he was more ruthless, establishing an early form of secret police to keep Catholics under control and to prevent attempts on the queen's life and his own.

Another highly visible member of Elizabeth's council was Robert Dudley, the earl of Leicester. Many scholars believe that Elizabeth wished to marry him, and when his first wife died under suspicious circumstances, it was widely suspected that Leicester had killed her in order to marry the queen. The scandal that resulted, as well as a number of other political problems, made the match impossible.

In addition to her advisers, Elizabeth had many favorites at court. Among them was Sir Walter Raleigh, a soldier, poet, and explorer. Raleigh may be best remembered for the legend that he once spread his

111

* *patron* supporter or financial sponsor

cloak on the ground so that Queen Elizabeth would not have to step in a puddle. But Raleigh lost the queen's favor with the arrival of Robert Devereux, the earl of Essex. Essex became a member of the Privy Council and attracted numerous admirers, including Shakespeare's patron* Henry Wriothesley, the earl of Southampton. After Essex led an unsuccessful expedition against Ireland, however, the queen banished him from court.

Despite these attachments, Elizabeth never married and came to be known as "the Virgin Queen." She had no children, and near the end of her reign, she named her cousin King James of Scotland heir to her throne.

ELIZABETH AND THE THEATER. Elizabeth I was famous for her great love of the theater. Not only did she prevent Puritans, who considered dramatic productions immoral, from shutting down the theaters, but her court provided an important source of security and even some income for the leading London acting companies. During the 1590s, when Shakespeare wrote the majority of his plays, performances became more and more frequent at Elizabeth's court.

Elizabeth was particularly fond of Shakespeare's acting company, the Chamberlain's Men, and they performed frequently for her. According to tradition the queen was so pleased with the character of FALSTAFF that she asked Shakespeare to write a play showing the comical knight in love. Shakespeare responded with *The Merry Wives of Windsor*, which many scholars believe was written for a performance before Elizabeth in 1597. (*See also* **Acting Companies, Elizabethan; Diplomacy and Foreign Relations; James I; King's Men; Merry Wives of Windsor, The; Poets and Playwrights; Shakespeare, Life and Career; Spanish Armada.**)

ELIZABETHAN THEATERS

* *Puritan* English Protestant who advocated strict moral discipline and a simplification of the ceremonies and beliefs of the Anglican Church

The Elizabethan theaters where Shakespeare's plays were first performed were quite different from modern auditoriums. There were two main types of theaters in Shakespeare's time: public, open-air playhouses such as the famous GLOBE THEATER, and private, indoor performance halls such as BLACKFRIARS.

LONDON's outdoor playhouses were located just outside the city's walls, beyond the reach of Puritan* authorities who wanted to shut down all the city's theaters. On the city's northern side stood the Theater, built in 1576, and the Curtain. The northwestern side held the Red Bull and Fortune theaters, while the southern side, just across the Thames River, was home to the Rose, the Swan, the Hope, and the most famous of all Elizabethan theaters, the Globe. In 1989 a construction crew unearthed the architectural remains of the Rose playhouse, and the remains of the Globe were discovered soon after. These two finds provided modern scholars with their best information yet about the structure of these Elizabethan playhouses.

Most of the outdoor theaters were roughly circular in shape (the Prologue to *Henry V* refers to the theater as a "wooden O"). Opposite the

London's public theaters were located outside the city walls to escape the authorities who wished to shut them down. This map shows the location of some of the better-known Elizabethan playhouses, including the Globe, where many of Shakespeare's plays were first performed.

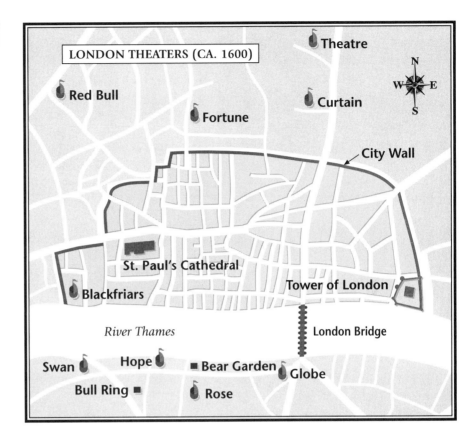

LONDON THEATERS (CA. 1600)

Theatre

Red Bull

Fortune

Curtain

City Wall

St. Paul's Cathedral

Tower of London

Blackfriars

London Bridge

River Thames

Swan   Hope   Bear Garden   Globe

Bull Ring   Rose

See color plate 13, vol. 1.

sixpence six pennies, or half a shilling

priory religious house

main entrance stood the raised stage, extending out from the wall into the center of the theater, partly covered by a roof or canopy. Behind it stood the tiring house, or dressing room. Two or more doors connected the tiring house with the stage, and in between there might have been a curtained-off recess, or "discovery space," in which characters or pieces of scenery were hidden. Above the stage doors was the stage balcony, which was used for scenes requiring an upper level.

An outdoor theater such as the Globe could hold as many as 3,000 people. The outer walls of the structure were lined with galleries, or seating areas, which were also roofed over. The large central yard at the base of the stage had no roof, letting in as much natural daylight as possible. A large group of spectators stood in this yard, with their bodies exposed to the weather and their heads approximately level with the actors' feet. These standing audience members, or groundlings, paid a penny for admission. Another penny purchased a seat in one of the covered galleries. Theaters might have more than one floor of gallery seating, and the upper galleries were generally more expensive to sit in than the lower ones. The best seats, called the lord's rooms, were located in private galleries directly above the tiring house. These expensive seats, costing sixpence* each, did not actually offer a very good view of the stage. People who sat in them were often more interested in being seen than in seeing what occurred below them.

The first indoor playhouse was Blackfriars, which opened in 1600 in an old London priory*. Others included the Whitefriars and St. Paul's.

These indoor theaters were much smaller than the outdoor playhouses, and their design was much more similar to that of a modern theater. Plays were performed in a large hall, much like a ballroom. The stage, with the tiring house behind it, occupied one narrow end of the long hall. The best seats were those closest to the stage, while the cheapest were on benches at the back of the auditorium. Even these seats, however, cost sixpence, and the most expensive cost half a crown—thirty times as much as the penny required to gain entrance at the outdoor playhouses. Some spectators actually sat on stools on the stage, where they could not only see the play well but also be admired by the audience. These highly visible spectators, mainly wealthy young gentlemen, could be very annoying to the other audience members if they smoked during the play or laughed at inappropriate moments, as the aristocratic audience does while watching the PLAY WITHIN THE PLAY in *A Midsummer Night's Dream.*

Because the indoor playhouses were much more expensive to attend, they attracted an audience of a higher SOCIAL CLASS than the outdoor theaters. Their location within the city limits also contributed to their appeal for wealthy Londoners. Another advantage was that, being indoors, they were entirely lit by torches and candles, making it possible to perform plays at night. (*See also* **Acting Profession; Inn Yards.**)

ENTERTAINMENT

See *Dance; Festivals and Holidays; Food and Feasts; Games, Pastimes, and Sports; Masques; Pageants and Morality Plays; Performances.*

ENVIRONMENT

See *Forests and Fields; Nature.*

EXPLORATION

At the time of Shakespeare's birth in 1564, England was nothing like the international empire it would eventually become. While Spain and Portugal had sponsored voyages of exploration since the late 1400s and had begun to profit handsomely from them, the English were just beginning to take an interest in the world beyond Europe. Developments during Shakespeare's lifetime changed English attitudes about exploration, however, and planted seeds of discovery that would bear fruit in the century that followed his death.

EARLY EXPLORATIONS

In the early 1500s, England had little interest in exploration and little incentive to engage in it. By 1550, however, the English were launching expeditions to gain access to overseas goods and markets.

Perhaps the most famous English explorer was Sir Francis Drake. In 1580 he returned to England after successfully raiding Spain's colonies in America and sailing homeward across the Pacific. Queen Elizabeth was so delighted by his achievement that she made him a knight.

BEGINNING OF ENGLISH EXPLORATION. English sailors began to explore the Atlantic as early as 1480, and by 1500 the explorer John Cabot, an Italian sailing under the flag of England, had reached the coast of North America. Later expeditions to this region discovered rich fishing grounds off Newfoundland, which attracted a few English ships. A 1527 voyage to North America proved fruitless, however, and King HENRY VIII —busy with domestic affairs—saw no reason to finance further English exploration.

The king's lack of interest was due in part to the fact that England already had a source of profitable TRADE in Europe. A company known as the Merchant Adventurers had established a trade in cloth with the city of Antwerp in the Netherlands (which at that time belonged to Spain). In exchange for high-quality English wool, the company obtained goods from other European merchants who had contacts in Asia, Africa, and the Near East. The English saw little need for long, risky voyages when they could acquire the goods they needed in nearby Antwerp.

In 1550, however, overproduction of finished cloth in the Netherlands caused the wool market to collapse. English merchants were forced to look for other markets for their wool. In the early 1550s some Englishmen began to compete with the Portuguese for trade in northern and western Africa. English explorer Richard Chancellor, seeking a northern trade route to Asia, sailed up to the north coast of Russia and from there to Moscow. He made contact with Czar Ivan IV, who granted trading

privileges to the English. Other ships prepared to undertake trade voyages to Turkey and the surrounding regions.

RIVALRY WITH SPAIN AND PORTUGAL. One of the obstacles to English exploration was the power of Spain and Portugal, both of which controlled huge overseas empires. After Christopher Columbus completed his first voyage in 1493, Spain and Portugal divided the unexplored portions of the world between themselves. Portugal claimed Brazil, as well as the regions of Africa and Asia not already claimed by other European powers, as its sphere of influence. Spain laid claim to everything west of Brazil, which turned out to include most of North and South America. England and the other European powers resented the arrogance of the Spanish and Portuguese but were too weak to challenge them.

After Mary Tudor became queen of England in 1553, she married King Philip of Spain, temporarily putting an end to any official rivalry with the Spanish. When Mary died in 1558, ELIZABETH I succeeded her on the throne. As a Protestant, Elizabeth had no interest in joining forces with Catholic Spain, but she knew that England was not strong enough to confront Spain directly. She offered no objection, however, when English ships found ways to harass the Spanish and Portuguese. Early in her reign, Elizabeth supported pirate raids carried out by French Protestants against Spanish vessels in the Caribbean. Attracted by the potential for riches, English sea captains soon began to join in these attacks.

John Hawkins, who tried to break into the slave trade between Africa and America, carried out assaults of another kind. Between 1562 and 1567, Hawkins made a series of voyages to Africa to gather slaves, whom he then took to Spanish ports in the Caribbean. Only Spanish vessels were legally allowed to trade at these ports, but the local landowners cared little for such formalities. Hawkins had slaves and cloth that the Spanish colonists needed. In 1567 Spanish treasure ships caught up with Hawkins and destroyed his small fleet. But this would not be the end of English raids against Spain.

ENGLAND AND AMERICA

The first English ventures into the Americas were not aimed at establishing colonies. Their goal, rather, was to prey on the Spanish colonies already established there. By the end of the Elizabethan era, however, the first English colonies had been founded in North America, and the roots of Britain's overseas empire were taking hold.

FRANCIS DRAKE. A few years into her reign, Elizabeth began licensing English captains as privateers, "legal" pirates who preyed on foreign vessels with the approval of the crown. The most successful of these was Francis Drake, who in 1573 led a daring raid against Panama and captured a rich cargo of Spanish treasure. Encouraged by his success, Drake planned an even more ambitious venture. In 1577 he sailed around the southern tip of South America, officially to explore the area as the site for a possible English colony. His real goal, however, was to raid the lightly

defended Pacific coast of Spain's American empire. His efforts were rewarded when he captured two Spanish treasure ships filled with gold and silver.

Drake then began to search for a way back to England. He sailed up the coast of California looking for a passage leading east to the Atlantic. When this proved unsuccessful, he landed near what is now San Francisco and gathered provisions so that he could continue his voyage. Equipped with Spanish charts of the Pacific, Drake sailed west, eventually reaching the Philippines. He then traveled through the East Indies (present-day Indonesia), trading with local rulers who up to this time had dealt only with the Portuguese. With their help Drake was able to continue across the Indian Ocean, around Africa, and reach home by the fall of 1580. The queen knighted him for his achievement. His ship was only the second to sail around the world, and Drake's success sent a message to Spain that it no longer dominated the Pacific. Drake's voyage also established contacts for future English trading ventures in Asia. In 1601 the newly formed East India Company made its first profitable trip to Asia. This enterprise would become the leading force for English imperial expansion in the early 1600s.

EXPLORATION IN CANADA. While Drake was sailing the Pacific, other Englishmen had their eyes on North America. In 1576 Martin Frobisher led an expedition to the northeast coast of Canada and brought back samples of rocks that seemed to contain gold. In 1577 a larger fleet gathered more of these rocks, but the promise of gold turned out to be merely an illusion. Nonetheless, Frobisher's voyages sparked interest in North America and led to further English expeditions into the New World.

In 1578 Sir Humphrey Gilbert acquired a license to capture and use land overseas. He promised plots of land to his investors, including a group of Catholics lured by the prospect of creating a settlement far from the authority of the Protestant queen. Gilbert's efforts to reach the region that is now New England were plagued by misfortune. In 1582 the wind kept his fleet bottled up in the English Channel. The next year he reached Newfoundland and claimed it for England, but his main ship sank on the return to England, taking Gilbert with it. Only one vessel returned home, but its captain gave a glowing report of the new land. Threats from Spain persuaded the Catholic participants in the plan to withdraw, and the venture was abandoned in 1584.

CHESAPEAKE COLONIES. In 1584 Sir Walter Raleigh sent an expedition to the coast of what is now North Carolina to look for a place to establish an English settlement. The following year Sir Richard Grenville led 100 settlers to the chosen location, Roanoke Island. At first the English and the local Indians lived together peacefully, but the colony's food ran short and the settlers began to demand corn from the Indians. The Indians refused to be bullied, and in 1586 Sir Francis Drake returned the colonists to England.

In the spring of 1587, another group of investors prepared an expedition to colonize the shores of the Chesapeake Bay in what is now

SHIPWRECKED AND TEMPEST-TOSSED

In the early 1600s an English ship, part of an expedition bound for Virginia, sank off the then-uninhabited island of Bermuda. On the island the crew discovered fresh water and food to sustain themselves. They also found cedar trees, from which they built two small vessels. They finally reached Virginia nearly a year after the rest of the expedition. Reports of the voyage were widely circulated in England and were probably well known to both Shakespeare and his audiences. It is possible that the tale inspired Shakespeare's play *The Tempest,* in which a shipwreck leaves several travelers stranded on a magical island in the Mediterranean.

Virginia (named by the English to honor their monarch—Elizabeth, the "Virgin Queen"). The expedition landed at Roanoke to collect the survivors from Grenville's colony, but by the time the fleet arrived, the settlers had left with Drake. The pilot of the fleet then refused to continue to Chesapeake Bay. Some of the colonists were left on the island, while the rest continued inland, planning to travel overland. For various reasons Roanoke Island was left on its own until 1590, when a supply ship arrived to find it deserted.

As it turned out, the lost colonists had settled near the peaceful Chesapeake tribe in southern Virginia. They remained there until 1606, when they and their hosts were killed by Powhatan, the leader of an Indian confederation who ruled the region. Powhatan was afraid that the presence of the settlers would encourage more English to arrive. In this he was correct, for the very next year saw the establishment of Jamestown, the first permanent English colony in North America (named in honor of King JAMES I). Years would pass before the English developed a serious presence in North America, but these early efforts set the tone for English exploration and colonization during the 1600s. England was now on a course toward overseas expansion that would eventually plant the English flag on every continent. (*See also* **Diplomacy and Foreign Relations; Navigation; Ships; Transportation and Travel.**)

FAIRIES

Belief in fairies has a long, rich tradition in English history. For centuries popular folklore taught that fairies—sometimes called elves, pixies, or brownies—were evil creatures, capable of causing illness and other misfortune. Shakespeare, however, portrayed fairies as small, pleasant creatures who delight in playing harmless pranks on foolish humans.

In Shakespeare's romantic comedy *A Midsummer Night's Dream*, his fairies tease and laugh, dance, sing lullabies, and love flowers. Their strong connection with nature is apparent in the playful names he gave them: Cobweb, Moth, Mustardseed, and Peaseblossom. The most famous of his fairy creations is PUCK, the court jester of the fairy kingdom.

Shakespeare also changed popular notions about the size of the fairies. He wrote that they are small, so small that they can hide in an "acorn-cup." In *A Midsummer Night's Dream*, even OBERON and TITANIA, the king and queen of fairy land, are described as only about six inches taller than the rest of the fairies. Mercutio, Romeo's hot-tempered friend, tells of a fairy named Queen Mab. He says that Queen Mab rides in her chariot—made from an empty hazelnut and driven by a gnat—across men's noses as they lie asleep.

Ariel, in *The Tempest*, represents a conventional sprite through whom a magician achieves his spells. Rescued by Prospero, Ariel is bound to serve the magician for a specified period of time, after which he is freed. Although child actors played the fairies, Shakespeare's audiences still had to use their imaginations to picture such tiny creatures.

FALSTAFF, SIR JOHN

See color plate 9, vol. 2.

* *soliloquy* monologue in which a character reveals his or her private thoughts

* *coronation* act or ceremony of crowning a monarch

* *pension* sum of money given after a person has retired from service

Sir John Falstaff is one of Shakespeare's most famous characters. He appears in three plays: *Henry IV, Part 1; Henry IV, Part 2;* and *The Merry Wives of Windsor.* His death is reported in a moving scene in *Henry V* (II.iii). An obese, irresponsible, and often hilarious knight, Falstaff has inspired numerous operas, symphonies, and films.

Critics have argued for centuries over the meaning and appeal of Falstaff's complex personality. In fact, the aging knight (somewhere between 55 and 70 years old) has been controversial since his creation. Originally, the character was called Sir John Oldcastle, the name of an actual soldier who died in the early 1400s. Oldcastle's powerful descendants disliked the way their ancestor was depicted, however, and put pressure on Shakespeare to change the character's name.

Falstaff first appears in *Henry IV, Part 1* as the companion of Prince Hal, the son of King Henry. Falstaff's sharp wit and common sense may be admired, but the old knight is clearly not a proper friend for a young prince. He drinks heavily, steals, and believes in neither courage nor honor. Although Hal seems to enjoy spending his days in taverns with Falstaff, he admits in a soliloquy* that he must eventually reject him and become a responsible leader.

The relationship between Falstaff and Hal changes in *Henry IV, Part 2.* After his coronation*, Hal rejects Falstaff, declaring "I know thee not, old man" (V.v.47), and forbids his presence at the royal court. Mercifully, Hal tempers his harshness by providing a pension* for his old friend to ensure that he will not steal for a living. Despite Falstaff's advanced age, he is a symbol of youthful indulgence and must therefore be put aside before Hal can become a strong and responsible ruler.

According to legend Queen Elizabeth requested that Shakespeare write a play in which Falstaff would be a major character. In response, he wrote *The Merry Wives of Windsor,* a comedy in which the jovial knight attempts to seduce two wealthy married women. In this play, however, Falstaff functions as a buffoon and is the target of a succession of practical jokes. (*See also* **Plays: The Histories.**)

FAMILY

See Marriage and Family.

FATE AND FORTUNE

Most Elizabethans firmly believed that their lives were influenced by supernatural forces. This view was prominent both in the popular culture of the time and in the doctrines of the Church of England.

Elizabethans considered astrology* a legitimate science, believing that fate was tied to the movements of the planets and stars. According to the common PHILOSOPHY of the age, all of nature was bound together in a great

In the Middle Ages, fortune had often been imagined as a constantly turning wheel, as shown here in a woodcut from Alexander Barclay's *The Shyp of Folys of the Worlde* (1509). The turning of fortune's wheel could bring happiness out of despair, but it could also plunge a happy person into misery.

* **astrology** study of the supposed influences of the stars and planets on human events
* **salvation** deliverance from the consequences of sin
* **Puritan** English Protestant who advocated strict moral discipline and a simplification of the ceremonies and beliefs of the Anglican church

"chain of being," with the consequence that events in the heavens had a profound effect on the earth. Just as plant growth depended on the sun, and tides were influenced by the moon, the arrangement of heavenly bodies could determine a person's character. Being born under the wrong star or at a time when the planets were not favorably aligned foretold a difficult life or a tragic fate. All types of people consulted astrologers to determine the most and least favorable dates for undertaking various actions. Queen Elizabeth's court astrologer, John Dee, was one of her most influential advisers.

The Church of England reinforced the idea that life on earth was controlled by forces beyond human understanding. One of the church's basic beliefs was in predestination—the idea that God determined the fate of all living things at the beginning of the world. According to this belief, human actions were insignificant. If God had willed something to happen, it would occur despite all human efforts to the contrary. Even salvation and damnation were foreordained. Those chosen for salvation* need only to accept Christ as their savior to earn a place in heaven, while those destined for hell could do nothing to change their fate.

Although both astrology and religion promoted the idea that outside forces controlled one's fate, conflicts still arose between the two belief systems. Puritans*, for example, felt that knowledge of the future was reserved to God alone. Those who sought to predict future events betrayed a lack of faith in God's plan. As the Puritan William Fulke put it, "Those things that are above us pertain nothing unto us; and those things which are above our reach are not to be sought for with much curiosity." Others objected that people used the influence of the stars as an excuse for their own sins.

Shakespeare's plays are filled with references to the popular belief in astrology. In *King Lear,* for example, the earl of Kent remarks, "It is the stars, the stars above us, govern our conditions" (IV.iii.32–33). But the plays also express the contrary viewpoint through such characters as Cassius in *Julius Caesar,* who says that "The fault . . . is not in our stars, / But in ourselves" (I.ii.140–41). Shakespeare's own view, and that of the average Elizabethan, was probably somewhere between the two notions. Although the stars did not dictate all the actions of a person, it was not unreasonable to believe that they might predispose people to act in certain ways. (*See also* **Astronomy and Cosmology; Church, The; Religion; Supernatural Phenomena.**)

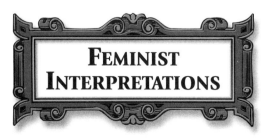

FEMINIST
INTERPRETATIONS

In 1980 a book called *The Woman's Part: Feminist Criticism of Shakespeare* was published. This collection of 18 essays—all about women, and all but two written by women—marked a major new direction in the field of Shakespeare criticism. Feminist readings of the plays not only directed the reader's attention toward Shakespeare's female characters but also shifted the entire focus of literary analysis from the "universal" to the "individual."

ORIGINS OF FEMINIST CRITICISM. Until the 1970s the famous Shakespeare critics were almost exclusively male, and they wrote almost exclusively about male characters, particularly about tragic heroes such as Hamlet, Othello, King Lear, and Macbeth. They also made generalizations about "mankind," ignoring the fact that this term often tends to exclude the experiences of women. For example, Theodore Spencer's 1942 book *Shakespeare and the Nature of Man* talks extensively about what the author calls "human experience as a whole" yet says almost nothing about women. Spencer dismisses the character of Cressida in *Troilus and Cressida* as "worthless," and his chapter on *Antony and Cleopatra* completely ignores Cleopatra, saying merely that her character is "beyond our present scope."

In 1975 the British critic Juliet Dusinberre published *Shakespeare and the Nature of Woman,* a volume whose striking title is clearly a response to Spencer's. The revolutionary central argument of her book is that Shakespeare was a feminist. Dusinberre claims that, as Puritans* gained influence in British society, women were increasingly viewed as household partners rather than simply as the property of their husbands. She then suggests that the drama of the period, including Shakespeare's work, reflected this new status. She also emphasizes the importance of discussing women as women rather than assuming that such categories as "man" and "human" cover the experience of women as well. Although Dusinberre's book was influential, it was widely criticized for taking too positive a view of Shakespeare's work, paying attention only to the evidence that supported her theory while ignoring passages that displayed more negative attitudes toward women.

The new movement in Shakespearean criticism truly began in 1976, when the Modern Language Association of America held a Special Session on Feminist Criticism of Shakespeare. A year later the editors of *The Woman's Part*—Carolyn Ruth Swift Lenz, Gayle Greene, and Carol Thomas Neely—began gathering the essays for their book. The authors of these essays had varying approaches to feminism, but all were persuasive writers whose main focus was on women. This collection, with its many points of view, effectively launched feminist criticism of Shakespeare. It forced literary critics, especially those in the United States, to think about Shakespeare's plays in new ways.

ISSUES IN FEMINIST CRITICISM. One issue of central concern to feminist critics is how limited Shakespeare's portraits of women are. Actresses have long known that there are very few great roles for them in Shakespeare's plays. This may be partly because of the limits placed on female roles in real life. But it was probably also because there were no female actors on stage during Shakespeare's time with the consequence that women's roles were played by boys. In many plays women are notably absent, particularly mothers, who do not appear in several plays that feature fathers. When women are present they often are hardly characters at all. King Lear's three daughters, for example, exist mostly as instruments to advance the plot. Meanwhile, even Shakespeare's more fully developed female characters usually reflect the rigid gender roles of his

***Puritan** English Protestant who advocated strict moral discipline and a simplification of the ceremonies and beliefs of the Anglican Church

society. That is why characters like Juliet in *Romeo and Juliet*, DESDEMONA in *Othello*, and Hermia in *A Midsummer Night's Dream* would have been expected to obey their fathers, and their refusal to do so would have been quite shocking to some Elizabethan viewers.

Many of Shakespeare's most memorable women are the bright, spirited central characters of his comedies. Portia in *The Merchant of Venice*, ROSALIND in *As You Like It*, Beatrice in *Much Ado About Nothing*, Viola in *Twelfth Night*, and Helena in *All's Well That Ends Well* all dominate their plays, entertaining audiences and intriguing the scholars who have written about them. Critics who have praised these characters, however, have also noted that they all end their careers in marriage, forcing them into the Elizabethan mold of women as wives and mothers. In response some feminist critics have begun exploring new interpretations of the plays, imagining the possibility that Isabella might refuse Duke Vincentia's offer of marriage at the end of *Measure for Measure* or that Hippolyta in *A Midsummer Night's Dream* might not be a happy bride to Theseus, who has, as he claims, "woo'd her with his sword" (I.i.16).

Feminist critics are also concerned with the attitudes of Shakespeare's male characters toward women. Some of them—especially young lovers such as Valentine in *The Two Gentlemen of Verona*—offer eloquent praise of "their" women. Others, including such major characters as Hamlet, Lear, Macbeth, Othello, and Posthumus (in *Cymbeline*), view the female sex with extreme distrust. Feminists see a kind of horror of female sexuality in Hamlet's speeches about women who paint their faces an inch deep and in Leontes' warning to his son in *The Winter's Tale* about unfaithful wives. Other feminist scholars have noted that mothers are usually portrayed, when they are portrayed at all, as a bad influence on the development of male heroes in the plays. Coppelia Kahn in *Male Identity in Shakespeare* and Janet Adelman in *Suffocating Mothers* have discussed at length the negative effects of maternal influence, and they note that such effects can be seen even when the mothers are not physically present in the plays.

Another issue of interest to feminist scholars is how Shakespeare's female characters are portrayed on the stage. Irene Dash's *Wooing, Wedding, and Power* has shown that stage productions of the 1700s frequently cut or modified women's roles to fit the values of the time. The first half of *The Winter's Tale* was dropped, for example, eliminating the strong female characters of Hermione and Paulina, while in *King Lear* Cordelia was saved from death and married off to Edgar. The lines of other women, moreover, were regularly shortened or rearranged to focus attention more clearly on male protagonists*.

Some of Shakespeare's most interesting female characters are seldom presented on the stage at all. In *Engendering a Nation: A Feminist Account of Shakespeare's English Histories*, Jean Howard and Phyllis Rackin analyze women's roles in the histories and note that extraordinary female characters appear in two of the plays that are least often performed or analyzed by scholars. Thus in *Henry VI, Part 1*, Queen Margaret and Joan of Arc are both powerful military leaders whose lines have been either eliminated

* *protagonist* central character in a dramatic or literary work

or drastically reduced even in the rare instances in which the play is performed. *King John*, probably Shakespeare's least performed play, features Constance, the widow of John's brother, who fights desperately, and eloquently, to save her son, Arthur. She is the only fully developed exception to the notable absence of mothers. Even when women are not neglected in the texts, they have been ignored when the plays in which they appear are rarely if ever performed.

INFLUENCE OF FEMINIST CRITICISM. Feminist criticism has drawn attention to Shakespeare's female characters and to how they have shaped modern ideas about women. It has shown how the playwright's limited, if fascinating, portraits of women reflect the ideas of a male-dominated Elizabethan society that was significantly different from the modern world. It has also drawn attention to the inappropriateness of certain ideas in traditional critical works, such as the assumption that "mankind" means the same thing as "womankind," or the view that there are "universal" traits that apply to all humans of either gender.

Feminist critics are redefining both tragedy and comedy. Shakespeare's tragic heroes, such as Othello, Macbeth, Lear, and Hamlet, no longer seem to be universal figures whose downfall is due to some identifiable tragic flaw. Likewise, marriage is no longer the inevitable happy ending of comedy. In demonstrating the narrow range of possibilities available to Shakespeare's female characters, feminist critics have opened up new ones. Modern stage productions have experimented with the idea of gender in the plays, presenting actresses in such male roles as Richard II, Hamlet, and King Lear—sometimes even changing the gender of these central figures. Such revisions allow the plays to reflect human experience more fully. Rather than attempting to show "universal" experiences, they draw attention to and celebrate the differences among individuals.

Feminist critics have greatly broadened and enriched the study of Shakespeare. Although early feminist interpretations met with resistance, even the most articulate opponents of feminism now acknowledge its importance in Shakespearean scholarship. As modern society changes, both male and female audiences are learning to respond more critically and creatively to the richness of Shakespeare's portrayal of men and women in a wide range of conditions and situations. (*See also* **Characters in Shakespeare's Plays; Gender and Sexuality; Marriage and Family; Shakespeare's Work, Adaptations of.**)

FESTIVALS AND HOLIDAYS

The modern concept of a vacation—an extended period of time away from work—was unknown in Elizabethan England. Nonetheless, there were many breaks from the daily routine in the form of traditional festivals and holidays that dotted the calendar. At these times nearly everyone enjoyed a day of relaxation, special foods, and general merrymaking.

Festivals and Holidays

Elizabethans celebrated May Day by erecting a maypole on the village green and dancing wildly around it. These festivities were relics of ancient pagan rituals.

* *pagan* referring to ancient religions that worshiped many gods, or more generally, to any non-Christian religion

* *secular* nonreligious; connected with everyday life

Most English holidays were descended from ancient pagan* festivals that marked the key events of country life, such as the coming of spring. The Catholic Church had linked these holidays to religious feast days, so that by Shakespeare's time many of the old festivals were celebrated under names such as Saint Catherine's Day and Saint Agnes' Eve. Before King HENRY VIII broke with the Roman Catholic Church in the early 1530s, there were more than 70 religious and secular* holidays on the calendar. With so many breaks from the daily routine, there was a real concern that not enough time was being devoted to necessary business. Under Protestant rule the number of holidays was significantly reduced, but more than 25 annual feast days were still celebrated in England during the late 1500s. On those occasions Elizabethans celebrated with a fury: feasting, drinking, dancing, dressing in costumes, and abandoning the seriousness and hard work that marked their everyday routines.

WINTER FESTIVALS. The most important holiday on the Elizabethan calendar was Christmas. Although its official purpose was to mark the birth of Christ, it evolved from midwinter celebrations of the ancient pagan religions. Unlike most holidays, which lasted a single day, Christmas continued for nearly two weeks, from Christmas Eve to Twelfth Night

(the evening of January 5). Because there was little or no farmwork to be done at that time of the year, Christmas became an extended break from life's labors. New Year's Day, not Christmas Day, was the traditional date for exchanging gifts. Some people gave presents on Twelfth Night, traditionally considered to be the day on which the wise men visited the infant Jesus.

The Christmas season was a time of constant feasting, especially at the houses of the wealthy. A lord's Christmas feast might feature such fancy dishes as boar's head and roasted peacock, trimmed with its own feathers. In addition to the family and their guests, beggars of all sorts would appear outside the fine houses looking for handouts, and they were rarely disappointed.

Entertainment featured mummers, costumed performers who staged plays based on popular tales, such as the legend of Robin Hood. In each town or village, a local resident known for his high spirits and good humor was proclaimed the Lord of Misrule. Along with a "court" of about 20 friends, he was responsible for leading the mummers and other revelers throughout the holiday season. It was his duty to make sure that the celebration continued at a high level of merrymaking.

At the royal court and in many of the noble houses, MASQUES were held. These were more elaborate and ritualized versions of mummers' plays. They featured costumed players dressed in the richest and most fantastic outfits imaginable. Queen Elizabeth I was known to be extremely fond of masques.

SPRING FESTIVALS. Spring was ushered in by Easter. Leading up to this festival were the 40 days of Lent, during which Christians were forbidden to eat meat and other rich foods. On Shrove Tuesday, the last day of feasting and partying before Lent began, people ate as much fat as possible. Pancakes were served throughout England for Shrove Tuesday. Easter Sunday, marking the end of Lent, also featured lavish feasting. People celebrated by wearing their newest and brightest clothing.

The other major festival of spring was May Day (May 1). While Easter was clearly religious in nature, May Day was pure paganism. The night before, people of all ages and stations dashed to the woods to collect spring greenery and decorate their homes. They also searched for a great tree that would become the maypole. Many spent the entire night outdoors with their sweethearts, a custom much frowned on by Puritans* and other moralists of the day. The following morning the great maypole (an ancient pagan symbol of fertility), brightly painted and decorated with streamers, was erected on the village green. Energetic dancing and drinking took place around the base of the maypole while the Lord of Misrule and his party entertained the revelers. The most beautiful and popular young woman was chosen as the May Queen to preside over the festivities.

SUMMER FESTIVALS. A couple of months after Easter came Whitsunday, which marked the beginning of the church season called Pentecost.

ROAST GOOSE FOR MICHAELMAS

For a delicious Michaelmas tradition, soak aromatic herbs (such as parsley, bay leaves, sage, and rosemary) and garlic in vinegar. Place the herbs and garlic in the cavity of a goose, rub the skin with olive oil, and sprinkle with salt and pepper. Put the goose in a roasting pan, and place the pan in a 400° oven. Roast for two to three hours, or until the bird is tender and has turned a deep golden brown. Serve with a sauce made from pan drippings and the juice of an orange, lemon, or lime.

Feuds

Whitsunday was traditionally a day when churches held ales, or large parties featuring the sale of strong ale, that were intended to raise money for the work of the congregation. Many churches also held ales on the anniversary of the church's founding or on the feast day of its patron saint. These occasions were sometimes known as wakes (wakes were also associated with funeral feasts).

The next major celebration was Midsummer Eve, or Saint John's Day, held June 23 or 24. For ancient pagans this day had marked the passing of the summer solstice, when the nights begin to lengthen again. Superstition held that on this day the souls of people who would die in the following year left their bodies to seek the place they would be buried. As in ancient times, great fires were lit both in the countryside and in town and city lanes. Dancers often leaped through the fires, another echo of long-ago pagan tradition.

Midsummer Eve was another occasion for feasting, mummery, and general rowdiness. In London the most splendid event of the evening was the Midsummer Watch. This was a procession through the city streets that featured many of the most prominent figures in the city in all their finery. They were accompanied by dancers, musicians, and mummers, as well as by companies of armed men. The watch displayed the power and majesty of the English crown, and also patrolled the streets to make sure the celebration did not become too unruly.

AUTUMN FESTIVALS. Holidays celebrated in the fall were essentially harvest festivals linked by the church to religious figures. On Michaelmas (September 29) families feasted and gave thanks to Michael, prince of the angels, who was celebrated as the provider of the blessings of the table. The traditional food of Michaelmas was the goose. All Hallow's Eve, still celebrated today as Halloween, was the Elizabethan version of a pagan "night of the witches," although to the church it was simply the evening before the feast of All Saints (November 1). On this night according to tradition, ghosts and other supernatural creatures could be seen by mortals. The holiday was celebrated with mummery and dancing. Closing out the fall was Saint Martin's Day (November 11), which marked the final grain harvest. These and other holidays and festivals served as reminders that life, though difficult, held joys to be celebrated both in the glory of springtime and in the gloom of winter. (*See also* **Country Life; Dance; Food and Feasts; Weather and the Seasons.**)

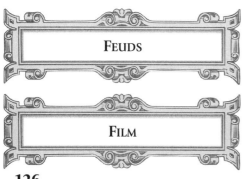

FEUDS

See *Duels and Feuds.*

FILM

See *Shakespeare on Screen.*

FIRST FOLIO

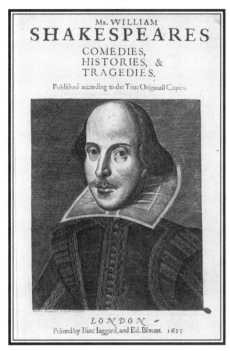

MR. WILLIAM
SHAKESPEARES
COMEDIES,
HISTORIES, &
TRAGEDIES.

Published according to the True Originall Copies.

LONDON
Printed by Isaac Iaggard, and Ed. Blount. 1623.

Martin Droeshout's engraving, printed on the title page of the First Folio, is the earliest known portrait of Shakespear. It is the best indication modern readers have of what the playwright looked like.

The first collected edition of Shakespeare's plays—and one of the most famous books in the world—is known as the First Folio. Because Shakespeare wrote his plays primarily to be performed rather than read, they were not collected and published until 1623, seven years after his death. The word *folio* refers to a printing format that consisted of large sheets of paper, each folded once in the middle and yielding four pages.

The First Folio was compiled by John Heminges and Henry Condell, two actors who had worked with Shakespeare as members of his acting company, the Chamberlain's Men, later known as the KING'S MEN. Approximately half of Shakespeare's plays had been published before, but some of these earlier versions contained serious errors and alterations. Heminges and Condell wrote that they published the First Folio because they wanted people to have an edition of the plays that was "Truely set forth according to their first original." They gathered the plays from various sources, including manuscripts and PROMPT BOOKS, copies of the works that contained detailed stage directions.

The First Folio consists of 36 plays, 18 of which had never before been published. The works are organized, (though not by Shakespeare himself) into three sections—Comedies, Histories, and Tragedies—and the title page features a portrait of the playwright. Preceding the title page is a poem written by Shakespeare's friend and fellow dramatist Ben JONSON. In it Jonson cautions readers not to rely solely on Shakespeare's portrait but to look instead at "his Booke."

Although errors were accidentally introduced as the First Folio was compiled and printed, it remains the most authoritative source for most of Shakespeare's dramatic works. In all likelihood somewhere between 750 and 1,200 copies of the First Folio were published, and about 230 of them still exist. A copy in excellent condition is worth well over a million dollars in the current market. (*See also* **Museums and Archives; Printing and Publishing; Quartos and Folios**.)

FLETCHER, JOHN

See *Henry VIII; Playwrights and Poets; Two Noble Kinsmen, The.*

FLORIO, JOHN

ca. 1553–1625
Translator

John Florio was a well-known Elizabethan translator and a teacher of the Italian language. Scholars believe that Shakespeare's use of Italian words and phrases was directly influenced by Florio's writings, and that Florio may have been the model for Holofernes in *Love's Labor's Lost*.

Florio's parents were Italian Protestants who left Italy to escape religious persecution. They settled in England, where John was born. After graduating from Oxford University, he wrote two Italian grammar books and a large Italian-English dictionary. The Italian sentences that appear in *The Taming of the Shrew* came from Florio's grammar books. The success

* *patron* supporter or financial sponsor of
an artist or writer

of these books gained Florio a position as tutor to the earl of Southampton, who was one of Shakespeare's patrons*. Florio's association with the earl and his friendship with Ben JONSON, a playwright and friend of William Shakespeare, have led many scholars to conclude that he also knew Shakespeare.

In 1603 Florio translated the essays of French writer Michel de Montaigne. His translation of this work influenced the language Shakespeare used in *The Tempest* and *King Lear*. The thoughts expressed in Montaigne's essays also influenced some of the prince's soliloquies* in *Hamlet*. In addition to being inspired by Florio's publications, Shakespeare may have used the translator's large library of Italian books as the sources for such works as *The Merchant of Venice* and *Two Gentlemen of Verona*. (*See also* **Translations of Shakespeare**.)

* *soliloquy* monologue in which a character
reveals his or her private thoughts

FOLGER LIBRARY

See *Museums and Archives.*

FOOD AND FEASTS

Elizabethans loved to eat, and during Shakespeare's day they enjoyed a great amount and variety of food. This abundance was the result of growing wealth (which enabled people to buy more) and increased overseas trade (which brought exotic new foods to English dining tables). Although the wealthy ate larger and more diverse meals than the poor, all SOCIAL CLASSES enjoyed many of the same types of food and drink. In addition they observed essentially the same table manners. Occasionally, nobles and peasants even ate together at the most lavish of all Elizabethan meals, a holiday feast.

FOOD AND DRINK

The diet of Elizabethans consisted principally of bread, meat, and ale. Depending on a person's wealth and social class, however, other foods were available for sustenance and enjoyment.

See
color plate 9,
vol. 1.

ONE MAN'S MEAT. The general word for solid food in Elizabethan England was *meat*, a term applied even to foods no longer called by that name today. Milk, cheese, and eggs were referred to as white meat, and for many of the poor, these dairy products formed the bulk of their diet. Those who could afford to do so, however, ate mostly animal flesh. Compared to the citizens of other countries, such as France and Spain, the English relied on meat (in the modern sense) to an astounding degree. In fact French people referred to English soldiers as beefeaters, a name that is still used today to refer to the royal guards at the TOWER OF LONDON.

* _mutton_ flesh of fully grown sheep, as opposed to lamb

* _capon_ rooster that is castrated to make its flesh more tender

An average meal in a well-off household might include beef, pork, lamb, mutton*, calf, deer, and rabbit—all at the same time. Meat was usually seasoned with a variety of spices and served in rich sauces. These sauces not only added flavor to a dish but often hid the fact that the meat had begun to spoil, a common occurrence in an age without refrigeration. Because it was impossible to feed large herds of livestock during the winter, animals were slaughtered in the fall and their flesh was preserved either by salting or smoking.

In addition to red meat, various types of fowl were also popular. Chicken, capon*, goose, swan, pigeon, pheasant, and duck were among the most commonly served. Being an island nation, England had fish in abundance, including salmon, pike, trout, and carp. Fish was seldom served, however, except on days when religious restrictions forbade the eating of red meat. Abstaining from red meat and fowl was a form of self-denial that was meant to demonstrate remorse for sins. During the

Feasts provided an opportunity for wealthy Elizabethans to gather together and enjoy a shared meal. This menu features some of the dishes that might have been served at a typical feast.

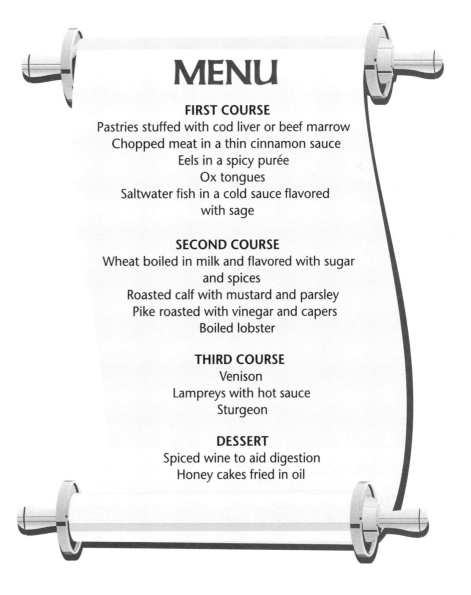

MENU

FIRST COURSE
Pastries stuffed with cod liver or beef marrow
Chopped meat in a thin cinnamon sauce
Eels in a spicy purée
Ox tongues
Saltwater fish in a cold sauce flavored
with sage

SECOND COURSE
Wheat boiled in milk and flavored with sugar
and spices
Roasted calf with mustard and parsley
Pike roasted with vinegar and capers
Boiled lobster

THIRD COURSE
Venison
Lampreys with hot sauce
Sturgeon

DESSERT
Spiced wine to aid digestion
Honey cakes fried in oil

* **garnish** edible ornament, such as a sprig of parsley, used as decoration on a dish of food or in a drink

* **chip** to flake off

MEDICINAL PEARS

Elizabethan feasts usually ended with baked fruits and other desserts. Pears especially were thought to have medicinal properties, and as such they were considered ideal fare for sick people. One Elizabethan cookbook suggests putting the pears "out into fine silver dishes; then they are borne to the sick person."

To bake pears, wash the fruits and remove the cores. Place whole pears in a pan and bake at 400° for 30 to 45 minutes, until they have turned a deep brown. Sprinkle with cinnamon and sugar, and garnish with honey.

reign of Queen ELIZABETH I, Mondays, Wednesdays, and Fridays were all meatless days by law. In addition to compelling people to observe religious tradition, these regulations were intended to ensure the prosperity of the English fishing industry.

VEGETABLES, BREADS, AND SWEETS. Although the English grew peas, cucumbers, sweet potatoes, lettuce, asparagus, radishes, and other vegetables, these foods were unpopular. A salad of raw or cooked vegetables was often served before the meat courses, but vegetables that accompanied meat were typically served as garnish* for a dish. The poor, who were unable to afford expensive meat or fowl, usually ate more vegetables than their wealthier neighbors.

For many English families, bread was the staff of life, the staple, or most important part of their daily diet. Barley and rye were the flours used for the bread eaten in humble households. The poorest people also made bread from beans, oats, and even acorns in particularly lean times. The wealthy preferred bread made from white flour, which was refined so that the coarse, dark outer shell of the grain was removed. Whether light or dark, however, bread had to be chipped* before serving to remove the burned outer portion of the loaf.

The English loved sweets, and not just for dessert. Cooks often boiled meat until it fell apart and then mixed it with sugar, eggs, and cream and served it as pudding. For desserts, Elizabethans enjoyed eating apples, pears, plums, and strawberries raw, stewed with spices, or baked in pies and pastries. Candied fruits, called sweetmeats, were so popular that a great many people suffered from rotted, blackened teeth, including Queen Elizabeth.

DRINKS FOR KINGS AND COMMONERS. Ale was the most common drink, served at all hours of the day, including breakfast. This alcoholic beverage was not considered intoxicating. For an intoxicating effect, people drank ale that had been double brewed to increase its potency. These beverages went by such names as Mad Dog and Dragon's Milk. Wealthy people consumed a good deal of ale, but they also liked wine.

Because England is unsuited to the growing of grapes for fine wines, domestic vintages were made from raspberries and other fruits. Most fine wines were imported from Spain, France, Italy, and Germany. The most popular vintage was sack, a dry, sweet-tasting wine from Spain or France. Sack contained a large amount of sugar. Spices were also added to the wine, which was heated before being served. Elizabethans believed that this potent brew made them livelier, braver, and more intelligent.

MEALS AND BANQUETS

Eating played an important part in Elizabethan social life. Breakfast, dinner, and supper brought small groups of people together each day. On the other hand, banquets—which could be either full feasts or light desserts of fruits, wine, and sweets—provided an opportunity for large groups to gather together and enjoy life's pleasures.

ELIZABETHAN TIMES

Plate 1

Elizabethan England had two universities, Oxford and Cambridge, each located about 50 miles outside of London. The universities were organized into smaller "colleges" where students lived and studied. This detail from *The Life and Death of Sir Henry Unton* shows Sir Henry (a nobleman) as a student at Oriel College, Oxford, in 1574.

Plate 2

This painting by an unknown artist depicts a meeting that took place in 1604 at a London palace called Somerset House. Scholars believe that the men shown in the picture may be a group of advisers to Queen Elizabeth or King James. They can clearly be identified as gentlemen by their clothing, which includes high starched ruffs. Some of the older men wear small black caps known as coifs, which were fashionable during the Reformation.

Plate 3

Shakespeare's wife Anne was the daughter of Richard Hathaway, a wealthy farmer in the village of Shottery. The house where she grew up is a popular site for tourists and Shakespeare scholars. Known as Anne Hathaway's Cottage, the dwelling was purchased by the Shakespeare Birthplace Trust in 1892.

Plate 4
The new Globe, which stands on a site just east of the original theater, opened in 1997. Like Shakespeare's Globe, the new playhouse has a large open yard for the audience to stand in, although the price of a standing-room ticket is now £5, rather than the penny charged in Shakespeare's day. The new Globe can accommodate only about 1,700 people, compared to the estimated 3,000 who could sit or stand in the old theater.

Plate 5
Elizabethans almost never drank water—which was probably wise, since the water supply was polluted. The most common drink at all hours of the day was ale. Elizabethans also drank wine and stronger spirits, known as aqua vitae (literally, "water of life"). Whiskey, which is shown being distilled in this 16th-century illustration, was less common. In fact, the word *whiskey* does not appear even once in Shakespeare's plays.

Plate 6
Elizabethan weddings, like the one shown in this painting by Joris Hoefnagel (ca. 1600), were festive events. The ceremony itself was often held before noon, which was considered the luckiest time of day for a wedding. It was followed by a feast, which might last anywhere from several hours to several days, depending on the families' means.

Plate 7
England in Shakespeare's day had no regular police force. Catching and punishing criminals was the job of local officials known as constables and magistrates. Some of these local law enforcers were more effective than others. In Shakespeare's *Much Ado About Nothing,* the bungling town constable, Dogberry, advises his night watch to avoid thieves, since they might be a bad influence. This 1608 woodcut shows a night watchman making his rounds in London.

Plate 8

Ceremonies marking important life events—such as christenings, weddings, and funerals—gave the rich an opportunity to display their wealth. The death of an important person was likely to include a splendid funeral procession. When Queen Elizabeth died in 1603, the horses that drew her coffin were draped in black and the mourners who followed it carried large banners.

Plate 9

Elizabethan feasts were rowdy affairs quite unlike the formal meals referred to as banquets today. Elizabethans commonly ate with their fingers and tossed food scraps onto the floor for the household dogs. Conversation at the dinner table was encouraged, although it was considered rude to discuss business matters during a meal. Gentlemen were also expected to avoid mean-spirited jokes and scholarly subjects considered too confusing for ladies.

Plate 10

Children in Shakespeare's day were not required to attend school, but those whose parents wished them to attend could do so at little or no cost. Grammar schools, which focused on the teaching of Latin grammar, were open mostly to boys between the ages of 8 and 14 years. Students who misbehaved or failed to learn their lessons were often beaten with sticks, as shown in this woodcut from Raphael Holinshed's *Chronicles of England, Scotland, and Ireland.*

Plate 11

Hunting was one of the most popular sports for upper-class Elizabethans. The most common form of hunting involved the use of trained dogs to track a deer while the hunters pursued the prey on horseback. A more difficult sport was hawking, which made use of trained hawks to bring down game birds, such as pheasants. This cushion cover, embroidered with silk and silver threads, dates from the late 1500s and shows scenes of both hunting and hawking.

Plate 12

The enormous span of London Bridge, shown in this 1616 view of London by Cornelius Visscher, connected the city of London with the suburbs on the south bank of the Thames. The bridge was not merely a roadway, but a whole neighborhood, with buildings and shops along its length. Across the bridge in the district of Bankside, many businesses flourished that were not permitted within the walls of London. These included houses of prostitution, bearbaiting arenas, and theaters.

Plate 13

Before public theaters existed in England, actors performed mainly in the enclosed central courtyards of inns and taverns. A simple platform stage rested at one end of the yard and audience members either stood around the stage or sat on the balconies surrounding the yard. The balcony directly above the stage could be used as part of the performance area; the rooms directly behind the stage served as dressing rooms for the actors. Many of the features of the inn yards were incorporated into the design of the first Elizabethan playhouses.

Plate 14

The defeat of the Spanish Armada—a fleet sent by King Philip of Spain to attack England in 1588—established England as the leading naval power in Europe. One of the most brilliant tactics of the English navy was its use of fire ships—small boats coated with pitch that were set on fire and launched directly toward the Spanish vessels. The Spaniards were forced to break their formation or risk being set ablaze or blown to bits by the exploding gunpowder in their cannons.

Plate 15

Making music was a popular pastime for Elizabethans. Many people could sing a piece of music "at sight" (without having heard it previously) and follow their parts in the complicated vocal harmonies of the 1500s. Music played such an important role in Elizabethan life that Shakespeare makes more than 500 references to it in his works. Common Elizabethan instruments included the viola da gamba, which resembled a modern cello, and the lute, a stringed instrument that was plucked.

A King's Warning on the Dangers of Smoking

First imported from North America in the mid-1500s, smoking tobacco quickly became a popular after-supper pastime among fashionable English men and women. London teachers even taught their students the proper way to blow smoke through their nostrils. In addition to finding smoking enjoyable, the English considered it a remedy for diseases of the lungs and an antidote for infected wounds. However, some disapproved of the new habit. In 1602 King James I wrote that he considered smoking "a custom loathsome to the eye, hateful to the nose, harmful to the brain, and dangerous to the lungs."

MEALS. Breakfast was usually a simple meal, consisting of bread, butter, and ale for the noble and a thick stew of meat and vegetables for the peasant, who needed heartier fare. The main meal, called dinner, was served between 11 o'clock in the morning and noon. When not entertaining guests (which called for a more elaborate menu), a wealthy person might have roast mutton, boiled rabbit, bacon, fish, and bread, washed down with ale and followed by sweets for dessert. The dinners of peasants and laborers were much simpler. The last meal of the day, called supper, was usually served in upper-class homes around 5 or 6 o'clock. A peasant ate supper when he finished with his labors, which might be as late as 7 or 8 o'clock. For both rich and poor, supper was a much lighter meal than dinner.

FOOD FOR ALL. Lavish dinners were common affairs in Elizabethan England. They provided an occasion for the prosperous and highborn to show off their wealth, taste, and generosity. Invitations might be sent to dozens of guests or extended to anyone who showed up. Thus, nobles and peasants sometimes dined at the same table. A massive silver dish filled with salt normally marked the boundary between the two classes of diners.

Large feasts typically began with a salad or vegetable dish, followed by a first course that included several kinds of meat, fowl, and fish, such as ox tongues, calf meat with mustard and parsley, roasted chicken, pike roasted with vinegar and capers, and boiled lobster. Guests were not expected to eat from every dish offered but rather to sample those that appealed to them. Fancy meals provided a chance for cooks to show off their skills, and they prepared some dishes just for show. For example, whole peacocks were served with their feathers included as decoration. Desserts that followed the main course often included apples, pears, and cakes fried in oil and spread with honey. Dessert was usually accompanied by sweet wines, such as port. Meals often concluded with prayers.

Full banquets tended to be crowded, noisy events. Wealthy guests brought their own servants and some even brought tasters, servants who tested their masters' food to make sure it was not poisoned. Most people also brought their own knives to cut their food. Cups were kept on a sideboard rather than on the table, and servants ran back and forth filling them with ale and wine. Guests sat on long benches and ate off hard slabs of unleavened bread or off square wooden plates called trenchers. Forks were still rare in England at that time, and food was brought to one's mouth on the flat part of the knife or eaten with one's fingers.

Because guests handled the food with their fingers, a wash bowl and towels were always ready. Diners washed their hands frequently during the meal. Scraps, however, were tossed on the floor, where the household dogs gnawed on the bones. Regardless of how much the servants prepared, no food went to waste. Hosts distributed leftovers, and crowds of poor people often gathered outside the home of the family hosting a lavish banquet. (*See also* **Festivals and Holidays.**)

Fools, Clowns, and Jesters

FOOLS, CLOWNS, AND JESTERS

Various types of humorous characters appear in Shakespeare's plays, among them the fool and the clown. In addition to adding comic relief, these characters often serve as insightful commentators on the behavior of the play's main characters. Although fools and clowns are both amusing, the nature of the comedy they provide differs significantly.

SHAKESPEAREAN FOOLS. In most Shakespearean plays the fool is a jester, a professional entertainer whose job is to amuse the king or queen. A quick wit, the fool often taunts and satirizes the main characters. The fool is typically a perceptive observer, and his remarks often contain unwelcome truths about human nature. His comments also frequently mirror the audience's own attitude toward the behavior of the main characters. Because it is the fool's job to be clever and irreverent, he is rarely punished for his lack of respect to social superiors. Fools are free, in a way that other characters are not, to speak their minds regardless of whom their words might offend.

Fools did not figure prominently in Shakespeare's early plays, but they appear extensively in his later comedies. One of the most famous Shakespearean fools is Feste, a jester who appears in several scenes in *Twelfth Night.* Feste uses his sharp wit to point out the foolishness of the noble men and women who believe themselves to be wise. He observes that "Those wits that think they have thee [wit] do very oft prove fools; and I that am sure I lack thee, may pass for a wise man" (I.v.33–35). Feste also sings, and several of his songs comment on the action of the play and introduce a sad note that suggests that, even in a comedy, life is often gloomy.

Several of Shakespeare's tragedies feature fools who not only provide an objective view of the action but introduce a lighter element into the dramatic mix. The Fool in *King Lear* is perhaps the best example of a "tragic fool." Seeing that Lear is unwise to place himself under the care of his ungrateful daughters Goneril and Regan, he scolds the king and tells him, "Thou shouldst not have been old till thou hadst been wise" (I.v.44–45). Fools are featured less often in Shakespeare's romances, and those who do appear are generally less likable.

FOOLISH BEHAVIOR

Fools and jesters used a variety of antics to entertain audiences. Some played musical instruments, made up riddles, told stories, and even composed poems. Many professional fools and jesters, however, acted more like today's clowns. They told crude jokes, made silly faces, and played practical jokes. Some also carried a long stick called a bauble, which had a pig's bladder attached at one end. When they wanted a quick laugh, fools and jesters slapped the face of an audience member with the bauble. Elizabethans called this *slapstick,* a word still used to refer to broad, unsophisticated humor.

SHAKESPEAREAN CLOWNS. Clowns appear in Shakespeare's earliest plays. They serve a purpose similar to that of fools, but they do so in a very different way. While the fool is a professional comedian, the clown is typically a peasant or a common laborer who is portrayed as thick-witted. His humor comes not from his keen insight into human nature but from his clumsiness and ignorance. While fools are intentionally funny, clowns are funny because they stumble through the world in a state of confusion.

One way the clown's awkwardness is expressed is through the use of incorrect words or expressions. Dogberry, a constable* in *Much Ado About Nothing,* is famous for such errors. For example, instead of saying he "apprehended two suspicious persons," Dogberry says he "comprehended two aspicious persons" (III.v.46). Although clowns are typically portrayed

* *constable* public officer responsible for keeping the peace

Will Kempe of the King's Men often played the roles of clowns in Shakespeare's plays. He also became famous for his "Nine Days Wonder," in which he danced all the way from London to Norwich, a distance of about 100 miles.

WILLIAM KEMP DANCING THE MORRIS.
Kemp's "Nine Daies Wonder." 1600.

as dim, they often possess a basic common sense that more intelligent characters lack. Like the fool, the clown is free to comment truthfully on what he observes, but for a different reason. The clown's freedom comes from the fact that his social position is so low that few of his superiors are threatened by, or even pay attention to, what he has to say.

Like fools, clowns appear in tragedies as well as comedies. One of the best known is the gravedigger in *Hamlet*. In addition to providing comic relief in this very dark play, he expresses a matter-of-fact attitude toward death. As he happily digs a grave, throwing dirt into the air, he sings "But age with his stealing steps / Hath clawed me in his clutch, / And hath shipped me into the land [buried me], / As if I had never been such" (V.i.71–74).

The gravedigger reminds both Hamlet and the audience that death is inevitable. His simple and uncomplicated outlook on life, seemingly a sign of his lack of sophistication, actually reveals his basic wisdom. (*See also* **Characters in Shakespeare's Plays; Humor in Shakespeare's Plays; Plays: The Romances.**)

FOREIGNERS

Like most Elizabethan playwrights, Shakespeare probably lacked the time and money for overseas travel. Instead, he most likely gained his information about foreign lands and peoples from books and from the accounts of explorers and traders. Sources that Shakespeare may have used include the published records of missionaries* and popular narratives, such as Richard Hakluyt's *Principall Navigations Voiages and*

Forests and Fields

* **missionary** person who travels to a foreign country in order to convert nonbelievers to Christianity

Discoveries of the English Nation, which appeared in 1589. Shakespeare may also have acquired information from conversations with acquaintances who had journeyed to other lands. He could have listened to the tales of well-traveled sailors at London's harbor taverns, for example, or chatted with the servants of foreign diplomats who spent time in Queen Elizabeth's royal court. He almost certainly gained his knowledge of languages such as French and Italian from translators, such as John FLORIO.

Shakespeare's depiction of foreign characters often reflects common Elizabethan stereotypes. For example, the English considered the French fickle, as illustrated in this line from *Henry VI, Part 1:* "Done like a Frenchman—turn and turn again!" (III.iii.84–85). In *The Merchant of Venice* a young woman characterizes a Scottish lord as a habitual money borrower and a German duke as a drunkard. Such impressions of Scots and Germans were common in Shakespeare's time. His use of stereotypes, however, does not mean that his non-English characters lack individual and admirable characteristics. In *Henry IV, Part 1*, for example, the playwright depicts the Scottish noble Lord Douglas as a courageous and honorable fighter: "His valors shown upon our crests today / Hath taught us how to cherish such high deeds, / Even in the bosom of our adversaries" (V.v.29–31). (*See also* **Diplomacy and Foreign Relations; Geography; Race and Ethnicity; Shakespeare's Sources.**)

FORESTS AND FIELDS

* **courtier** person in attendance at a royal court

* **hamlet** small village

For many Elizabethans COUNTRY LIFE was preferable to COURT LIFE. For them the life of a country gentleman was interesting, busy, and useful. The life of a courtier*, by contrast, was boring, idle, and useless. These attitudes are reflected in the hundreds of references Shakespeare made to country life in his works. In *As You Like It*, for example, Duke Senior asks: "Hath not old custom made this life more sweet / Than that of painted pomp? Are not these woods / More free from peril than the envious court?" (II.i.2–4).

The English countryside of Shakespeare's time consisted of two distinct types of landscape: forests and fields. In fact, the terms *woodland*, or forest, and *champion*, or field, had long been used to contrast these two major types of English countryside. Woodlands were mostly forested or grassy areas, and the majority of their inhabitants settled in hamlets* and lived by hunting or herding. In contrast, champions were areas of open, plowed land where people lived mostly in villages and engaged in farming.

In personality as well as lifestyle, people of the forests and fields were believed to be as different as the regions they inhabited. People of the fields were considered to be more civilized, law-abiding, and prosperous. Woodlanders, on the other hand, were often depicted as poorer but prouder and freer.

During his childhood Shakespeare lived in STRATFORD-UPON-AVON, a town that straddled the boundary between the Forest of Arden and the fields of Warwickshire in central England. He was familiar, then, with

both aspects of the English countryside, and many of his plays have scenes that take place in forests or on farms. (*See also* **Arden, Forest of; Gardens and Gardening; Nature; Pastoralism; Shakespeare, Life and Career.**)

FREUDIAN INTERPRETATIONS

See *Psychology; Shakespeare's Works, Changing Views.*

FRIENDS AND CONTEMPORARIES

hakespeare was a native of STRATFORD-UPON-AVON, a small town in the English Midlands, but it was in LONDON that he made his living and gained fame as a playwright. Dividing his time between these two places, Shakespeare acquired friends and acquaintances from different walks of life. As a prominent local figure, he came to know some of Stratford's leading citizens, many of whom were lawyers and businessmen. His circle of friends in London probably consisted primarily of theater professionals and publishers. His importance as a literary figure also enabled him to associate with some of the major political figures in the court of Queen ELIZABETH I.

HOMETOWN FRIENDS. In his will, Shakespeare named as beneficiaries several of his neighbors from Stratford-upon-Avon. One of these was Francis Collins, a lawyer and deputy town clerk. Collins drafted and witnessed SHAKESPEARE'S WILL, which called for Collins to receive just over £13, an amount equivalent to about $5,000 today. This sum, which probably included Collins's fee, suggests that he was a close friend.

Another person named in the will was Thomas Combe, who received Shakespeare's sword. This bequest suggests a strong friendship, but little else is known of the relationship between the two men. Shakespeare was also a friend and business partner of other members of the Combe family. John Combe, a prosperous moneylender and landowner, was said to be the wealthiest man in Stratford-upon-Avon. He and his uncle William sold Shakespeare 127 acres of land near the village of Welcombe. When he died, John Combe bequeathed to Shakespeare the sum of £5 (about $1,800).

Other friends in Shakespeare's Stratford circle included Anthony Nash, the Sadlers, and William Walker. Nash was a wealthy farmer who served as a legal witness for some of Shakespeare's business deals and managed some of the playwright's farm holdings. Shakespeare bequeathed small sums to Nash, Nash's brother John (an innkeeper in town), and five other friends, to buy commemorative* rings. Nash's eldest son, Thomas, later married Shakespeare's granddaughter, Elizabeth Hall.

Hamnet Sadler, a local baker, and his wife, Judith, were probably the godparents of Shakespeare's twins, who were named after these two friends. Significantly, Sadler named one of his sons William. Sadler's

* *commemorative* preserving the memory of a person or event

name appears in official records as both Hamnet and Hamlet, and some observers have speculated that he, and the son named for him, inspired Shakespeare's portrayal of the title character in what many regard as his greatest tragedy.

Shakespeare was also close to William Walker, his godson. Walker was the son of a wealthy cloth merchant, and after the playwright's death, he served for a time as bailiff, or mayor, of Stratford.

FRIENDS AND ASSOCIATES IN THE CITY. Most of Shakespeare's friends and acquaintances in London were part of the theatrical and literary communities. One notable exception was Thomas Russell, a landowner from Warwick (located a few miles north of Stratford-upon-Avon). Shakespeare named Russell (along with Collins) an overseer of his will and left him £5. Russell was a widower, living in London and courting his future second wife, Anne Digges. Shakespeare had once lived near Anne Digges in Stratford-upon-Avon, and he almost certainly knew her sons, Leonard and Dudley. Leonard, a poet and translator, wrote a verse dedicated to Shakespeare in the FIRST FOLIO, the earliest published collection of Shakespeare's plays. Dudley, a politician and strong supporter of overseas exploration, may have provided Shakespeare with some of the information about the New World* that he drew on for *The Tempest.*

Among Shakespeare's professional friends in London was the printer Richard Field, who was a native of Stratford-upon-Avon. Field's father was a tanner* who had known Shakespeare's father. Rather than follow his father's trade, however, young Field became an apprentice* to a London printer in 1579. When his master died in 1587, Field assumed control of the business and married the printer's widow. Field published the first editions of *Venus and Adonis, The Rape of Lucrece,* and *The Phoenix and the Turtle.* He later sold the printing rights to *Venus and Adonis* and *The Rape of Lucrece,* but the man who bought those rights hired Field to print later editions of *Venus and Adonis* and the first quarto* of *The Rape of Lucrece.* Some scholars believe that Shakespeare referred to Field in *Cymbeline* (IV.ii), where Imogen says she works for a "very valiant Briton" named Richard du Champ, which is French for "Richard Field."

Not surprisingly, Shakespeare befriended many in the acting community. Two of his most significant relationships were with Henry Condell and John Heminges. These two actors gathered 36 of Shakespeare's plays (18 of which had never before been printed) and published them in the First Folio in 1623. Without this labor of love, many of the plays might have been lost to posterity. Both men are listed in the First Folio among the 26 "Principal Actors in all these Playes." Condell acted in the Chamberlain's Men (the company for which Shakespeare wrote many of his plays) from its founding in 1594. He continued to work with the company that succeeded it—the KING'S MEN. A founding partner of the BLACKFRIARS theater, Condell later acquired a share of the GLOBE Theater.

Richard Burbage was the leading player in the Chamberlain's Men and was considered one of the greatest actors of the Elizabethan era. He was the first actor to play the title role in *Richard III,* the play that established

* *New World* landmass of North and South America

* *tanner* person who converts animal hides into leather
* *apprentice* person bound by legal agreement to work for another for a specified period of time in return for instruction in a trade or art

* *quarto* referring to the format of a book; to produce each gathering of such a volume, a sheet of paper is folded twice, yielding four leaves or eight pages

See color plate 12, vol. 3.

* *protagonist* central character in a
dramatic or literary work

* *courtier* person in attendance at a royal
court
* *astrology* study of the supposed
influences of the stars and planets on
human events
* *atheist* person who denies the existence
of God
* *allusion* indirect reference to historical or
fictional characters, places, or events

A RING FOR REMEMBRANCE

An English custom popular since
the Middle Ages was the wearing of mourning jewelry. Lockets, brooches (pins), and rings
were fashioned to contain a lock
of hair from the deceased. In his
will, Shakespeare bequeathed a
sum slightly greater than 26
shillings, or about $400, to each
of seven friends for the purpose
of buying a ring to commemorate the friendship.

These bequests were made
to four Stratford friends: Anthony and John Nash, William
Reynolds (a landowner), and
Hamnet Sadler. He made the
same bequest to three theater
friends and colleagues: Richard
Burbage, Henry Condell, and
John Heminges.

Shakespeare as a writer of tragedy. Evidence suggests that Shakespeare
had Burbage in mind when he created many of his protagonists*, among
them Philip the Bastard, the illegitimate son in *King John.*

Burbage, who was also a painter, worked with Shakespeare outside
the theater as well. They collaborated on an emblem for the earl of Rutland's coat of arms. Burbage designed the picture that appears on the
emblem, or impresa, and Shakespeare wrote the poem that explained its
significance.

FRIENDS IN HIGH PLACES. Although Shakespeare was not a member
of the court of either Queen Elizabeth I or King JAMES I, he knew some of
the most prominent courtiers* of the time. Of these, one of the most famous was Sir Walter Raleigh. The son of an unknown country squire,
Raleigh gained fame and fortune as a soldier, sea captain, and explorer.

In addition to his adventurous side, Raleigh had a talent for poetry. In
fact, he was such an accomplished writer that some of his work was mistakenly attributed to Shakespeare. He was also interested in magic, astrology*, and other mystical "sciences," which led many people to condemn
him as an atheist*.

Some scholars believe that the long-winded, pompous Don Armado
in *Love's Labor's Lost* was modeled on Raleigh and that Shakespeare's reference to the "school of night" (IV.iii.251) is an allusion* to Raleigh's small
intellectual society, which was known by that name. Some even argue that
Shakespeare used Raleigh as the basis for the character of Tarquin, a Roman prince who sexually assaults a woman in *The Rape of Lucrece.*

If Shakespeare alluded unfavorably to Raleigh, it may have been to
please Robert Devereaux, the earl of Essex, who was Raleigh's enemy and
a friend of Shakespeare's patron, the earl of Southampton. At one time
Essex was Queen Elizabeth's favorite, but he lost her good will after marrying against her wishes. On one occasion Essex was so rude to Elizabeth
that she struck him, causing him to draw his sword in response. Surprisingly, he managed to regain the queen's favor, and she eventually commissioned him to lead an expedition to suppress a rebellion in Ireland.
In *Henry V,* whose Chorus to Act V was apparently written in 1599 just as
Essex departed for Ireland, the playwright anticipates the earl's triumphal
return:

> Were now the general of our gracious Empress,
> As in good time he may, from Ireland coming,
> Bringing rebellion broached [impaled] on his sword,
> How many would the peaceful city quit,
> To welcome him!
>
> (V.Prologue.30–34)

As it happened, Essex failed to subdue the Irish rebels, and after coming home in disgrace, he attempted to incite a rebellion against Elizabeth
and the councilors closest to her. The attempt was a dismal failure, and
Essex was executed for treason in 1601. (*See also* **Acting Companies, Elizabethan; Actors, Shakespearean; Government and Politics; Heminges,
John; Patronage of the Arts; Printing and Publishing.**)

Friendship

FRIENDSHIP

Shakespeare's poems and plays deal extensively with the subject of friendship. Like many Elizabethan writers, Shakespeare idealized close friendships between men, often contrasting the steadfast devotion of a male friend with the fickle love of a woman. The theme of friendship is central to the SONNETS and many of the plays, in which the poet dramatizes some close and loving relationships between women.

FRIENDSHIP IN THE SONNETS. Shakespeare's most extensive treatment of friendship is found in his 154 sonnets, at least 126 of which appear to address the relationship between the writer and a young man generally referred to now as the Friend or the Fair Youth. In these poems the narrator not only expresses his devotion and love for his young associate but also generalizes about the nature of friendship. In particular he compares friendship favorably with romantic love. In Sonnet 20, for example, he describes his male friend's devotion as more constant than the affection of a woman, saying the Fair Youth has "a woman's gentle heart, but not acquainted / With shifting change, as is false woman's fashion." Similarly, in Sonnet 144 the poet contrasts his loyalty to his friend with his passion for a strong-willed female lover, the mysterious DARK LADY. He calls the Fair Youth his "better angel," the purer of his "two loves," while the Dark Lady is his "worser spirit," tempting him to do evil.

Sonnet 144 is one of several poems in the collection that deal with the speaker's conflicting feelings over his friend's romantic involvement with the Dark Lady. Though hurt by this betrayal, the poet tries his best to forgive his friend's wrongdoing. In Sonnet 40 he even goes so far as to urge the Fair Youth to "Take all my loves, my love," because whatever the poet has belongs to those he loves. In Sonnet 42 he describes the loss of his friend as a "greater grief" than the loss of his female lover but claims to find comfort in the pretense that these two "loving offenders" have chosen to love each other because he loves both of them. He concludes at last with the fiction that his friendship with the young man is so close that "my friend and I are one; / Sweet flattery! Then she loves but me alone."

For Shakespeare the joys of friendship seem at times to provide enough comfort to make all the ills of the world bearable. In Sonnet 29 the poet's lamentation over his "outcast state" is transformed to joy by thoughts of his friend: "For thy sweet love rememb'red such wealth brings / That then I scorn to change my state with kings." Similarly, in Sonnet 30 his friend's love is enough to silence the poet's regrets over all the missed opportunities of his life: "But if the while I think on thee, dear friend, / All losses are restor'd and sorrows end." In Sonnet 112 the poet's attachment to the Fair Youth gives him strength to endure the scorn of others; he can disregard everyone else "who calls me well or ill" because his friend's opinion is the only one that really matters.

FRIENDSHIP IN THE PLAYS. While the sonnets appear to express Shakespeare's personal views of friendship, the plays dramatize friendship in action. *The Merchant of Venice* provides a significant expression of

the lengths to which true friends will go for each other. The play focuses on a merchant named Antonio and his friend Bassanio, who wishes to court a rich lady in Belmont. When Bassanio asks his friend for money to finance his journey, Antonio—who has no cash on hand because his fortunes are all tied up in overseas ventures—agrees to seek a loan to help Bassanio, no matter how much his credit is "racked" (stretched) as a result. Antonio even scolds Bassanio for hesitating to ask for such a favor, saying Bassanio wrongs him most by doubting that he would do anything in his power to help his friend. As it turns out Antonio hazards much more than his credit. The moneylender SHYLOCK, who holds a grudge against him, agrees to provide the necessary funds only if Antonio will offer a pound of his flesh as security for the loan. Bassanio urges Antonio to refuse, even though it means Bassanio will have to give up his courtship. But Antonio insists he will go to any length, even risk his own life, to help a friend in need.

Minor characters in several other plays also exemplify the ideal of true friendship. *Romeo and Juliet* presents two companions of Romeo with contrasting attitudes toward friendship. Mercutio teases Romeo about his lovesickness but later leaps to his friend's defense when he is insulted by Tybalt, Juliet's cousin. Mercutio fights a duel with Tybalt and is killed, provoking Romeo to slay Tybalt in revenge. Mercutio's response to Tybalt's challenge and the two deaths that result transform the play from a comedy to a tragedy. By contrast Romeo's cousin Benvolio attempts throughout the play to break up angry brawls between the feuding families and to reason with Romeo and others about their self-destructive passions.

The plays portray ideal friendships between women as well. In *As You Like It* when Duke Frederick banishes his niece ROSALIND from his court, his own daughter, Celia, immediately vows to follow her cousin into exile, saying "I cannot live out of her company" (I.iii.86). In *A Midsummer Night's Dream*, Helena describes her "school-days' friendship" with Hermia as so close that they were "two seeming bodies, but one heart" and criticizes her friend for "join[ing] with men in scorning your poor friend" (III.ii.192–221). This description conveys the kind of sorrow that results whenever the affection of a friend gives way to the attractions of romantic love. (*See also* **Loyalty.**)

GAMES, PASTIMES, AND SPORTS

For many in Elizabethan England, life was short and filled with grueling labor, harsh poverty, and potentially fatal disease. Games, pastimes, and sports offered a welcome break from the daily routine. In addition to providing an opportunity for relaxation, leisure activities taught important skills. Even the nobility required amusements to relieve the stress of managing large estates and carrying out important responsibilities. Meanwhile, the affluent used entertainments to display their wealth and status. In fact their social and economic rank often determined how Elizabethans spent their free time.

Games, Pastimes, and Sports

Hunting for sport was essentially limited to the upper classes. Only the monarch and his or her companions were permitted to hunt in the royal forests. Anyone else who killed a deer there could be arrested for poaching.

OUTDOOR RECREATION. During Shakespeare's day, bowling was an outdoor activity. Elizabethans bowled on well-tended lawns called bowling greens rather than on the indoor wooden lanes that are used today. The English played several variations of lawn bowling, including kayles, in which a player threw a stick at wooden pins, and loggets, in which a player attempted to knock down a pile of bones with another bone. These games were enjoyed by all SOCIAL CLASSES.

Tennis was another popular sport. The game ball was stuffed with hair, and at first players struck it with their bare hands or while wearing stringed gloves. Racquets were introduced later. Tennis was especially fashionable with the nobility, who played on private courts. In LONDON, however, public courts were built to accommodate ordinary city dwellers. In the countryside open fields often served as tennis courts for the peasants.

Football (the forerunner of what Americans now call soccer) was already popular during Shakespeare's day, but it was a rough sport shunned by the upper classes. The game was played with an inflated pig's bladder or a leather ball. Typically, a pasture between two villages served as the playing field. The goals were sometimes miles apart, and the sporting ground often included obstacles such as forests and rivers. The teams sometimes consisted of virtually all the men in a community. There were few rules, and severe injuries, such as broken arms and dislocated knees, were common. Injuries provoked many to criticize the game, among them King JAMES I, who wrote that football was "meeter [more fit] for laming than making able the users therof."

Other Elizabethan authorities also opposed allowing commoners to play football and similar games. Rather than objecting to the violence, however, these critics were concerned that people were not spending enough time preparing for war.

WAR GAMES. Virtually every adult man in Elizabethan England trained with the bow and arrow, but not solely for amusement and exercise. A law required all healthy adult males under 60 to practice archery. Despite the growing use of gunpowder, the longbow was still the most important weapon in the arsenal of the country's infantry*. English military preparedness was well served by having a vast number of trained archers to call on when necessary. Wealthy gentlemen practiced on their own property, but most people shot at public butts, bales of hay on which targets were mounted.

Fencing, another sport with origins in warfare, gained popularity during Shakespeare's lifetime. Swordplay became fashionable because of the introduction of the rapier, a sword with a long, thin blade made in Italy. Before the arrival of the rapier, the Englishman's weapon of choice was the broadsword. Fencing was considered a gentleman's sport, and matches were held at the royal court. Duels could be fatal, however, and a law passed in 1613 made murder by swordplay punishable by death.

In addition to being the principal method of transportation, horseback riding was a highly valued skill, especially among the nobility. Members of the upper class practiced dressage*. Noblemen also participated in jousts and TOURNAMENTS. During these events men on horseback fought each other with swords and lances. Another popular sport on horseback was charging a quintain, which was a target hung from a revolving bar with a mace tied to one end. If the rider was unskilled and did not move quickly enough, the mace swung around and knocked him off his horse.

THE HUNT. For those who had sufficient wealth and free time, hunting was an opportunity for exercise and entertainment. The favorite prey of Elizabethan hunting parties was the red deer. Many noblemen maintained deer parks in which they raised and kept the animals for the hunt. The gamekeeper would release the day's quarry, which was tracked by the master's hounds. Once the dogs scared the deer from its hiding place, the hunters pursued the animal on horseback. The dogs were not only an indispensable part of the hunt but also cherished members of the owner's

* **infantry** soldiers trained and armed to fight on foot

* **dressage** training of horses to perform precision movements in response to a rider's barely perceptible commands

See color plate 11, vol. 1.

141

household. Many noblemen pampered their favorite hounds and even gave them free run of their homes.

The poor were prohibited from hunting deer. Many forests that would otherwise have been considered common land were set aside as royal forests in which hunting was restricted to the king or to those authorized by the king. Nevertheless, poaching* on restricted lands was common, especially among country folk who were unable to obtain meat in any other way. A famous, but unproved, story about William Shakespeare maintains that he was forced to leave his boyhood home in STATFORD-UPON-AVON after being caught poaching in a nearby forest.

More specialized though less expensive than hunting, hawking was another sport engaged in by the wealthy. Hawks were trained to hunt game birds, such as pheasant, quail, and grouse. This sport, however, required expert knowledge that could be acquired only through study and practice. Some noblemen took the time and effort to become skilled at hawking, but most kept professional falconers at their estates to train the birds. Hawking was not limited to the upper classes, but only the rich could afford the largest birds, such as peregrine falcons. Less affluent hawkers trained smaller birds, such as sparrow hawks. Like hunting, hawking provided not only enjoyment but another source of food for the family.

INDOOR GAMES AND SPECTATOR EVENTS. Board, card, and dice games were fashionable in Elizabethan times and were played in much the same way as they are today. Board games included draughts (checkers), chess, shuffleboard, billiards, and table (a type of backgammon). Cardplayers wagered on the outcome of such games as maw (a two-player game played with 32 cards) and ruff (a four-player game played with 52 cards). Among the wealthy, primero was a favorite gambling game. Wagering on dice was a well-established pastime among all classes. Like several other games, dicing and playing cards were forbidden to the lower classes, but the prohibition did little to stop the poor from dicing. In part these laws reflected a desire of the privileged to dictate the pastimes that were considered proper for the different classes. Like one's house or clothes, the games people played were meant to indicate their social rank.

Among the spectator events favored by Elizabethans of all social classes were blood sports: cockfighting, bearbaiting, and bullbaiting. Cockfights were held in outdoor pits in which trained roosters, called gamecocks, battled to the death, using their spurs (sharp, bony spines on their legs) as weapons. Breeding gamecocks was an important industry in Norfolk and in other parts of England.

Baiting involved tying or chaining an animal (either a bear or a bull) to a stake and then setting dogs to attack it. The English bulldog, with its short snout and powerful jaws, was bred specifically for such contests. These events were held outdoors in public squares and on village greens as well as in indoor arenas. Interestingly, London's most popular baiting arena was located next to the GLOBE THEATER, where Shakespeare premiered many of his plays.

* *poaching* trespassing for the purposes of stealing fish or game (wild animals hunted for food)

SPORTS TALK, SHAKESPEARE STYLE

Shakespeare's plays include many references to popular games, pastimes, and sports. During a famous scene in *Hamlet,* the troubled prince sees a gravedigger removing the bones from an old grave to make room for a new occupant. When the gravedigger tosses out the bones, Hamlet reprimands him, saying, "Did these bones cost no more the breeding, but to play at loggats with them?" (V.i.91–92). In another bowling reference Shakespeare coined the famous phrase "Ay, there's the rub" (III.i.64). In bowling a rub is an obstruction on the green that makes it difficult to hit the target. By saying this, Hamlet refers to an impediment preventing him from deciding whether to kill his uncle and thereby avenge his father's murder.

Elizabethans considered blood sports and theatergoing to be equally worthy pastimes. Plays during Shakespeare's day were not highbrow cultural events. Instead, they were rowdy affairs that drew boisterous crowds and often featured violence and brash forms of humor. (*See also* **Dance; Duels and Feuds; Festivals and Holidays; Gardens and Gardening; Shakespearean Theater: 17th Century; Tournaments.**)

GARDENS AND GARDENING

Elizabethan gardens provided fruits, vegetables, and nuts for the table as well as herbs for medications. In addition, these well-tended plots of land provided quiet places to relax, receive guests, and take long strolls. Gardens figure prominently in Shakespeare's work: 29 scenes in his plays are set in gardens, and his characters make hundreds of references to the cultivation of fruits, vegetables, flowers, and other plants. Shakespeare displayed such an impressive knowledge of horticulture*, in fact, that some scholars believe he may have served as an apprentice* to a gardener before he became a playwright.

GARDENING GAINS RESPECT. There were several reasons for the great popularity of gardens and gardening in Shakespeare's England. One reason was the availability of new land that had formerly belonged to monasteries or to the crown. Another reason was the availability of numerous books on horticulture, such as Thomas Hill's *Profitable Arte of Gardeninge* (1563). These publications presented gardening as a noble occupation rather than as an occupation that depended on the drudgery of peasants, which is how gardening had been viewed in England until about 1500. A third reason was the influence of continental Europe, where gardening had been popular for some time.

Starting with Henry VIII, who reigned from 1491 to 1547, English monarchs and courtiers* made it fashionable to eat fruits and vegetables and grow them in gardens. The trend quickly spread from courtly circles into the countryside. Since gardens did not require much land or money, rich and poor alike could try their hand at them. By the end of the 1500s, people in every shire, or county, and in every walk of life were gardening.

GARDENS IN SHAKESPEARE'S TIME. The scale of a garden and the diversity of plants it included depended on the prosperity of the owner. Wealthy country estates usually included a huge formal garden, which was normally surrounded by a high, clipped hedge or an impressive stone wall with large, ornamental gates. In *Measure for Measure*, one of Shakespeare's characters describes such a setting: "He hath a garden circummur'd [walled round] with brick" (IV.i.28).

Formal gardens were filled with flowers, which were planted to form designs called knots. They also included shrubs, some of which were pruned to resemble geometric shapes or exotic animals, such as peacocks or elephants. Statues and fountains decorated the landscape, and broad walks enabled visitors to stroll the grounds of the enclosure. Outside the

THE RISE AND FALL OF THE ARTICHOKE

When Henry VIII first tried artichokes, he developed a gluttonous appetite for them. The popularity of the vegetable soon spread from the royal court, and by the early 1600s many country estates had whole gardens devoted solely to growing artichokes. Artichokes became increasingly plentiful, and soon they were available at markets throughout England. By the middle of the 1600s, there were so many artichokes that their price decreased sharply. When that happened, fashion-conscious Elizabethans no longer considered artichokes desirable, and the vegetable fell out of favor.

Gardens and Gardening

Elizabethans enjoyed gardening not only as a pastime but also as a source of fresh vegetables and useful herbs. Many books published during the 1500s described the pleasurable and practical value of home gardens.

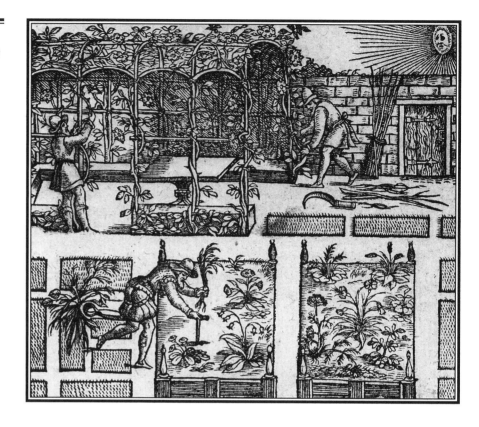

* **horticulture** science or art of growing fruits, vegetables, flowers, and plants, especially for display

* **apprentice** person bound by legal agreement to work for another for a specified period of time in return for instruction in a trade or art

* **courtier** person in attendance at a royal court

* **graft** to insert a shoot or bud from one kind of tree into a slit in a closely related tree so that it will grow there

* **aesthetics** branch of philosophy dealing with the nature of beauty

walls of the formal garden were kitchen gardens, so-called because the vegetables grown there provided the household with fresh produce. Fruit and nut trees were grown in the orchards, and a large expanse of lawn provided space for bowling.

The gardens of the wealthy also had a variety of unusual plants, many of which were imported from North America, South America, and other foreign lands. These plants produced apricots, melons, peaches, figs, oranges, almonds, and olives. In addition, wealthy gardeners experimented with agricultural techniques such as grafting* to produce new varieties of native plants. Some horticulturists could produce several different kinds of roses from the same bush.

Poorer people grew plants more for their uses than for their beauty. They grew vegetables to feed their families and herbs to make medicinal teas, ointments, and salves. Like all gardeners, however, they wanted their gardens to look attractive. They sometimes combined aesthetics* and utility by planting flowers between rows of vegetables.

GARDENS IN SHAKESPEARE'S PLAYS. Gardens provide backdrops for scenes in many of Shakespeare's plays. He used some of them in the same ways that Elizabethans used their own gardens: as peaceful settings for after-dinner walks, afternoon naps, quiet conversations, reading, listening to music, dancing, and participating in sports.

Because the shrubs and walls of Elizabethan gardens offered privacy, people felt free to talk in them without being overheard. In Shakespeare's plays, gardens provide ideal settings for secret meetings between lovers or conspirators. Many of these secret meetings are overheard, of course, often with comic results, as in *Twelfth Night* (II.v) and *Much Ado About Nothing* (II.iii).

Shakespeare also used gardens as a symbol of the realm. For example, in *Richard II*, John of Gaunt compares England to a "sea-walled garden," which because of Richard's misrule

> Is full of weeds, her fairest flowers chok'd up,
> Her fruit-trees all unprun'd, her hedges ruin'd,
> Her knots disordered, and her wholesome herbs
> Swarming with caterpillars.
>
> (III.iv.44–47)

(*See also* **Agriculture; Forests and Fields; Herbs and Herbal Remedies.**)

GENDER AND SEXUALITY

Gender and sexuality have always been of great interest to readers of Shakespeare, partly because so many of his heroines bend and break the rules of behavior established for Elizabethan women. Characters such as ROSALIND *(As You Like It)*, Portia *(The Merchant of Venice)*, and Viola *(Twelfth Night)* are much more clever, articulate, and outspoken than the modest, quiet woman Elizabethans appear to have upheld as an ideal. Many of Shakespeare's women rebel against the male-dominated worlds of their plays by cross-dressing: assuming male clothing and masculine identities in order to explore the greater freedom available to men. Through such actions these female characters test the limits of Elizabethan ideas about gender.

GENDER ROLES IN ELIZABETHAN SOCIETY. It is difficult to know what attitudes ordinary men and women held toward each other in Elizabethan England. The literature of the time, however, tends to depict men as physically, intellectually, and morally superior to women. Whereas men were expected to be assertive and ambitious, women were supposed to remain chaste*, silent, and obedient to their fathers' or husbands' wishes.

Legally, women's roles in Elizabethan society depended on their relationships to men. A legal manual of the time divides women into three groups: women not yet married, wives, and widows. According to English common law, a married woman was considered a *femme covert*, or "covered woman," meaning that her husband was legally responsible for her. A married woman could neither make a contract nor sue for damages in her own name. Furthermore, all her property, with the exception of any land she inherited, became her husband's. These laws placed women at a great social and financial disadvantage, although many women managed to prosper by taking advantage of loopholes in the notoriously complicated and irregular English law.

The well-known phrase "a man's home is his castle" was taken quite literally in the 1500s, when the rule of a husband over his wife and family

* chaste sexually pure

* **microcosm** miniature representation of a larger whole; literally, "small world"

was thought to be fundamental to the structure of society as a whole. The family was seen both as the original form of government and as a microcosm* of the state. Just as the king was a kind of father to his people, the father was to be regarded as the lord of his household. Any threat to an individual home, therefore, was seen as a threat to the state and to the natural order. Women who murdered their husbands were charged not simply with murder but with *petit treason*, a crime against the state that carried a more severe penalty than murder. Though such cases were rare, stories of wives who plotted with lovers to kill their husbands were the basis of many popular plays and tabloid-like pamphlets during and shortly after the reign of ELIZABETH I (1558–1603).

A woman's primary role in the Elizabethan family was to produce children who would inherit their father's name and property. It was important, therefore, for the father to be certain that any infants his wife bore were his own, making extramarital* sex a major threat to the family. The Elizabethan theater was obsessed with infidelity*, which was a central theme in both tragedies and comedies. Anxiety over sexual activity can be seen clearly in Shakespeare's *The Winter's Tale*, where a king becomes convinced that the child his pregnant wife carries is the offspring of his childhood friend. His jealousy over an affair that seems highly improbable is so extreme that he orders the baby to be cast adrift at sea.

* **extramarital** outside of marriage
* **infidelity** sexual unfaithfulness

GENDER ROLES IN THE ELIZABETHAN THEATER. Sexual intrigue was not only a major theme in Elizabethan drama; it was also associated with the theater itself. Many Elizabethans, particularly Puritans*, believed that theatrical performances corrupted the morals of all who watched or participated in them. Puritan officials therefore banned public playhouses from central London, forcing the major ELIZABETHAN THEATERS to be built outside the city limits, often in disreputable neighborhoods alongside gambling houses and brothels*.

* **Puritan** English Protestant who advocated strict moral discipline and a simplification of the ceremonies and beliefs of the Anglican Church

* **brothel** house of prostitution

Many critics of the theater were particularly concerned about its effect on women in the audience. Foreigners who visited London were shocked to see women attending the theater without male escorts—indeed, without even going so far as to wear veils to conceal their faces. There was also concern that respectable women might be forced to sit or stand next to prostitutes or immoral men who would try to seduce them.

Another problem that alarmed many moralists was the fact that all the female characters in Elizabethan and Jacobean* public theaters were played by boys. Women were forbidden to act on the stage because it was considered improper for them to display themselves in front of men. As it happens, many writers found the solution just as threatening as the problem it was supposed to correct. They feared that having boys play female roles would break down the rigid gender distinctions so important to Elizabethan society. These distinctions were vital because, according to Renaissance ideas of human anatomy, the physical differences between the sexes were fairly minor. The male reproductive organs were thought to be essentially the same as the female reproductive organs, with the primary difference being that they were thrust outside the male body by its supposedly higher temperature. On the fringes of medical belief, there

* **Jacobean** referring to the reign of James I, king of England from 1603 to 1625

Work in Elizabethan England was typically determined on the basis of gender. Men generally worked outside the home in the fields or in the marketplace, while women handled most household tasks, such as spinning.

were even stories of rare, spontaneous sex changes—women who had turned into men later in life.

Such stories reveal a fundamental uneasiness about gender differences in Elizabethan society, which may explain why it was considered so vital for society to reinforce those gender distinctions. If the biological line between men and women was very thin, then it was only the society's strict enforcement of acceptable gender roles that kept the sexes in separate categories at all. For this reason Elizabethans placed a great deal of emphasis on sumptuary laws, which determined what CLOTHING could be worn by people of different social classes and genders. The theater, which relied on COSTUMES to alter an actor's appearance, could easily have been seen as a threat to established class and gender rules.

It is difficult to say how much the audience's experience was affected by the knowledge that boys were playing the women's roles. It is possible that spectators simply acknowledged the boy actors as women in much the same way as they accepted the GLOBE THEATER's bare stage as the "vasty fields of France" (*Henry V,* Prologue, line 12). On the other hand, Shakespeare's extensive use of cross-dressing in his plays may have been a kind of inside joke with his audiences, who knew that the female characters in men's clothing were being played by male actors in women's clothing. One way or the other, Shakespeare's plays encourage audiences to consider the interesting possibility that gender itself may be a performance as much as it is a biological destiny. (*See also* **Law; Marriage and Family.**)

GENRE

See *Plays: The Comedies; Plays: The Histories; Plays: The Romances; Plays: The Tragedies.*

GEOGRAPHY

England occupies the largest part of the island of Great Britain, with Scotland to the north and Wales to the west. The island of Ireland lies westward across the Irish Sea, while France and the rest of the European continent lie to the east across the frequently stormy English Channel.

England's territory covers more than 50,000 square miles of greatly varied terrain. Geographers commonly divide England into lowlands and uplands. The lowlands are mainly in the east, center, and south of the country. The typical lowland is marked by plains, forests, and hills. The lowlands also include the Fens, a region on the east coast that was marshland in Shakespeare's time but has since been drained.

The uplands comprise the western region near Wales and the northern reaches of the country near Scotland. The uplands include mountain ranges, such as the Pennines, and vast bogs known as moors. The soil in these areas is marshy and less fertile than it is in the lowlands, but it contains coal and other important minerals. The highest point in England,

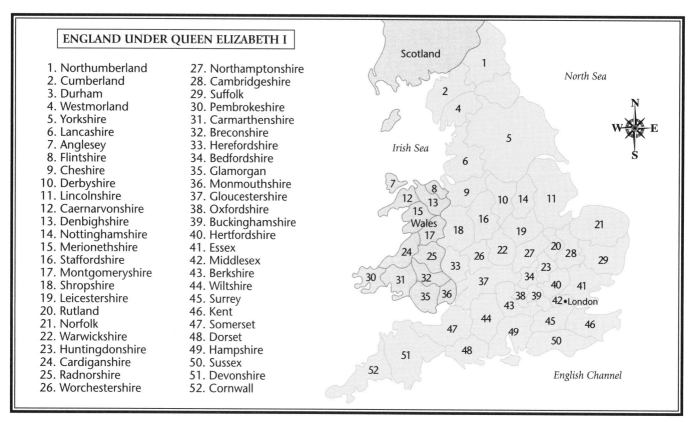

ENGLAND UNDER QUEEN ELIZABETH I

1. Northumberland
2. Cumberland
3. Durham
4. Westmorland
5. Yorkshire
6. Lancashire
7. Anglesey
8. Flintshire
9. Cheshire
10. Derbyshire
11. Lincolnshire
12. Caernarvonshire
13. Denbighshire
14. Nottinghamshire
15. Merionethshire
16. Staffordshire
17. Montgomeryshire
18. Shropshire
19. Leicestershire
20. Rutland
21. Norfolk
22. Warwickshire
23. Huntingdonshire
24. Cardiganshire
25. Radnorshire
26. Worchestershire

27. Northamptonshire
28. Cambridgeshire
29. Suffolk
30. Pembrokeshire
31. Carmarthenshire
32. Breconshire
33. Herefordshire
34. Bedfordshire
35. Glamorgan
36. Monmouthshire
37. Gloucestershire
38. Oxfordshire
39. Buckinghamshire
40. Hertfordshire
41. Essex
42. Middlesex
43. Berkshire
44. Wiltshire
45. Surrey
46. Kent
47. Somerset
48. Dorset
49. Hampshire
50. Sussex
51. Devonshire
52. Cornwall

This map shows the counties of England during the reign of Elizabeth I. Counties were known for the products they produced. Cumberland and Derbyshire, for example, were famous for their rich deposits of lead, while Worcestershire, Oxfordshire, Wiltshire, and Somerset were known for wool production.

at 3,210 feet above sea level, is in a northern upland known as the Lake District, famous for its natural beauty.

In Shakespeare's time England was divided into about 40 shires, or counties. Among them were York in the north; Cornwall, Devon, and Dorset in the southwest; and Norfolk, Suffolk, Essex, and Kent in the east. Middlesex county, in the southeast, included LONDON, by far the largest urban center in the country, resting on the banks of England's most famous river, the THAMES. (*See also* **Agriculture; Cities, Towns, and Villages; Forests and Fields; Population.**)

GHOSTS AND APPARITIONS

Belief in ghosts (spirits of the dead) and apparitions (spirits of other types) was common in Shakespeare's time. It is not clear whether Shakespeare himself believed in such spirits, but he certainly found them useful as dramatic devices. They appear in many of his plays. Typically, these spirits are seen by some characters but not others, since it was commonly believed that ghosts and apparitions could limit their visibility. For example, in one scene the ghost of Hamlet's father can be seen by Hamlet but not by his mother, Gertrude.

All of the characters described as ghosts in the plays present themselves as the spirits of people who have been murdered. In three plays the victims confront their murderers, reminding them of their guilt. The

See color plate 1, vol. 2.

ghost of Banquo appears to Macbeth, the ghost of Julius Caesar appears to BRUTUS, and King Richard III, in a dream, sees the ghosts of 11 people he has killed just before the battle in which he loses his own life. In *Hamlet* the ghost of the murdered king appears not to his killer but to his son, urging the prince to avenge his death. Only in *Cymbeline* do ghosts seek mercy rather than revenge. When Posthumus is imprisoned, the spirits of his dead family members appear and plead with the god Jupiter to help him. Shakespeare identified these characters in the text as apparitions rather than ghosts.

Other types of apparitions appear in four plays. In *Macbeth* the Weyward* Sisters (witches with powers of prophecy) summon three apparitions—an armed head, a bloody child, and a child with a crown—to foretell Macbeth's future. Likewise, in *Henry VI, Part 2*, the witch Margery summons an apparition called Asnath to predict Henry's future.

* *Weyward* name given to the witches in the First Folio text of *Macbeth;* modern editions refer to them as "Weird Sisters"

Apparitions may be either malicious or benevolent. In *Henry VI, Part 1*, Joan La Pucelle calls on fiends that she addresses as "familiar spirits" to help save France from the English. In *Henry VIII*, by contrast, six apparitions dressed in white dance before the dying Queen Katherine, and she describes them as "spirits of peace." (*See also* **Gods and Goddesses; Supernatural Phenomena; Witches and Evil Spirits.**)

GLOBE THEATER

The Globe is the theater principally associated with the production of Shakespeare's plays. Richard Burbage, a leading actor of the day, and his brother, Cuthbert, built the theater in Southwark, on the bank of the River Thames, during the winter of 1598–1599. It was constructed largely from the timbers of the Burbages' old playhouse, known simply as the Theater, which had been built in 1576. The Globe came to be co-owned by the Burbages in association with five shareholding actors in the Chamberlain's Men, among them William Shakespeare. The playwright may have been referring to the newly completed theater when he wrote the Prologue for *Henry V:* "Can this cockpit hold / The vasty fields of France? Or may we cram / Within this wooden O the very casques / That did affright the air at Agincourt?" (lines 11–14).

Although no architectural plans for the Globe exist, its features were probably similar to those of other playhouses of the time. Among these were a polygonal* shape, three galleries (seating areas), and a thatched roof. A central yard was open to the sky. The stage, or platform (as it was commonly called), was roofed over by the Heavens, an overarching canopy that was supported by pillars that rested on the stage. The Heavens both protected the players from inclement weather and housed the stage machinery that raised and lowered large props, such as a royal throne. Beneath the stage, which was accessible through several trap doors, was an area called Hell, from which characters could enter.

* *polygonal* having three or more sides

In some Elizabethan playhouses, a rail was built around the platform to keep spectators from climbing onto the stage. Wealthy spectators, who paid more than a penny or two for admission, were seated in

See color plate 4, vol. 1.

Like other large playhouses, the Globe was a roughly circular structure with an open roof that let in the daylight. In the prologue to *Henry V,* Shakespeare refers to the theater as a "wooden O."

the gallery sections alongside the stage. These areas became known as the gentlemen's rooms. Above the stage was a balcony, also called the gallery, where musicians played. Some scenes, such as the balcony scene in *Romeo and Juliet,* may have been performed from this section. Behind the stage was a tiring house, where the players' costumes, props, and scripts were stored. This was also where the players dressed, changed costumes, and waited for their cues to enter the stage. The stage wall, at the back of the platform, had several doors, which were probably covered with curtains. Little else is known of the Globe's design or its decoration.

In June of 1613 during a performance of Shakespeare's *Henry VIII,* a cannon was fired and a flaming wad of paper landed on the Globe's thatched roof. The building caught fire, and within two hours it burned to the ground. An eyewitness stated that nobody had been injured. One man reported that his trousers caught fire but that another spectator quickly put out the blaze with the ale he had been drinking. By the following summer the King's Men had erected another playhouse, also called the Globe, on the same site. By this time, however, Shakespeare had retired to his native home of STRATFORD-UPON-AVON. Little remains of the first Globe playhouse. In 1989 archaeologists from the Museum of London located what appear to be small sections of the actual foundation of the second Globe. A few drawings of the first and second Globe theaters exist in early views or maps.

On a visit to London in 1947, the American actor Sam Wanamaker decided to rebuild the Globe. A new site, near the original one, was cleared in the 1980s, and the new Globe opened in 1997 with a production of Shakespeare's *The Two Gentlemen of Verona.* Unfortunately, Wanamaker died in 1993, before his dream had become a reality.

GODS AND GODDESSES

* *classical* referring to the tradition of ancient Greece and Rome

Most people today have only a limited knowledge of the mythology of ancient Greece and Rome. Elizabethans, on the other hand, were quite familiar with classical* myths. Grammar schools, such as the one Shakespeare probably attended, offered a Greek and Latin curriculum, so anyone with a basic education was well versed in the tales of ancient gods and goddesses. Even those with no formal schooling had enough exposure to classical mythology to understand many of the references to the traditional figures and legends that appear in the works of Shakespeare and his contemporaries.

The names of gods and goddesses in Elizabethan literature functioned as a sort of shorthand for references to the natural world or to human characteristics. For example, because Neptune was the god of the sea, audiences would recognize the phrase "green Neptune's back" (from *Antony and Cleopatra*) as a reference to the sea. In addition various deities were associated with particular moral qualities or personal attributes. The supreme god—known variously as Zeus, Jupiter, or Jove—was a symbol of power, dignity, and authority. When Hamlet says his murdered father

had "the [forehead] of Jove himself" (III.iv.56), therefore, the audience knew something about the man Hamlet describes. With a single phrase, the prince calls to mind his father's dignity and majesty, the power and respect he commanded, and the legitimacy of his rule—as contrasted with that of Claudius, Hamlet's stepfather.

According to the critic R. K. Root, classical references tend to be more frequent in Shakespeare's comedies and earlier plays than in his tragedies and later works. Many of these allusions* are short and simple, such as the use of the name *Aurora* to refer to the dawn. In other cases gods and other mythological figures appear as characters in the plays. In the final act of *As You Like It,* for example, Hymen (the Roman god of marriage) arrives to bless the four couples who marry at the end of the play. While most of Shakespeare's works refer to classical deities in a purely symbolic way, a few—such as *Pericles*—deal directly with the relationship between human beings and the gods. In this play Diana, the divine patroness of chastity*, appears to Pericles in a dream and directs him to go to her temple at Ephesus to offer a sacrifice. There he is reunited with his long-lost wife, Thaisa, who has become one of Diana's priestesses.

Any notion of the gods as all-powerful and all-knowing is turned on its head in *King Lear.* While reliance on the classical deities is the only hope for the characters in *Pericles,* in *King Lear* the gods appear to have abandoned those who believe in them the most. In the play's first scene, Lear repeatedly calls on various divinities to support him in actions that, unknown to him, will lead to his destruction and to that of his truly loving daughter, CORDELIA. After Cordelia refuses to flatter her father in order to secure a portion of his kingdom for herself, he disowns her, swearing,

> For by the sacred radiance of the sun,
> The mysteries of Hecate and the night;
> By all the operation of the orbs
> From whom we do exist and cease to be,
> Here I disclaim all my paternal care.
> (I.i.109–13)

The earl of Kent protests Lear's decision, saying, "Now, by Apollo, king, / Thou swear'st thy gods in vain" (I.i.160–61), suggesting that it is useless for Lear to appeal to the gods to justify and favor him for so foolish an action.

In the following scene Edmund, the duke of Gloucester's illegitimate son, calls on the gods to look kindly on his plan to steal his legitimate brother's inheritance. He cries "Now, gods, stand up for bastards!" (I.ii.22). For a while it seems that Edmund's prayers have been answered. His plot succeeds, and other crimes are piled on top of it. Lear's ungrateful daughters cast him out into the wilderness, then Gloucester is blinded and stripped of his title for attempting to help the king. Approaching despair, Gloucester expresses his loss of faith in the idea that the gods reward the just and punish the wicked: "As flies to wanton boys are we to the gods, / They kill us for their sport" (IV.i.36–37).

* *allusion* indirect reference to historical or fictional characters, places, or events

* *chastity* quality of moral virtue achieved by abstaining from unlawful sexual activity

Although Edmund's plot is eventually exposed and the play's evil characters are indeed defeated, most of the virtuous die as well. This conclusion differs from that of the original story on which Shakespeare based his tragedy. In at least one earlier version, Lear regains his throne, and Cordelia lives and prospers as queen of France. Shakespeare's rejection of a happy ending must have been a shock to his initial audience, and to many later observers it appeared to discredit the idea of divine justice. In due course a 1681 adaptation by Nahum Tate gave the play the kind of denouement* found in Shakespeare's comedies, and the playwright's tragic version was not staged again in its authentic form for almost 150 years. (*See also* **Fate and Fortune; Shakespeare's Works, Adaptations of; Symbolism and Allegory; Venus and Adonis.**)

* *denouement* outcome; unraveling of the plot

GOVERNMENT AND POLITICS

* *convention* established practice

Since 1066, when William the Conqueror, duke of Normandy, defeated the Anglo-Saxons at the battle of Hastings, England has been a monarchy, a government ruled by a king or queen. The monarchy of Shakespeare's time was a special kind. Although the monarch ruled without question, at the top of the political and social ladder, his or her power was subject to some well-defined limitations. Chief among these was the law of the land and its accepted conventions*. It was called common law because it applied to all the nation's people, including their king or queen.

THE ENGLISH MONARCHY. The primary powers of the English sovereign included the right to appoint government officials, administer justice, regulate trade, and punish traitors. Much of the ruler's time, however, was occupied with foreign relations, which were vitally important for the protection of the country and its people against attacks by enemies such as France and Spain. In addition to these responsibilities, the monarch was the head of the Church of England and, as such, had the final say on all religious questions.

An English king or queen could not create new laws, abolish old ones, or impose new taxes. In addition, English law gave every subject in the kingdom the right to challenge a monarch's decisions through a formal request called a petition. If a king unjustly seized an individual's land, the former landowner could petition to have the property restored. The power of the English monarchy was also limited by the absence of a large standing army or police force to compel obedience to a ruler's commands. As a result, he or she needed the voluntary cooperation of lower government officials.

CHAIN OF COMMAND. After the monarch the most powerful force in the government was the Privy Council, a governing body composed of advisers appointed by the king. In addition to advising, council members had the authority to make decisions about the day-to-day operations of the government. The issues they dealt with ranged from matters

See color plate 2, vol. 1.

Only the reigning monarch had the right to call Parliament into session. The monarch also had the right to veto any laws passed by the two bodies of Parliament: the House of Lords and the House of Commons.

* *alderman* high-ranking member of a town council

of national importance to cases affecting a single individual. During a typical week in 1592, for example, the Privy Council's agenda included issuing instructions to an army commander in France and providing relief for a poor man who was unable to pay his taxes.

The members of the Privy Council delegated much of their work to lower governmental departments. The oldest and most important of these was the Exchequer, which collected, spent, and accounted for the royal income. Except for times when the nation was at war, the major expense of the government was maintaining the royal household and court. Both ELIZABETH I and JAMES I maintained luxurious courts and extravagant lifestyles. Elizabeth tried to be frugal, but James spent vast amounts, leaving the government nearly bankrupt.

Other government departments included the Chancery, the Office of the Privy Seal, and the Signet Office. The Chancery, headed by the lord chancellor, drafted royal grants, treaties, appointments, and acts. The Office of the Privy Seal issued instructions to royal officials and used the seal of state to authenticate bonds, which were used to raise money for the crown. The Signet Office, headed by the secretary of state, played a role in diplomacy by authenticating the king's correspondences with foreign rulers. The Signet Office also issued orders for the arrest of people accused of being enemies of the state.

The royal chain of command extended into each county by way of commissions granting power to local officials to carry orders in the name of the king or queen. One of the most important commissions was that of the justices of the peace, who set up courts in every shire, or county. Local sheriffs were responsible for law enforcement and for arranging the election of representatives to Parliament, the English legislative body.

London and other cities and towns were governed by councils of aldermen*, who annually elected a lord mayor to govern them. These city governments kept order and established courts for settling disputes. Villages governed themselves through tribunals composed of prominent local citizens. All of these officials, whether at the county, city, or village level, were unpaid.

LAWS AND TAXES. Members of Parliament had the right to levy taxes, make new laws, and amend old ones. The monarch or Privy Council often introduced bills, but parliamentary approval was required for a bill to become law. Parliament's most important right, however, was the authority to impose new taxes. This "power of the purse" enabled members of Parliament to influence the decisions made by a king or queen by granting or denying his or her request for money.

Although Parliament had many powers, it also had some restrictions. The authority to convene Parliament belonged to the crown; therefore, the members did not meet on a regular basis. The English Parliament was part of the monarch's government, and he or she could summon members to a session or dismiss them at will.

Parliament underwent a transformation between 1484 and 1536. During this time it became an institution with three equal partners: the

MEN OF BUSINESS

With so many members of Parliament, agreement was often difficult to achieve. The king's ministers usually attended sessions to make sure that the purposes for which they were convened were carried through.

The ministers were helped by men who were not officeholders but were attached to leading councilors and worked on their behalf. These "men of business," as they were named in the late 1800s, still work in Parliament in much the same way that lobbyists do in the U.S. Congress.

monarch, the House of Lords (upper chamber), and the House of Commons (lower chamber). As head of state the king or queen was preeminent, and the Lords were socially and politically superior to the Commons. The monarch could veto what the other partners had agreed to, and each house could kill legislation passed by the other or introduced by the king or queen.

POLITICS AND PATRONAGE. Both Elizabeth I and James I used persuasion, negotiation, compromise, and other political tactics to ensure the carrying out of their orders. Queen Elizabeth and her closest advisers were highly skilled in the art of politics. Her secretary of state, William Cecil, kept a map of the English counties on which he listed the names of the leading families in each county. His job, in part, was to respond to the complaints and requests of these families to ensure their loyalty to the queen as well as their quick and willing obedience to her wishes. This strategy of enforcing and rewarding obedience is known as the patronage system.

Elizabeth was skilled at keeping her rivals in Parliament and other government agencies divided so that they would not gain support at her expense. King James, on the other hand, was a failure as a politician. He was unable to prevent his rivals from uniting against him, and he lost touch with the local leaders, whose cooperation he desperately needed. As a result his subjects often ignored his orders, and the division between the king and his subjects widened. (*See also* **Church, The; Court Life; Crime and Punishment; Diplomacy and Foreign Relations; Law; Royalty and Nobility; Spies.**)

GREENE, ROBERT

See *Groatsworth of Wit.*

GROATSWORTH OF WIT

* *debauchery* excessive indulgence in sensual pleasures

* *parody* to imitate for the purpose of humor or ridicule

In 1592 a famous verbal attack on Shakespeare appeared in a pamphlet written by Robert Greene. A playwright and contemporary of Shakespeare, Greene wrote several autobiographical pamphlets in which he expressed sorrow for the debauchery* of his early days. *Groatsworth of Wit* was one of these. In it he warned other playwrights—namely, Christopher MARLOWE, Thomas Nash, and George Peele—not to trust actors, and one actor in particular. He described this actor as conceited: he "thinks of himself as the onely Shake-scene in a countrey." Greene called him "an upstart Crow, beautified with our feathers, that with his *Tygers hart wrapt in a Players hyde,* supposes he is as well able to bombast out a blanke verse as the best of you."

In all likelihood, "Shake-scene" refers to Shakespeare. Greene himself highlighted the phrase *"Tygers hart wrapt in a Players hyde,"* which parodies* a line from Shakespeare's *Henry VI, Part 3* ("O tiger's heart wrapp'd in a woman's hide" [I.iv.137]). Many Shakespearean scholars believe that the phrase "beautified with our feathers" was meant to accuse Shakespeare of plagiarism. Others believe that Greene was simply accusing Shakespeare of being presumptuous in calling himself a playwright when he was merely an actor. Several months after Greene's death, his editor, Henry Chettle, issued a public apology to Shakespeare. (*See also* **Authorship, Theories About; Pamphleteers; Playwrights and Poets.**)

GUILDS

I n Elizabethan England, industry was controlled by guilds, organizations of workers in particular trades, such as wine making or glass working. Similar to modern labor unions, guilds set standards for their professions and protected the interests of their members. Guilds were also called livery companies because their members wore elaborate and distinctive clothing, called livery, to occasions such as ceremonial dinners and formal processions.

* *medieval* referring to the Middle Ages, a period roughly between A.D. 500 and 1500

FORMATION OF GUILDS. Most Elizabethan guilds began in medieval* times as loose associations of workers or merchants that gradually evolved into official organizations with royal charters. They formed when new products or improved methods of manufacturing led to the development of new occupations or to extensions of established trades or professions. The clockmakers' guild, for example, formed in the 1600s for the manufacture of fine indoor clocks for the home. Blacksmiths, who continued to make large outdoor church clocks as they had for centuries, remained in a separate guild.

Occasionally two guilds merged to form a single organization. This might occur if two related professions began to decline or lose members. More commonly, however, guilds divided as professions became more specialized. In the late 1300s, for example, bowyers (makers of bows) split off from the fletchers' guild (which represented makers of arrows) and formed their own professional society.

LONDON'S GUILDS. In Shakespeare's London, there were more than 70 different guilds. The largest of these were the 12 "great" guilds. Several

One responsibility of the trade guilds was to set standards for their members. This woodcut, created in 1600, lists the prices that could be charged for loaves of bread of different types and sizes based on the market price of wheat.

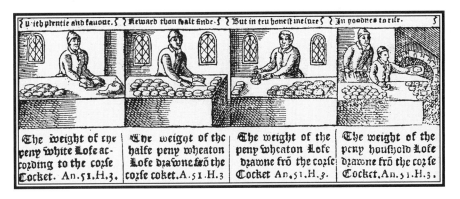

of them dealt in cloth goods. The Mercers' Company sold fine cloth, the Drapers' Company sold cheaper cloth, and the Haberdashers' Company sold men's clothing and accessories. Others supplied food. The Fishmongers' Company sold fish, the Salters' Company produced and sold salt, the Vintners' Company made and sold wine, and the Grocers' Company sold most other foodstuffs. Until 1617 when they created their own guild, apothecaries (druggists) belonged to the Grocers' Company. Still other great guilds were the Skinners' Company (preparers or sellers of hides), the Goldsmiths' Company (makers or sellers of gold items), and the Ironmongers' Company (sellers of iron and hardware).

London also had more than 60 smaller guilds, among them organizations for barbers, musicians, candlemakers, and stationers (printers and publishers). The Stationers' Register, which listed books and plays published, is one of the best sources of information about the years in which various Elizabethan plays were printed.

Members of the larger guilds tended to concentrate their shops in a particular part of the city. Fishmongers typically placed their stores on Bridge Street, near a pier on the Thames, where fish could be quickly unloaded from boats, and shoemakers set up shops on Shoe Lane. Many of these business districts can still be found in London today.

Individuals gained membership in a guild in several ways. The son of a guild member was admitted to the guild automatically. Membership could also be purchased for cash. Most people, however, earned their guild membership by successfully completing apprenticeships. They served master craftspeople for a specified number of years, usually seven, while they learned their trades. An apprentice then had to demonstrate his skill to the guild, take an oath, and pay his dues before being admitted as a full guild member. (*See also* **Craftworkers; Printing and Publishing; Work.**)

GUNPOWDER PLOT

* *dissident* one who disagrees with an established political or religious system

The Gunpowder Plot was a failed conspiracy to assassinate King JAMES I, the Scottish king of England. James was a Protestant, and he had attempted to halt the spread of Catholicism when he came to the throne in 1603. Two years later a group of Catholic dissidents*, including a man named Guy Fawkes, laid plans to blow up the Parliament building on November 5, when James would be there to open a new session. The conspirators had rented space in the cellar beneath the structure and had packed it with gunpowder. The scheme was discovered at the last minute, and the conspirators were promptly tried, convicted, and hanged. As a result of the plot, the government tightened its already firm control over Catholics.

King James himself was crushed by the event, which shattered his self-image as a monarch who was much loved by his subjects. Shakespeare, too, was greatly affected by the conspiracy. In the year following the plot, he wrote *Macbeth,* a tragedy about the assassination of an earlier Scottish king.

* **effigy** crudely made figure representing a detested person

Guy Fawkes Day is still commemorated in England every year on November 5. During this celebration effigies* of Guy Fawkes are burned and children chant rhymes such as "Remember, remember, the Fifth of November / Gunpowder, treason, and plot; / I see no reason why gunpowder treason / Should ever be forgot." (*See also* **Religion**.)

HAMLET

* **usurp** to seize power from a rightful ruler

* **rampart** broad embankment, usually with a wall on top, that serves as a barrier

Throughout the centuries that have passed since its initial appearance, *Hamlet* has remained among the most popular and frequently staged of Shakespeare's plays. The reasons for its popularity are obvious, for the tragedy's impact and influence are as powerful today as they have always been. *Hamlet* centers on the moral dilemma faced by the prince of Denmark, who discovers that his uncle has murdered his father and usurped* the throne. The prince wrestles with his conscience as he tries to reconcile an obligation to see justice done with a fear that he will place his own soul at risk if he avenges his father's death himself. Anyone who has faced an ethical struggle can relate to Hamlet's struggle. Young people, in particular, have identified with the prince's sense of helplessness as he strives to find a way to address the corruption he sees around him.

PLOT SUMMARY. The play is set at Elsinore Castle, the seat of Denmark's royal court. Claudius, brother to the former king of Denmark, who has recently died, rules the nation. Claudius has married his late brother's widow, Queen Gertrude, and taken over the kingdom. The action opens on the castle ramparts*, where soldiers are alert for an expected invasion from Norway's prince, Fortinbras. With the soldiers is a scholar, Horatio, who has come to investigate reports that the ghost of Denmark's late king has been appearing nightly. The Ghost appears but refuses to speak. Horatio decides to reveal this news to his friend Hamlet, the late king's son, who is still in mourning for his father—much to the displeasure of Claudius and Gertrude. When he learns of the Ghost's appearance, Hamlet agrees to join Horatio and the guard the following midnight.

Meanwhile Laertes, another young man at the court, is preparing to return to his studies in Paris. His father POLONIUS, chief councilor to the king, sends Laertes on his way with a long-winded speech in which he advises his son about proper and prudent behavior. As he departs, Laertes warns his sister OPHELIA not to trust Hamlet, who has been sending her love letters. Polonius picks up this subject and forbids his daughter to see the prince. Ophelia reluctantly agrees, adding a further indignity to those that Hamlet has already suffered.

That night Hamlet confronts the Ghost, who claims to be the dead king's spirit. He discloses that Claudius murdered him and orders Hamlet to avenge his death. But at the same time, the Ghost says, "howsomeever thou pursues this act, / Taint not thy mind, nor let thy soul contrive / Against thy mother aught. Leave her to heaven" (I.v.84–86). The Ghost's command plunges Hamlet into a quandary, because he must find a way

Hamlet

to avenge his father's death without clouding his own judgment or doing anything to harm his mother. He tells Horatio and Marcellus that he will put on an "antic disposition"—pretending madness to cover his actions— and he swears them to secrecy.

Time passes, and Hamlet's "madness" becomes evident to everyone. Ophelia, in particular, is alarmed when Hamlet bursts into her room and stares at her in silence for several minutes. She describes the encounter to Polonius, who becomes convinced that his daughter's rejection of the prince's favors is the cause of Hamlet's strange behavior. Polonius presents his theory to the king and queen, who have been worried about the prince's behavior and have sent for Hamlet's old friends ROSENCRANTZ AND GUILDENSTERN in the hope that the prince will reveal his thoughts to them. They meet with Hamlet and attempt to learn what is troubling him, suggesting that his unhappiness must stem from frustrated political

Laurence Olivier directed the first popular motion picture of *Hamlet* in 1948, with himself in the title role. In this famous scene, the prince laments over the skull of his boyhood friend, the jester Yorick, and broods on the nature of mortality.

ambition. Hamlet quickly perceives that Claudius has sent for them and warns them that he is not as crazy as he appears. At this point a band of traveling players arrive at the court. Hamlet devises a plan to verify the Ghost's story by producing a play that mirrors Claudius's murder of his brother. He hopes his uncle's reaction to the drama will give clear evidence of his guilt, and he says, "The play's the thing / Wherein I'll catch the conscience of the king" (II.ii.604–5).

In the next scene Claudius and Polonius attempt to test Polonius's theory about Hamlet's lovesickness by eavesdropping on an encounter between the prince and Ophelia. At first Hamlet ignores Ophelia, delivering a lengthy monologue to no one in particular. In this famous soliloquy* he appears to contemplate suicide, asking whether it is nobler to suffer the pains of life or to take an active role in ending them. When he begins talking with Ophelia, he soon realizes that the encounter is a trap and makes a thinly veiled threat against Claudius. Disgusted with Ophelia's behavior, Hamlet curses her and advises her to go to a nunnery (convent)—a term that in Elizabethan slang could also refer to a house of prostitution. After Hamlet departs, Ophelia laments over his lost wits, giving the audience its first glimpse of her own mental breakdown. Polonius remains convinced that Hamlet's madness is due to disappointed love, but Claudius correctly suspects that his nephew's condition reflects a more serious and threatening state of mind.

That night, before the players perform, Hamlet takes Horatio aside and asks him to watch Claudius carefully. He praises his friend's sound judgment and acceptance of his fortune, calling him "one in suff'ring all that suffers nothing" (III.ii.66) and admiring his ability to take "Fortune['s] buffets and rewards" with "equal thanks." Hamlet's calm and rational remarks reveal a dramatic change of mood from the violence of the previous scene and the scenes that follow. The prince's wild mood swings show that he himself does not possess the qualities he admires in Horatio. Instead he is "passion's slave." As the players perform *The Murder of Gonzago*, the story of a king who is murdered by his kinsman, Claudius stops the show, visibly upset. Excitedly, Hamlet swears to his friend that he will "take the ghost's word for a thousand pound" (III.ii.286–87).

Rosencrantz and Guildenstern appear and summon Hamlet to his mother's dressing room. On his way Hamlet sees Claudius at prayer, alone and unguarded. Hamlet draws his sword and is about to kill the king when he stops to think that by doing so he will send the murderer not to hell, where he belongs, but to heaven. Hamlet therefore withdraws, hoping to find an opportunity to kill his uncle when he is "about some act / That has no relish of salvation in't" (III.iii.91–92). Hamlet's uncharitable thoughts indicate that he has failed to heed the Ghost's warning: he has allowed his lust for revenge to "taint," or corrupt, his mind. Ironically, after Hamlet leaves, Claudius reveals that he has, in fact, been unable to pray: "My words fly up, my thoughts remain below: / Words without thoughts never to heaven go" (III.iii.97–98).

In the queen's chamber, Polonius hides behind the drapery and eavesdrops as Hamlet harshly criticizes Gertrude for her sins. Frightened,

* *soliloquy* monologue in which a character reveals his or her private thoughts

HUMOROUS HAMLETS

Not only has *Hamlet* been performed countless times on stage and screen, but many other plays and films have been made about Shakespeare's play. The comedy *I Hate Hamlet,* by Paul Rudnick, tells the story of a television actor preparing to play Hamlet for the first time, with the help of John Barrymore's ghost. The 1995 film *The Fifteen Minute Hamlet* shows Shakespeare filming a production of his play, then cutting it down to 15 minutes. Another 1995 film, *Green Eggs and Hamlet*, presents the entire story of Hamlet in the style of children's author Dr. Seuss.

See
color plate 15,
vol. 2.

she cries out and is echoed by Polonius. Believing it is the king hiding behind the arras, Hamlet thrusts his sword into the drapery and kills the old man. For the moment, however, he is too upset with his mother to give any thought to the vileness of his deed. He continues to scold her, rousing himself to such a fury that the Ghost must appear once more to stop him from harming Gertrude. The Ghost criticizes Hamlet for not carrying out his commands and then leaves abruptly. Gertrude, who does not see the Ghost, thinks her son is mad. Reassuring her, Hamlet begs her to repent and not to sleep with Claudius again.

The death of Polonius marks a major turning point for several characters. Hamlet believes that it is the will of heaven "to punish me with this, and this with me" (III.iv.174) and realizes that he will be called to account for his deed. When Ophelia learns that her lover has killed her father, she goes mad and eventually drowns herself. For Claudius the killing provides an excuse to get Hamlet out of the way. He plans to send the prince to England, accompanied by Rosencrantz and Guildenstern, and have him executed. As Hamlet prepares to leave, he sees Fortinbras—who has listened to reason and abandoned or postponed his planned invasion of Denmark—leading his army through Danish territory to attack Poland instead. In a bitter soliloquy Hamlet compares himself unfavorably to the young Norwegian, who is willing to risk countless lives for the sake of honor, while Hamlet believes that he himself has failed to carry out a much more significant task.

Events move quickly after this. Laertes returns from Paris, hell-bent on revenging his father's death, and threatens a rebellion against Claudius. When he learns who actually killed his father, however, Laertes abandons his plan and instead plots with Claudius to kill Hamlet in a rigged fencing match. Meanwhile, Hamlet discovers the plot to have him slain and secretly substitutes new orders, making Rosencrantz and Guildenstern the victims instead. The ship carrying Hamlet to England is attacked by pirates, who take the prince prisoner and return him to Denmark. There he meets Horatio in a churchyard and, much to his horror, finds Ophelia's funeral in progress. He and Laertes exchange words and blows over Ophelia's corpse. Later, when Hamlet tries to excuse his behavior, Laertes only partially accepts the apology.

The fencing match between Hamlet and Laertes occurs in the play's last scene. Claudius has arranged for Laertes to be given an unblunted sword, smeared with poison, and Hamlet a conventionally dull-edged one. He has also prepared a lethal drink for Hamlet in case Laertes cannot hit him. Laertes injures Hamlet with the poisoned sword, but a scuffle follows in which the two men exchange swords. Hamlet then injures Laertes with the poisoned blade. Meanwhile, Gertrude accidentally drinks from the poisoned cup and dies. The dying Laertes forgives Hamlet and reveals Claudius's plot. Hamlet immediately stabs Claudius and forces what is left of the poisoned drink down his throat. Horatio threatens to kill himself, but Hamlet urges him to live on and tell the prince's story. As the play ends, Fortinbras arrives, fresh from his conquest in Poland. With his dying voice, Hamlet endorses the Norwegian prince as the new ruler of Denmark.

TEXT AND SOURCES. Accounts from Shakespeare's time indicate that an older play about Hamlet, referred to by scholars as UR-HAMLET, had been performed by 1589. Scholars are not certain whether Shakespeare based his *Hamlet* (written around 1600) on this play or on its original sources, but he probably knew of both. The story of murder and revenge goes back as far as the *Historica Danica* of Saxo Grammaticus (1180–1208), which sets the tale in pre-Christian Denmark. It was retold in a Christian setting by François de Belleforest in *Histoires Tragiques* (1576). Shakespeare may have read Belleforest's version in the original French.

As usual, Shakespeare adapted these sources to his own purposes. In the process, he radically changed the genre* of revenge tragedy. In earlier plays of this type, such as Thomas Kyd's *The Spanish Tragedy* (ca. 1587), punishing a murderer through blood vengeance was depicted as an absolute necessity. This convention* changed dramatically in works that followed *Hamlet*, such as Cyril Tourneur's *The Atheist's Tragedy* (1611) and George Chapman's *The Revenge of Bussy D'Ambois* (1613), although many other aspects of the genre, such as the appearance of a ghost, remained unchanged.

COMMENTARY. A central issue in *Hamlet* is the reason for the prince's repeated delays in carrying out the act of revenge. Throughout the play he spends far more time reflecting than acting. In his meditations he not only appears to question what he should do at particular moments but raises larger issues about human actions and motivations in general. His final soliloquy, in which he compares his own inaction with Fortinbras' willingness to lead his men into battle over a "quarrel in a straw" (IV.iv.55), sets side by side the two alternatives he faces. Particularly in his famous soliloquy, "To be, or not to be" (III.i.55–87), Hamlet wonders whether it is better to accept the torments of life passively or to take action to eliminate them.

The play never provides a clear answer to Hamlet's question, but a possible clue may be found in the character of Fortinbras. Of the three young men Claudius refers to in his first speech (I.ii.1–39)—Fortinbras, Laertes, and Hamlet—Fortinbras is the only one who survives. Hamlet, who has spent most of the play reflecting and reasoning rather than taking action, dies at the end. So does Laertes, who has shown himself ready to act without thinking—hurrying back to Denmark to overthrow the king the minute he hears of his father's death. The fact that Fortinbras not only lives but succeeds to the Danish throne is a tribute to his nature, which combines courage and strength with the ability to reason and control his passion for revenge.

Although Hamlet does eventually take his revenge, he never forms a plan of action against Claudius. Rather, he kills the king with a poison that Claudius himself has prepared. Ironically, it is Claudius who has made all the arrangements that lead to his own death. This seems to justify Hamlet's belief that destiny, rather than personal choice, shapes human actions: as he says to Horatio just before the duel scene, "There's a divinity that shapes our ends, / Rough-hew them how we will" (V.ii.10–11). In his act of avenging his father, Hamlet can be seen as the instrument of

* *genre* literary form

* *convention* established practice

fate or divine will, heaven's "scourge and minister." His acceptance of this role, however, comes at great expense. Purging Denmark of its corruption costs the lives of eight characters, and the play's tragic justice punishes the innocent (Ophelia) along with the guilty (Claudius).

PERFORMANCE HISTORY. *Hamlet* has probably been performed more often than any other Shakespearean play—both on stage and, more recently, on film and television. It is almost a requirement for every classical* actor to play the title role at least once in his career. Richard Burton, Nicol Williamson, Ralph Fiennes, Kevin Kline, and many others have attempted the role, with varying success. In the 1900s John Gielgud was one of the most celebrated Hamlets, noted for his rich and fluid speaking voice. John Barrymore, who played the prince in both America and England, is also viewed as one of the great 20th-century stage Hamlets.

Many stage and screen productions of this lengthy and complex play have cut portions of the text. Laurence Olivier, in his 1949 film—considered to be the first great motion picture version of the play—made considerable changes to the text, rearranging speeches and scenes and cutting a good deal. Director Franco Zeffirelli did likewise in his 1990 film with Mel Gibson in the title role. In 1980 BBC television produced a much fuller version of the play with Derek Jacobi as Hamlet. The longest version of the play on record, however, is the four-hour film directed in 1996 by Kenneth Branagh, who adapted the play by updating the setting to the 1800s. Another version that updated the play was the 1970 television production directed by Peter Wood and starring Richard Chamberlain. Adapted from a stage version, Wood's production was set in the English Regency period (1811–1820), during the height of the Romantic* era, as reflected in Chamberlain's emotional performance. (*See also* **Actors, Shakespearean; Directors and Shakespeare; Fate and Fortune; Play Within the Play; Playwrights and Poets; Shakespeare on Screen; Shakespeare's Sources; Shakespeare's Works, Adaptations of.**)

* *classical* referring to those who perform the classics, works of enduring excellence

* *Romantic* referring to a school of thought, prominent in the 1800s, that emphasized the importance of emotion in art

HATHAWAY, ANNE

1556–1623
Shakespeare's wife

Anne Hathaway was born in Shottery, England, a small village just a mile from Shakespeare's boyhood home in STRATFORD-UPON-AVON. The farmhouse at Hewlands Farm, where she lived, is now called Anne Hathaway's Cottage and has become one of the most popular attractions for tourists visiting the Stratford region. Anne's father, Richard Hathaway, was a well-to-do farmer, and Anne was one of seven children.

Anne Hathaway married William Shakespeare in 1582, when she was 26 and he was 18. She gave birth to their first child (a girl named Susanna) six months later and to twins (a boy named Hamnet and a girl named Judith) in 1585. Soon after the birth of the twins, Shakespeare moved to London, while Anne and the children stayed in Stratford-upon-Avon. Hamnet died in 1596, and the next year Shakespeare bought Anne and their two daughters a large estate, called New Place, in Stratford. Shakespeare continued to live and work in London but appears to have

See color plate 3, vol. 1.

made frequent visits to New Place. In 1611 he evidently retired to Stratford and remained there with Anne until his death in 1616. Anne died there seven years later at the age of 67.

Some scholars have argued that Shakespeare came to regret his marriage to Anne Hathaway. By the time he was 21, he had three young children and a wife who was almost 30. In several of his plays, Shakespeare advises young men to avoid marrying older women. There is no direct evidence, however, to indicate that the playwright was unhappy with his lot. (*See also* **Shakespeare, Life and Career; Shakespeare's Will.**)

HEMINGES, JOHN

died 1630
Actor

John Heminges was an English actor who spent most of his career working alongside Shakespeare. Heminges acted in and later managed Shakespeare's acting company, the KING'S MEN. He is probably best known for his work, with Henry Condell, compiling the FIRST FOLIO edition of Shakespeare's plays.

The date of Heminges's birth is not known, but a 1629 document identifies him as the "Sonne and Heire of George Hemings of Draytwiche in the Countye of Worcester." He apparently began his acting career in London with a company called the Queen's Men. By 1593 he had joined another troupe, Strange's Men. The next year, he joined the newly formed Chamberlain's Men, who became the King's Men after James I came to the throne in 1603. Heminges stayed with the company until his death. He started managing the King's Men in 1596, and in 1611 he quit acting to devote all his time to management. He was apparently on good terms with Henry Herbert, the MASTER OF THE REVELS. When the King's Men were unable to show him the "allowed book" (official version) of Shakespeare's *A Winter's Tale,* Herbert gave them permission to produce the play based on Heminges' word that "nothing profane [had been] added" to the original script.

Heminges' financial talents were apparently well known. Several members of his acting company, including Shakespeare, chose him to oversee the execution of their wills. His role as executor gave him the opportunity to purchase his fellow actors' shares in the company's two theaters—the GLOBE and the BLACKFRIARS—from their heirs after they died. By the time of his death, Heminges owned one-fourth of the shares in each theater. (*See also* **Acting Companies, Elizabethan.**)

HENRY IV, PART 1

Considered by many critics to be Shakespeare's most accomplished history play, *Henry IV, Part 1* presents a cross section of English society, from kings and earls to barroom cronies. Although the play is named for the historical king who ruled England from 1399 to 1413, the story is really about Henry's eldest son, Prince Hal, and the qualities of a good leader. Throughout the play Hal is confronted by the

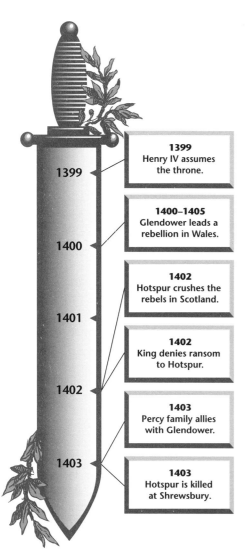

* *depose* to remove from high office, often by force

* *penance* act performed to show sorrow or repentance for sin

* *soliloquy* monologue in which a character reveals his or her private thoughts

1399
Henry IV assumes the throne.

1399

1400–1405
Glendower leads a rebellion in Wales.

1400

1402
Hotspur crushes the rebels in Scotland.

1401

1402
King denies ransom to Hotspur.

1402

1403
Percy family allies with Glendower.

1403

1403
Hotspur is killed at Shrewsbury.

conflicting values and models of behavior he sees in King Henry (his politically shrewd father), Hotspur (the hot-tempered rebel who opposes the crown), and Sir John FALSTAFF (an irreverent old knight). The play's dual actions—securing the throne against insurrection and the unfolding of the prince's character—reach a climax during an epic battle that dominates the last act.

PLOT SUMMARY. The play begins where RICHARD II, Shakespeare's preceding history play, ends. In that work the rebellious Henry Bolingbroke deposes* King Richard II and ascends the throne as King Henry IV. As *Henry IV, Part 1* opens, the king laments that he must delay a pilgrimage to the Holy Land, which he planned to undertake as penance* for seizing the throne and causing Richard's murder, because rebellions have erupted in Wales and Scotland.

The Welsh forces, led by Owen Glendower, have defeated the English and captured Edmund Mortimer, earl of March. The Scottish rebels, however, have been crushed by English troops led by Henry Percy (known as Hotspur). The problem is that Hotspur refuses to surrender his prisoners to the king. Although Hotspur disobeys the king by his refusal, Henry admires his fighting spirit. He even admits that he envies Hotspur's father and complains that his own son, Prince Hal, indulges in a life of "riot and dishonor."

Meanwhile, the prince is carousing with Sir John Falstaff, a fat, pleasure-loving old man. Hal and his jolly companion trade humorous insults, which reveal Falstaff's keen wit and his amusing ability to justify his carefree behavior. When Hal calls Falstaff a thief, for example, the latter replies "Why, Hal, 'tis my vocation, Hal, 'tis no sin for a man to labor in his vocation" (I.ii.104–5). Ned Poins, Hal's friend, invites Falstaff and the prince to join him in a highway robbery. A reluctant Hal agrees to go along only when Poins suggests that the exploit will include a practical joke to expose Falstaff's cowardice. Although the prince appears lazy and indifferent, he reveals in a soliloquy* that he intends to reform. He says that his irresponsible past will make him seem more virtuous when he improves and that he will be "like bright metal on a sullen [dark] ground" (I.ii.212).

Back at court Hotspur, his father (the earl of Northumberland), and his uncle (the earl of Worcester) explain their positions to the king. Hotspur infuriates Henry by refusing to hand over his captives unless the king agrees to pay Glendower to release Mortimer. Henry refuses to ransom Mortimer, whom he calls a traitor, and tells Hotspur, "Send us your prisoners, or you will hear of it" (I.iii.124). After the king's departure Worcester suggests that Henry has refused to pay the ransom because Mortimer is the rightful heir to Richard's stolen crown. The scene ends with the three outraged men planning a war to remove King Henry from the throne.

In Act II, Falstaff and his fellows rob some wealthy travelers. As planned, Hal and Poins don disguises and rob Falstaff, who runs away in a fright. Back at the Boar's Head tavern, Falstaff returns and tells Hal and Poins a tall tale. As he boasts of his valiant defense against his attackers,

THE REAL-LIFE FALSTAFF

The rowdy, boozy, cowardly old soldier who is Prince Hal's companion was originally named Sir John Oldcastle. But a real Sir John Oldcastle had existed, although he was unlike the figure Shakespeare created. Known as a "valiant captain and a hardy gentleman," he was burned to death as a religious martyr in 1417. When Shakespeare's play opened, Oldcastle's descendant William Brooke, Lord Cobham, objected to the way in which his ancestor had been portrayed and forced Shakespeare to change the name. Not to be outdone, however, Shakespeare inserted the original name in Act I, where Prince Hal calls Falstaff "my old lad of the castle."

* *conscript* one who has been drafted for military service

Falstaff exaggerates their numbers until they become a virtual battalion. When Hal and Poins reveal that the two of them were the only bandits, Falstaff, ever unflappable, says, "By the Lord, I knew ye as well as he that made ye . . . was it for me to kill the heir-apparent?" (II.iv.267–69).

A message arrives from the king, summoning Hal to court, and Falstaff suggests that the prince rehearse his response to his irate father. Taking the part of the king, the old knight condemns all of Hal's friends except, of course, "a goodly portly man" (himself). When Hal assumes the king's role, however, he singles out for special condemnation "that villainous abominable misleader of youth, Falstaff, that old white-bearded Satan" (II.iv.462–63).

In Act III, Hotspur, Worcester, Mortimer, Glendower, and their fellow conspirators gather in Wales to discuss how they will divide the realm after they overthrow Henry. Meanwhile, at court, the king rebukes Hal for engaging in "barren pleasures" and keeping "rude society." The prince promises to regain his father's trust by conquering the rebels and defeating Hotspur. When he returns to the Boar's Head tavern, Hal speaks excitedly of the next day's battle. Falstaff promises to be there, too, although he would rather spend the day in the company of his drinking companions.

As Act IV opens, Hotspur receives word that illness prevents Mortimer from joining the rebellion and that Glendower and his troops are delayed. Although the king's forces greatly outnumber the rebels, Hotspur refuses to postpone the battle. Meanwhile, a ragged group of conscripts* arrive on the battlefield led by Falstaff, who is moving slowly in the hope that he will miss the fighting. Back at the rebel camp, Hotspur has sent Worcester to negotiate a peace with the king.

In Act V, Henry offers to pardon the rebels if they disband, and Prince Hal proposes that he and Hotspur settle the disagreement in single combat. Falstaff, on the other hand, is unwilling to risk his life for the sake of an idea, commenting, "Can honor set a leg? . . . What is honor? A word. What is in that word honor? . . . Air" (V.i.131–35). Worcester returns to the rebel camp but conceals from Hotspur the king's offer of amnesty.

During the battle Hal fights bravely, saves his father's life, and kills his hotheaded rival. At the other extreme, Falstaff once again proves his cowardice by pretending to be dead in order to escape injury. He explains his actions with the oft-quoted observation that "the better part of valor is discretion" (V.iv.119–20) and then lies that he killed Hotspur. As the play ends, the king announces plans to move against the surviving rebels, Mortimer and Glendower.

SOURCES AND HISTORY. Most scholars believe that Shakespeare completed *Henry IV, Part 1* in 1596. His main source for the play was the 1587 edition of Raphael Holinshed's *Chronicles,* a work compiled by the English historian in 1577. He also borrowed from a poem called "The Civil Wars Between the Two Houses of York and Lancaster," published in 1595 by Samuel Daniel. Shakespeare followed Daniel's version by having the prince challenge Hotspur to single combat and by making Hotspur approximately the same age as Hal. The historic Hotspur was much older than the prince.

In describing Hal's wild youthful exploits, Shakespeare was following an English tradition, which maintained that Henry V (Prince Hal) had been a rowdy young man. An anonymous play called *The Famous Victories of Henry V*, written sometime before 1594, provided details of such activities as the mock highway robbery. These incidents also appeared in several histories that Shakespeare may have consulted.

COMMENTARY. In *Henry IV, Part 1*, three groups of characters—the king and his advisers, Falstaff and his cronies, and Hotspur and his fellow rebels—force Hal to deal with conflicting demands for his attention and loyalty. Each has virtues and weaknesses, and Shakespeare's remarkable achievement is that he portrays them all so vividly that the audience can identify and sympathize with each in turn.

The king and his advisers at court are careful, calculating, shrewd, and practical. They are motivated less by emotions, such as love or hate, than by the need to restore order to the kingdom. King Henry evaluates each person or situation in terms of the advantage or danger it presents. He is mature and generally conscientious but also weary of the burdens and cares of his office.

Falstaff and his tavern friends, on the other hand, pay no attention to time, law, or order. They are concerned only with drinking, eating, and other pleasures. Falstaff is admirable, even lovable, for his humor, his self-mockery, and his rejection of pomposity. He knows that "honor" and "duty" are sometimes cloaks for selfish deeds, but he refuses to acknowledge that they are often necessary to the maintenance of social order.

The tempestuous Hotspur, so devoted to valor that he sacrifices himself to it, is a remnant of England's heroic, chivalric* past. His death on the battlefield symbolizes the end of the medieval* warrior-leader, a hero who is ill equipped to maneuver in a more complex world of politics, shifting loyalties, and negotiation.

Hal is measured against each of these groups. In his shrewd plans for his future "reformation," he proves himself a calculating politician like his father. In the humorous insults he trades with Falstaff, he demonstrates his sharp wit and his capacity for enjoyment. Similarly, in his fight against Hotspur and others on the battlefield, he proves his courage and demonstrates his honor.

During the play Hal uses the freedom he finds with Falstaff to try different roles—robber, joker, and even king. By the play's end he has become what he is supposed to be: a prince.

PERFORMANCE HISTORY. The earliest known performance of *Henry IV, Part 1* was given in 1600. Over the next 40 years it was frequently staged, with Falstaff's character remaining especially popular. In fact the play was sometimes humorously titled *The First Part of Sir John Falstaff*.

When the 1642 law banning theaters was lifted in 1660, *Henry IV, Part 1* was among the first works to be performed in the reopened English playhouses. In the late 1600s Thomas Betterton, an actor and theater

* *chivalric* referring to the rules and customs of medieval knighthood

* *medieval* referring to the Middle Ages, a period roughly between A.D. 500 and 1500

manager, staged productions in which he cast himself as Hotspur and, years later, as Falstaff. This established the tradition of lead actors taking the Falstaff role. During the early 1700s David Garrick, a theater manager, also played both Hotspur and Falstaff. Producers at this time often cut scenes to focus more attention on the comic knight.

During the late 1800s, *Henry IV, Part 1* lost popularity—largely because Victorian* audiences considered Falstaff too vulgar—and the play was seldom performed. Interest revived in the early 1900s, however, and in many notable productions Falstaff was portrayed as a fallen man or an aging vaudevillian*. In 1945 Ralph Richardson was highly praised for his portrayal of Falstaff as a figure of great mental agility and wisdom. Laurence Olivier appeared as Hotspur in the same production. Orson Welles took the role of Falstaff in his 1965 film *Chimes at Midnight*, which is based on *Henry IV, Part 1* and *Henry IV, Part 2* and is considered by many to be the finest Shakespearean film ever made.

Among the more recent productions was that of the English Shakespeare Company (1986), which presented the full cycle of eight histories. The cast performed all eight plays in repertory on the weekends. One could attend morning, afternoon, and evening shows on Friday, Saturday, and Sunday to see the entire cycle. Television versions of *Henry IV, Part 1* include a 1997 American production called *Young Prince Hal*. (*See also* **Henry IV, Part 2; Henry V; History in Shakespeare's Plays: England; Holinshed's Chronicles; Plays: The Histories.**)

* *Victorian* referring to the reign of Victoria, queen of England from 1837 to 1901

* *vaudevillian* one who performs vaudeville, a staged variety act that might include song, dance, slapstick, or acrobatics

HENRY IV, PART 2

Shakespeare's two plays named for King Henry IV are part of a series of histories that explore the causes and consequences of the English civil wars of the 1400s. Beyond their focus on political and military events, these plays examine the responsibilities of kingship and the qualities that make a suitable, or unsuitable, ruler.

The two Henry IV plays devote less attention to the title character than to his son and heir, Prince Hal, who will one day rule as King Henry V. In *Henry IV, Part 2*, Hal completes the developmental process that transforms him from a seemingly wild, undisciplined, and pleasure-seeking young man into a dutiful monarch. The play examines the question of what Hal gains and gives up along the way. Central to that issue is the prince's relationship with his old tavern companion, the clever and rowdy old knight Sir John Falstaff, one of Shakespeare's most popular and enduring characters. The many scenes in which Falstaff appears contribute to the play's rich portrait of 15th-century English life, making it obvious that ordinary folk are a vital part of the history that kings and nobles shape in palaces and on battlefields.

PLOT SUMMARY. *Henry IV, Part 2* opens where *Henry IV, Part 1* ends: in the midst of a bloody insurrection against King Henry. The climax of the first play is a battle at Shrewsbury in which the royal forces defeat a rebel army and Prince Hal kills Hotspur, a rebel leader. At the beginning of the

second play, the earl of Northumberland, Hotspur's father, hears from Lord Bardolph, another plotter against the king, a rumor that his son has been victorious. This is merely the first of many "false reports"—lies, misunderstandings, misplaced hopes, and misguided fears—that obscure the truth and exemplify the chaos of the time.

Northumberland soon learns that his son's rebel army has been defeated and that royal troops under Prince John of Lancaster, the king's second son, are coming to capture him. His fellow conspirators tell him, however, that the revolt against Henry continues. The archbishop of York is raising troops to attack Henry for deposing* King Richard II and ordering his execution, events that Shakespeare dramatized earlier in *Richard II*. The archbishop's men plan to continue the fight, claiming that the people have turned against Henry for his murder of Richard.

Meanwhile, Falstaff has ignored a legal summons and offended the lord chief justice, a high government official. He has also decided to pass off his limp, the result of a disease caused by unhealthy living, as a war injury so that the government will reward him for his service.

Act II is set mainly in the Boar's Head tavern, Falstaff's usual haunt, and shows the fat jokester in yet another confrontation with the justice. With his customary wit, he talks his way out of money owed to Mistress Quickly, hostess of the tavern, and even wangles an invitation to dinner with the hostess and Doll Tearsheet, a prostitute. Prince Hal and a friend, disguised as servants, spy on the dinner party until a message from the king calls Hal to join the army that is preparing to fight the rebels. Bardolph, a tavern crony of Falstaff and Hal who appears in *Henry IV, Part 1*, is here as well. (He is unrelated to Lord Bardolph, the conspirator.)

The two scenes of Act III contrast serious matters of state with Falstaff's comical antics in a town outside London. In Westminster Palace the king ponders his many worries and the burdens of his office. He also speaks of the days when he was merely Henry Bolingbroke, cousin to King Richard, and reflects on the changes that time and circumstances bring to one's loyalties. Falstaff, meanwhile, arrives in a village for the purpose of recruiting men for the royal army. Two rustic officials, Shallow and Silence, meet him. Between their incompetence and Falstaff's willingness to accept bribes for releasing the most able-bodied men from service, the episode reminds viewers that a discrepancy often exists between real life and the ideals of heroism and military valor.

Act IV brings an end to the rebellion. Northumberland abandons the fight, and Prince John captures the other rebel leaders by trickery. He pretends that the king will respond to their grievances if they will dismiss their troops, but once they have done so he arrests them. Falstaff speaks disapprovingly of Prince John, not because he is treacherous but because he does not drink and carouse—"this same young sober-blooded boy doth not love me," he complains; "nor a man cannot make him laugh" (IV.iii.87–88).

In Act IV, Scene v, King Henry lies dying at Westminster. He criticizes Hal for being with his low tavern companions instead of at his side. The prince arrives and finds the king asleep. Thinking that his father has died, he places the crown on his own head. Henry wakes and accuses

* *depose* to remove from high office, often by force

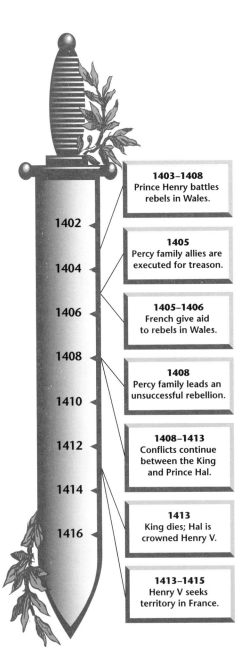

1403–1408
Prince Henry battles rebels in Wales.

1405
Percy family allies are executed for treason.

1405–1406
French give aid to rebels in Wales.

1408
Percy family leads an unsuccessful rebellion.

1408–1413
Conflicts continue between the King and Prince Hal.

1413
King dies; Hal is crowned Henry V.

1413–1415
Henry V seeks territory in France.

1402
1404
1406
1408
1410
1412
1414
1416

In this Royal Shakespeare Company production of *Henry IV, Part 2* (1982), Falstaff (Joss Ackland) gestures dramatically as he recounts one of his outrageous lies.

Hal of wishing him dead so that he can become king. Hal defends himself and convinces Henry of his love and goodwill. Henry then gives advice to his son, warning him that the unrest that has troubled his reign—because he came to the throne illegally and by violence—will continue after his death. He advises Hal to engage in foreign wars, which will keep potential rebels occupied elsewhere and prevent strife at home. Then he is carried off to die.

In Act V, after Hal has become King Henry V, he meets with the lord chief justice, who had once arrested him for a wild youthful escapade. After the justice speaks movingly of "the majesty and power of law and justice" (V.ii.78), the new king vows to be guided by him, give up his self-indulgent habits, and make England equal to "the best govern'd nation" (V.ii.137) in Europe.

Falstaff, meanwhile, has been drinking with Shallow and Silence. He boasts of the rewards and privileges that he, as Hal's old friend, expects to receive from the new king, and he promises to avenge himself on the lord chief justice. Falstaff with his blustering sidekick Pistol hurries to London, thrusts himself into Henry's coronation parade, and addresses him familiarly as "most royal imp of fame" and "my sweet boy." To the impudent knight's dismay, Henry replies formally, "I know thee not, old man, fall to thy prayers" (V.v.42–47). The new king orders that Falstaff and his other tavern companions be arrested until they can be shown out of London, and he advises them to mend their ways. To make their transition as humane as possible, however, he promises them a pension*. The play ends with Prince John and the chief justice discussing the possibility of war in France.

* *pension* sum of money given after a person has retired from service

SOURCES. Shakespeare drew on many of the same sources for *Henry IV, Part 2* as for the two history plays that preceded it, *Richard II* and *Henry IV, Part 1*. Chief among these were the 1587 edition of HOLINSHED's CHRONICLES and a 1595 poem by Samuel Daniel called "The Civil Wars Between the Two Houses of York and Lancaster." The latter emphasized the deathbed reflections of King Henry IV and the notion that he blamed the troubles of his reign on his unlawful seizure of Richard's throne.

Shakespeare used additional source material to develop the character of the lord chief justice. The story of Prince Hal's two encounters with this character appeared in two books on English history that Shakespeare may have known: Thomas Elyot's *The Boke called the Gouvernor* (1531) and John Stow's *Annales of England* (1592).

COMMENTARY. For more than 300 years, critics and commentators have argued about Henry's treatment of Falstaff at the end of *Henry IV, Part 2*. Samuel Johnson, a leading scholar and editor of the 1700s, found Falstaff "corrupt" and "despicable," "a character loaded with faults" but also with a dangerous charm, "an unfailing power of producing laughter." Johnson felt that Henry's rejection of his old friend—and of his former way of life—was necessary if the prince was to become a king. Critic William Hazlitt wrote in the early 1800s that "we never could forgive the Prince's treatment of Falstaff, though perhaps Shakespeare knew what was best," and argued that Falstaff was a "better man" than Henry.

Critics and audiences have fallen into two camps. Many see Henry and his whole family as cold and heartless politicians, willing to sacrifice much to maintain a public image. Others see them as public servants who realize that private sentiments have no place in public life, especially when they threaten the social order.

Shakespeare set the stage for Henry's rejection of Falstaff by allowing the characters of both men to develop from *Part 1* to *Part 2*. Falstaff remains clever, comical, and full of insatiable appetites, but the dishonest and manipulative elements of his personality emerge more fully, painting a darker picture of this charmer. His associates are not merely fun-loving rogues but stupid men, whores, and violent criminals. At the same time, the prince who becomes Henry—who proved himself a military hero in the first play—must demonstrate that he will be a wise and just king. He appears less often with Falstaff in the second play than in the first, a sign that the distance between them is steadily increasing. To fulfill his destiny, he must reject Falstaff, who has become a symbol not only of pleasure but also of lawlessness. Henry's alliance with the lord chief justice can be seen either as a sincere embrace of maturity or as a shrewd political move to create an appropriate public image. The scene exemplifies how skillfully Shakespeare handles ambiguity* and the mystery of human behavior and motives.

On one level *Henry IV, Part 2* is about a prince becoming a king. On another it deals with the larger issues that have been raised in the earlier history plays: justice, guilt, and the consequences of one's actions. King Henry IV is certain that his troubles, including Hal's unprincely conduct, are his punishment for what he did to Richard. Although he seized the

ANIMAL KINGDOM

Shakespeare used animal imagery to convey both positive and negative meanings. In *Henry IV, Part 2*, disturbing analogies symbolize social and political disorder. Early in the play Northumberland says that civil war is "like a horse / Full of high feeding" (I.i.9–10) that has broken loose and trampled everything in its path. In his gloomy deathbed speech Henry IV calls his son's companions "apes of idleness" (IV.v.122). He fears that when Hal is king order will break down: "the wild dog / Shall flesh his tooth on every innocent" (IV.v.131–32), and the country will be "a wilderness again, / Peopled with wolves" (IV.v.136–37).

* *ambiguity* quality of being unclear or able to be interpreted in more than one way

throne to restore order to the kingdom, he is now tragically aware that his actions created new disorder, which he fears will continue into the future. Shakespeare's genius in the two parts of *Henry IV* was in portraying history not as an abstract political chess game between great men but as a web connecting men and women of all stations, high and low, shaping their lives in both large and small ways.

PERFORMANCE HISTORY. References exist to performances of *Henry IV, Part 2* before 1600, but no details survive. Although *Part 2* has been produced less frequently than *Part 1*, perhaps because it has generally held less appeal for audiences, it appears to have been staged several times during the 1600s, either together with *Part 1* or in versions that merged scenes from both plays.

The first performance of *Henry IV, Part 2* for which detailed information exists was in 1700, with a text altered by Thomas Betterton. The well-known actor Colley Cibber revived this production several times in the early 1700s. The play remained popular throughout the 18th century. King George II astounded London audiences by acting in it, playing Henry IV in 1753. Moreover, the coronation celebrations of both George III (in 1761) and William IV (in 1821) included productions of *Henry IV, Part 2*. William Charles Macready played Henry IV in New York City in 1827.

More recently the play was produced as part of cycles of the history plays at STRATFORD-UPON-AVON in 1906, 1951 (with Richard Burton as Hal), 1964 (with Hugh Griffith as Falstaff and Ian Holm as Hal), and 2000. In 1945 the British actor Ralph Richardson won acclaim for his performance as Falstaff in both *Part 1* and *Part 2*. *Henry IV, Part 2* has been produced for television several times, most notably in 1979 by the British Broadcasting Corporation (BBC). (*See also* **Actors, Shakespearean; Henry IV, Part 1; Henry V; History in Shakespeare's Plays: England; Plays: The Histories.**)

HENRY V

Shakespeare's *Henry V* can be enjoyed either on its own or as the climax of three previous history plays: *Richard II; Henry IV, Part 1;* and *Henry IV, Part 2*. Together the four works dramatize the story of King Richard's overthrow and murder by Henry IV and the subsequent emergence of Henry V from a pleasure-seeking young man into one of England's greatest kings.

Henry V also continues Shakespeare's examination of the qualities of a great leader. Some theater historians claim that the playwright portrays Henry V as an ideal leader who conquers France, England's longtime enemy. Others believe that Shakespeare depicts Henry as a cunning, and at times brutal, warrior who starts an unnecessary war for selfish purposes, disregarding the lives and limbs that will be lost on the battlefield. Most agree, however, that the work is complex enough to encompass a variety of viewpoints.

Henry V

* **Chorus** character in Elizabethan drama who recites the prologue and epilogue and sometimes comments on the action

* **dauphin** eldest son of a French king; spelled "Dolphin" in Shakespeare's play

PLOT SUMMARY. *Henry V* begins with a prologue, an introductory speech that apologizes for "this unworthy scaffold [stage]," which cannot adequately present the play's subject matter. The Chorus* acknowledges that a wooden playhouse is far too small a setting to accommodate France's vast battlefields or the hundreds of soldiers who fought there. To compensate for this, the Chorus asks the members of the audience to use their imaginations and "Think, when we talk of horses, that you see them / Printing their proud hoofs i' th' receiving earth" (Prologue. 26–27).

Act I opens with the archbishop of Canterbury and the bishop of Ely, two high-ranking church officials, worrying about Parliament's proposal to seize the church's wealth. The archbishop reveals that, in order to guarantee Henry's support of the church, he has promised him a large sum of money to finance a war against France that Henry wishes to undertake. He says that before the king could accept the offer, however, French ambassadors arrived, interrupting the conversation.

Before meeting with the ambassadors, King Henry summons Canterbury for another conference. During this meeting Canterbury gives a lengthy explanation of French law to prove, he says, that Henry has a legal claim to the French throne. Satisfied that a war against France would be justified, Henry summons the ambassadors. They deliver a message from the dauphin*, who dismisses Henry's claims to French dukedoms and advises the young king to stay at home and play games. As an added insult, the dauphin sends a barrel of tennis balls as a gift. Infuriated, Henry declares war on France and orders the ambassadors to tell their leader that his disrespectful joke "hath turn'd his balls to gun-stones [cannonballs]" (I.ii.282).

In the prologue to Act II, the Chorus describes England's preparations for war. He also warns the audience that three traitors are plotting to assassinate King Henry in Southampton before he sails for France.

In this Royal Shakespeare Company production of *Henry V* (1985), the king (Kenneth Branagh) seeks help from his uncle, the duke of Exeter (Pete Postlethwaite).

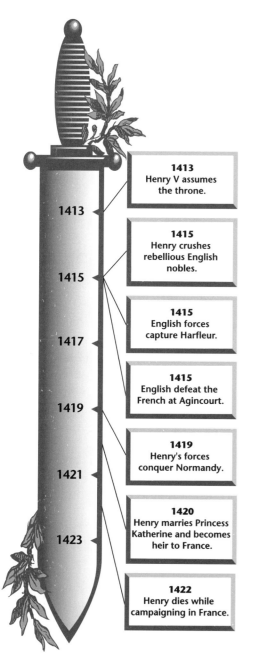

1413
Henry V assumes
the throne.

1415
Henry crushes
rebellious English
nobles.

1415
English forces
capture Harfleur.

1415
English defeat the
French at Agincourt.

1419
Henry's forces
conquer Normandy.

1420
Henry marries Princess
Katherine and becomes
heir to France.

1422
Henry dies while
campaigning in France.

* *siege* long and persistent effort to force a surrender by surrounding a fortress with armed troops, cutting it off from aid

* *Saint George* patron saint of England and Christian martyr, who lived in the A.D. 200s

As Act II opens, Bardolph, a lieutenant, and Nym, a corporal, are speaking. Nym vows revenge on Pistol, a former friend who stole his fiancée, Mistress Quickly. Bardolph urges reconciliation and, when Nym and Pistol prepare to duel, threatens to kill the first man to draw blood. A servant of Sir John Falstaff arrives with news that the once jovial knight is seriously ill. Concerned, all depart to visit their ailing friend.

Meanwhile in Southampton, King Henry speaks with the earl of Cambridge, Lord Scroop, and Sir Thomas Grey, the three traitors who are planning to kill him. Unaware that their treason is known, they advise Henry to punish a soldier who denounced him. Moments later when they themselves are arrested, Henry rejects their pleas for leniency, reminding them of their harsh judgment of the other soldier: "The mercy that was quick [alive] in us but late, / By your own counsel is suppress'd and kill'd. / . . . For your own reasons turn into your bosoms [against you], / As dogs upon their masters . . ." (II.ii.80–83). After the three traitors are led away to be executed, Henry muses that the failure of their plot is a sign that God approves his plan to conquer France.

Back in London, Falstaff's companions mourn his death. Mistress Quickly says that the sinful old knight repented on his deathbed and went to heaven, but the others are less sure about the fate of the old man's soul. Drying their eyes, the men depart for the war, hoping to plunder as much wealth as possible.

Meanwhile in France, King Charles orders his son to prepare strong defenses against Henry's invasion. The dauphin, however, belittles Henry's leadership, calling him "a vain, giddy, shallow, humorous [indecisive] youth" (II.iv.28). The discussion breaks off when Henry's ambassador arrives with orders that Charles either relinquish his throne or be conquered in battle. Charles says he will give Henry an answer the following day.

In the prologue to Act III, the Chorus asks the audience to imagine the English navy departing and explains that French ambassadors have offered Henry a proposal of marriage to Princess Katherine, along with a few minor dukedoms. Because Henry has rejected the offer, the war begins.

During a siege* of the French town of Harfleur, Henry praises his soldiers' bravery and encourages them to continue fighting, saying, "Once more unto the breach, dear friends" (III.i.1). He then leads them on with the battle cry "God for Harry, England, and Saint George*" (III.i.32).

Not all the English soldiers, however, are willing to risk their lives for their king and country. Bardolph, Nym, Pistol, and their boy servant retreat until they are driven forward by Fluellen, a Welsh captain. Before rejoining the battle, Fluellen speaks with Gower (an English officer), Macmorris (an Irish officer), and Jamy (a Scottish captain), about the tactics of siege warfare. Harfleur's citizens finally surrender after Henry warns them that if they refuse, they will see their old men's "heads dash'd to the walls; / [Their] naked infants spitted [impaled] upon pikes" (III.iii.37–38).

Back at the French palace, Princess Katherine receives English lessons, while in another chamber King Charles and his court marvel at the ferocity

Henry V

* *pax* tablet decorated with a sacred image, such as the Crucifixion

FALSTAFF'S FAREWELL

One line in *Henry V* underwent what may be the best-known editorial change in all of Shakespeare's works. In Act II, Scene 3, Mistress Quickly, the tavern hostess, tells of Falstaff's death. Lines 15 and 16 of the First Folio read: "his nose was as sharp as a pen, and a Table of green fields." Lewis Theobald, an early editor of Shakespeare, thought that Shakespeare meant "his nose was as sharp as a pin, and a' [he] babbled of green fields." Some readers have interpreted the "green fields" as the "green pastures" mentioned in the Lord's Prayer, which Falstaff may have recited as he lay dying. Most modern editors and critics have praised Theobald's version of the line. But in recent years, some have argued for a restoration of the original phrasing, in which *Table* can be interpreted to mean "picture" (as in the French *tableau*).

* *soliloquy* monologue in which a character reveals his or her private thoughts

of Henry's attack. The constable of France assures Charles that his vast army will frighten Henry into negotiating a truce.

Meanwhile at the English camp, Pistol asks Fluellen to save Bardolph, who has been condemned to hang for stealing a pax* from a church. The Welsh captain refuses, however, and is cursed by Pistol. Soon thereafter, a messenger arrives and delivers Charles's warning that if Henry rejects a truce and is defeated, France will take all of England's wealth. Although Henry admits that his troops are sick and outnumbered, he refuses to surrender.

The prologue to Act IV describes the night before the battle, asking the audience to envision overconfident French soldiers playing dice while English soldiers contemplate impending death. King Henry, the Chorus says, is seeking to raise the soldiers' morale by visiting them.

As Act IV begins Henry moves among his troops in disguise. He quarrels with Williams, a soldier who claims that God will hold the king responsible for the men killed in the war on France and that on Judgment Day

> all those legs, and arms, and heads, chopp'd off in a battle, shall join together at the latter day and cry all, "We died at such a place,"—some swearing, some crying for a surgeon, some upon their wives left poor behind them, some upon the debts they owe, some upon their children rawly left [unprovided for].
>
> (IV.i.135–41)

He and Henry exchange gloves so that they can recognize each other later and settle their quarrel in single combat. Afterward, in a soliloquy* Henry speaks of the burdens of kingship. He also prays for help in defeating the French and asks God to overlook his father's sin of deposing Richard II.

Before the battle Henry rouses his soldiers by telling them that those who fight alongside him are his kinsmen: "We few, we happy few, we band of brothers; / For he to-day that sheds his blood with me / Shall be my brother" (IV.iii.60–62).

During the battle of Agincourt, Pistol captures a French soldier and threatens to murder him unless he pays a large ransom. Meanwhile, Henry orders his troops to slit the throats of all their prisoners after learning that French reinforcements have arrived. French troops have also acted brutally, executing unarmed boys. Realizing that they have been outmatched, the French admit defeat. Henry gives Fluellen Williams's glove to wear, and when Williams strikes the Welshmen, the king intercedes. As a sign that he holds no grudge against Williams, Henry returns the soldier's glove after filling it with coins.

In the prologue to Act V, the Chorus describes Henry's triumphant return to England. Henry soon returns to France, however, to negotiate a peace with King Charles.

Act V opens at the English camp in France, where Fluellen beats Pistol for insulting him and Wales. Disgraced but unrepentant, Pistol says he will return to England to steal and, once there, will claim he received

his scars in battle. At the French palace the queen says that she wishes for peace with England, but Henry says that the French "must buy that peace" by agreeing to his demands. As the French and English diplomats negotiate, Henry courts Princess Katherine. The diplomats and King Charles return and announce that they have agreed to all of Henry's demands. Among other things, Charles gives Henry Katherine's hand in marriage and names him heir to the French throne.

The play concludes with an epilogue* in which the Chorus tells the audience that conquered France was left to Henry VI, who inherited the crown when he was still an infant. The Chorus also notes that Henry VI will lose all that his father has won.

SOURCES AND HISTORY. A historical reference in the prologue to Act V indicates that Shakespeare wrote that portion of *Henry V* during the spring or summer of 1599. In the prologue the Chorus speaks about the impending triumphant return of the earl of Essex, who embarked on a mission to crush an Irish rebellion in March of 1599. In September, Essex returned in defeat, and for that reason scholars infer that this prologue must have been written during the months when the earl was away.

Shakespeare's main source for the play was the 1587 edition of Raphael Holinshed's *Chronicles,* a work completed by the English historian in 1577. The playwright also borrowed from *The Union of the Two Noble and Illustre Famelies of Lancastre and York,* written by the English historian Edward Halle and published in a second edition in 1548. Scholars believe that Shakespeare took the stories of the dauphin's gift of tennis balls, Pistol's capture of the French soldier, and Henry's courtship of Katherine from *The Famous Victories,* a play about Henry V written anonymously around 1586.

COMMENTARY. *Henry V* can be interpreted in two distinct ways: as a patriotic story about a heroic English conqueror or as a satire* on the immorality of war. The play provides evidence to support both viewpoints.

In Shakespeare's day people viewed Henry V as a hero, a bold and successful king who conquered England's greatest enemy. In the play Henry displays many admirable qualities. He refuses to invade France until the archbishop of Canterbury assures him that doing so will be legal and justified. He also seems humble and religious, admitting that defeating the French will be difficult and asking for God's help. During the war Henry often behaves mercifully toward his enemies, warning his soldiers not to rob or curse the French. Even after winning the battle of Agincourt, Henry remains humble, refusing to take credit for the victory: "Praised be God, and not our strength, for it!" (IV.vii.87).

The king, however, also displays a darker side. Although he seems religious, he often uses "the will of God" to justify getting what he wants, such as when he asks for divine assistance in punishing the dauphin for his insulting gift of tennis balls. He displays brutality when he orders the execution of French prisoners and tells Harfleur's citizens that his soldiers will kill their elderly, impale their infants, and rape their young women unless they surrender. Henry is also unyielding in peace,

* ***epilogue*** speech to the audience at the end of a play

* ***satire*** literary work ridiculing human wickedness and foolishness

175

demanding King Charles's daughter and the French throne in exchange for an end to the war.

Most people agree that *Henry V* is neither a purely nationalistic* play nor an absolute satire. Instead, it is a complex work that depicts an unmistakably successful ruler and what he must do, and not do, to succeed.

PERFORMANCE HISTORY. Although the KING'S MEN most probably staged *Henry V* the year it was written, the earliest known performance was given at the court of King JAMES I in 1605. In 1723 the English poet Aaron Hill wrote an adaptation that omitted Bardolph and Pistol and added a new subplot. Hill's version was frequently performed until 1735, when the authentic *Henry V* regained popularity. During the mid-1700s John Philip Kemble, an English actor and theater manager, was highly praised for his portrayal of King Henry. By the late 1700s elaborate productions and stage sets had become customary. In 1776, for example, a theater company's production included a model of Westminster Abbey, the church where English kings are crowned. Productions during the 1800s were also spectacular. An 1849 rendering by Charles Kean, for example, featured 550 actors on the stage to enact Henry's victory march after Agincourt.

Henry V's patriotic subject matter has made it popular in England during wartime. In 1900, when the English were fighting Dutch settlers in South Africa, London audiences stood and cheered during a performance of *Henry V.* The play was often staged during World War I (1914–1918) and World War II (1939–1945). Some modern productions, especially since the 1950s, have treated *Henry V* as an antiwar play by emphasizing its portrayal of the selfish motives of warmongers and its descriptions of atrocities.

Henry V has twice been produced on film. In 1944 Sir Laurence Olivier made a movie version of the play at the request of Prime Minister Winston Churchill, who wanted a popular film that would encourage the English to fight harder against Adolf Hitler during World War II. Olivier starred in and directed the film, which featured a replica of the GLOBE THEATER and impressive battle scenes. In 1989 another British actor, Kenneth Branagh, directed and starred in a darker, more ambiguous* version of *Henry V.* The play was also filmed for television in 1957, 1966, and 1979. (*See also* **Henry IV, Part 1; Henry IV, Part 2; History in Shakespeare's Plays: England; Plays: The Histories; Richard II.**)

HENRY VI, PART 1

The first play of Shakespeare's tetralogy* that recounts the events of the WARS OF THE ROSES, the struggle for the English crown that occurred during the second half of the 1400s, is *Henry VI, Part 1.* The other three plays are *Henry VI, Part 2; Henry VI, Part 3;* and *Richard III. Henry VI, Part 1* focuses on the origins of the conflict, showing how King Henry's ineffective leadership enabled ambitious nobles to divide England. The play also shows how England's weakness led to its defeats during

* **nationalistic** characterized by devotion to a nation, especially praising one nation above all others

* **ambiguous** unclear; able to be interpreted in more than one way

* **tetralogy** four-part series of literary or dramatic works

* **siege** long and persistent effort to force a surrender by surrounding a fortress with armed troops, cutting it off from aid

* **parley** conference between opponents or enemies

The story of the plucking of the roses to explain how the red and white roses came to represent the houses of Lancaster and York, appears to be Shakespeare's own invention. Henry A. Payne captured the scene in this modern-day painting.

the Hundred Years' War, a conflict between the English and the French for control of France. As Shakespeare's first history play, *Henry VI, Part 1* reveals the young playwright's developing talent for dramatizing past events and writing powerful verse.

SUMMARY. The play opens with the funeral of King Henry V, who has died unexpectedly and left his young son to rule. Before the ceremony ends, an argument erupts between two high-ranking nobles: the duke of Gloucester and the bishop of Winchester. The quarrel is interrupted by the news that French rebels, led by Charles VII, have defeated English troops in several battles in France. These defeats are blamed on the English nobles, whose disagreements have weakened the army.

Meanwhile in France, Joan de Pucelle, also known as Joan of Arc, asserts that she has God-given powers and offers to help Charles expel the English from France. Charles accepts her help, and together with the dukes of Alençon and Anjou, they raise the siege* of the French city of Orléans.

In Act II, Lord Talbot, an English general, recaptures Orléans from the overconfident French. After the battle a French countess attempts to trap Talbot, who escapes with the help of his soldiers. Back in London a quarrel erupts between Richard Plantagenet and the earl of Somerset. In an effort to resolve the dispute through a vote, Plantagenet asks each of his supporters to pluck a white rose, and Somerset asks each of his followers to pluck a red one. When Somerset sees that he is outnumbered, however, he reminds the others that Henry V executed Plantagenet's father, the duke of York, for treason.

Distressed, Plantagenet visits his uncle, Edmund Mortimer, a prisoner in the TOWER OF LONDON. Mortimer reveals that he was the heir to the throne before Henry Bolingbroke deposed King Richard II. He explains that Richard's father attempted to place him on the throne but was executed in the attempt and that he himself was imprisoned. Just before he dies, Mortimer names Richard as his successor.

Act III opens in Parliament, where Gloucester and Winchester exchange angry words until King Henry establishes a fragile peace between them. The young ruler then restores to Richard Plantagenet the title of duke of York and departs for Paris to be crowned France's king. Meanwhile in France, Joan and four soldiers enter Rouen disguised as tradesmen and seize the city. As Talbot did at Orléans, however, he quickly recaptures the lost territory from the French.

Joan calls a parley* with the duke of Burgundy, a French nobleman allied with the English. Appealing to Burgundy's patriotism, Joan persuades him to abandon the English. Meanwhile in Paris, Henry knights Talbot for his faithful service.

Act IV opens with Henry's coronation as king of France. The ceremony is interrupted, however, by the news that Burgundy has deserted the English. The duke of York (formerly Richard Plantagenet) and Somerset, who have joined the king in France, argue again. Attempting to be evenhanded, Henry divides the English army, giving York command of the infantry and Somerset command of the cavalry. When Talbot enters a battle against Burgundy and calls for reinforcements, York and Somerset

refuse to cooperate with each other. Because of their dispute, Talbot is overwhelmed and killed by the French.

In Act V, King Henry agrees to marry a French noblewoman in order to secure peace. In France, York takes Joan prisoner, and the earl of Suffolk captures Margaret, the duke of Anjou's daughter. Suffolk, who is married, falls in love with Margaret and promises to make her England's queen if she agrees to be his lover. Back at the English camp, Joan begs for her life before being burned at the stake. In order to secure peace, Charles agrees to submit to Henry's authority. Meanwhile in England, Suffolk's description of Margaret's virtues convinces Henry to make her his queen despite his betrothal* to another French noblewoman. The play ends with Suffolk confessing in a soliloquy* his intention to "rule both her [Margaret], the King, and realm" (V.v.108).

SOURCES AND HISTORY. Lack of evidence has prevented scholars from determining exactly when Shakespeare wrote *Henry VI, Part 1*. Most agree, however, that the play was written between 1589 and 1592, with 1590 being the most widely accepted date.

Shakespeare's main sources for this play were Raphael Holinshed's *Chronicles* (1587 edition) and Edward Halle's *The Union of the Two Noble and Illustre Famelies of Lancastre and York* (1548). Shakespeare borrowed some details about the feud between York and Somerset from *The New Chronicle of England and of France* (1516) by English historian Robert Fabyan. The portrayal of Joan of Arc as a witch and a harlot came from *The Discoverie of Witchcraft* (1584) by English author Reginald Scot, as well as from Holinshed's *Chronicles*. Although Shakespeare borrowed from historical texts, he drastically altered the sequence of events, compressing more than 20 years of history into his five-act play. Many of the stories in the play, such as the plucking of the roses, are Shakespeare's creation.

COMMENTARY. *Henry VI, Part 1* is primarily concerned with how disorder among England's nobles enabled the French to rebel against English rule. This theme is established in Act I, when an argument between Gloucester and Winchester is interrupted by news of rebellions in France. Throughout the play disputes among ambitious noblemen are followed by French victories. The selfish nobles are contrasted with the selfless and courageous Lord Talbot, whose final defeat is the direct result of a quarrel between York and Somerset.

The play also suggests that England's misfortunes are a sign that God is displeased with England. Joan of Arc proclaims that she is God's instrument for punishing England: "Assign'd am I to be the English scourge" (I.ii.129). Nevertheless, her practice of witchcraft condemns her to be executed. Joan's character underscores the play's anti-French prejudice, an attitude shared by most Elizabethans.

Henry VI, Part 1 demonstrates Shakespeare's skill at converting chaotic events into an exciting and unified story. Even so, many critics argue that the play lacks the poetic technique, character development, and psychological insight that define the playwright's later works.

* *betrothal* mutual promise to marry in the future
* *soliloquy* monologue in which a character reveals his or her private thoughts

SAINT JOAN

Shakespeare's unflattering portrayal of Joan of Arc has troubled many readers. In fact Shakespeare altered historical facts concerning Joan. The play shows Joan convincing the duke of Burgundy to betray the English. But, in fact, Burgundy did not withdraw from the English alliance until years after Joan's death. Also, despite Shakespeare's depiction of Joan begging for her life to be spared, historical records indicate that her behavior at trial was dignified and honorable. Evidence suggests that the historical Joan has won out over Shakespeare's characterization. In 1920 the Roman Catholic Church declared her a saint.

PERFORMANCE HISTORY. Theater historians believe that *Henry VI, Part 1* was first performed in 1592 at the Rose theater, where it was a great success. The play lost popularity after Shakespeare's time, however, and the next known production was staged in 1738. In 1817 *Richard Duke of York*, an adaptation combining *Henry VI, Part 1* and *Henry VI, Part 2*, was performed in London. Combining the *Henry VI* plays remained a popular method of presentation. In 1963 Peter Hall was highly praised for *The Wars of the Roses*, an adaptation constructed from *Henry VI, Part 1* and the first half of *Henry VI, Part 2*. Although the play has not been made into a film to date, it has been adapted for television. In 1961 the British Broadcasting Corporation (BBC) produced *An Age of Kings*, which covers English history as told by Shakespeare in *Richard II; Henry IV, Part 1; Henry IV, Part 2; Henry V; Henry VI, Part 1; Henry VI, Part 2; Henry VI, Part 3; and Richard III*. (*See also* **History in Shakespeare's Plays: England; Plays: The Histories.**)

HENRY VI, PART 2

* *tetralogy* four-part series of literary or dramatic works

T he play *Henry VI, Part 2* continues Shakespeare's dramatization of how King Henry's ineffective leadership and the selfishness of England's noblemen lead to the loss of territory in France and to civil war at home. The play is part of a tetralogy* that presents the story of the WARS OF THE ROSES, a battle for the crown that was fought during the second half of the 1400s. The other plays in the series are *Henry VI, Part 1; Henry VI, Part 3;* and *Richard III*.

SUMMARY. The action begins in London, where the royal court is gathered to celebrate the arrival of Margaret of Anjou, Henry's French bride. The festive mood is broken when it is learned that the marriage terms require Henry to cede French territories to Margaret's father.

The loss of French lands causes the king's noblemen to argue. Soon the squabbling leaders break into two rival camps: those who wish to oust the duke of Gloucester from his position as King Henry's chief adviser, and those who support the duke. Among those plotting to destroy Gloucester are Cardinal Beaufort and the dukes of Suffolk, Buckingham, and Somerset. Gloucester's supporters are the earls of Salisbury and Warwick and the duke of York. During a soliloquy*, however, York reveals that his ultimate goal is to depose* Henry and seize the throne for himself.

* *soliloquy* monologue in which a character reveals his or her private thoughts
* *depose* to remove from high office, often by force

Although Gloucester is loyal to the king, his wife, Eleanor, is not. Using witchcraft, she calls on an evil spirit to predict the fates of Henry, Suffolk, and Somerset. The spirit foretells that Henry will be deposed by a duke, Suffolk will die by water, and Somerset will perish near a castle. Moments after the spirit departs, Gloucester's enemies burst in and arrest Eleanor. They hope that her humiliation will lead to Gloucester's downfall.

Act II opens in London, where York convinces Salisbury and Warwick that he is the rightful heir to the English throne. Meanwhile, Henry exiles Eleanor for witchcraft and for plotting against his life. Disgraced by his wife, Gloucester is forced to give up his office as chief adviser.

BAD QUARTOS

For many years most scholars believed that Shakespeare adapted *Henry VI, Part 2* and *Part 3* from an earlier play known as *The Contention.* Scholars pointed out that *The Contention* was published in 1594, whereas Shakespeare's plays about Henry VI were first printed 29 years later. In 1929, however, English scholar Peter Alexander presented convincing evidence that editions of *The Contention* were merely unauthorized and faulty versions of *Henry VI, Part 1* and *Part 2* based on an actor's recollections of the lines. These early editions became known as *bad quartos,* a term that is now disputed by some scholars.

In Act III, Margaret and Suffolk attempt to convince Henry that Gloucester is a traitor. The discussion is interrupted by news that England has lost its remaining territories in France. After Gloucester is arrested for treason, Suffolk, Margaret, Cardinal Beaufort, and York agree to have him killed before a trial can prove his innocence.

Meanwhile word arrives of a revolt in Ireland, and York is given an army and sent to suppress the rebels. In a soliloquy he rejoices that he now has an army to help carry out his plans to depose the king. He also reveals that he has hired a commoner named Jack Cade to incite a rebellion in England.

When Gloucester is murdered, an angry mob demands that Suffolk be punished for the crime. Henry agrees with the crowd and exiles Suffolk. During a sorrowful farewell scene between Suffolk and Queen Margaret, it becomes clear that they are adulterous lovers.

In Act IV a pirate named Walter (pronounced "water" by the Elizabethans) Whitmore captures and kills Suffolk, thus fulfilling the spirit's prediction that he would die by water. Meanwhile, Cade's rebellion plunges England into chaos. The rebels, who are weavers, butchers, and other laborers, seem to target the educated upper classes. They execute a man for being literate, and in a famous line one rebel says, "The first thing we do, let's kill all the lawyers" (IV.ii.76–77). When the insurgents reach London, however, Buckingham and Lord Clifford convince them to surrender; Cade flees, but he is soon slain.

In Act V, York returns from Ireland with his army and announces his intention to seize the crown. The battle between York and Henry at St. Alban's marks the beginning of the Wars of the Roses. During the battle, York's son Richard kills Somerset outside an alehouse called the Castle, thus fulfilling the spirit's prophecy. The play ends with Henry and Margaret retreating to London after losing the battle to York and his fellow rebels.

For plotting against the life of the king, the duchess of Gloucester is exiled and forced to do public penance. Officers of the law parade her around town dressed in a white sheet and carrying a lighted candle, as shown in this painting by Edwin Abbey (1900).

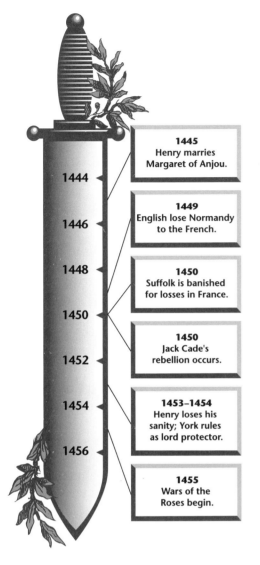

1445
Henry marries
Margaret of Anjou.

1444

1449
English lose Normandy
to the French.

1446

1450
Suffolk is banished
for losses in France.

1448

1450
Jack Cade's
rebellion occurs.

1450

1453–1454
Henry loses his
sanity; York rules
as lord protector.

1452

1454

1455
Wars of the
Roses begin.

1456

SOURCES AND HISTORY. Most scholars think that Shakespeare wrote *Henry VI, Part 2* sometime between 1590 and 1591. His main sources for this play were Raphael Holinshed's *Chronicles* (1587 edition) and Edward Halle's *The Union of the Two Noble and Illustre Famelies of Lancastre and York* (1548). Minor sources included John Foxe's *Acts and Monuments* (1563), Robert Fabyan's *The New Chronicle of England and of France* (1516), and John Hardyng's *English Chronicle*.

COMMENTARY. *Henry VI, Part 2* begins with Henry's marriage to Margaret. All the subsequent disasters—the loss of France, the murder of Gloucester, and the rebellion of York—are a consequence of this flawed union. The marriage terms, which cede hard-won territory to France, cause the nobles to quarrel. In addition Margaret and her lover, Suffolk, plot to destroy Gloucester, Henry's only loyal servant. Their murder of Gloucester, who was heir to the throne, removes an obstacle that might have prevented York from launching his rebellion. In the end Henry's marriage to Margaret results in the Wars of the Roses.

The play demonstrates Shakespeare's growing powers of characterization. He skillfully depicts Henry as a weak leader. When the king receives the news that all English-ruled lands in France are lost, for example, his reaction seems passive: "Cold news . . . but God's will be done!" (III.i.86) Margaret and Suffolk are richly drawn villains who prove equally capable of cold-blooded murder and passionate love. During his sorrowful farewell Suffolk tells Margaret, "If I depart from thee, I cannot live" (III.ii.88). Shakespeare also displays a growing command over a wide range of language, from the poetic speeches of Gloucester and York to the violent bluster of Jack Cade and his rebels.

PERFORMANCE HISTORY. Although *Henry VI, Part 2* was popular during Shakespeare's lifetime, no records of specific performances survive. The first recorded staging was in 1681. This and other productions during the 1600s and 1700s were adaptations, however, and the authentic play was not presented again until 1864. Its American premiere occurred in 1935 in Pasadena, California. British television incorporated the play into its acclaimed series, *An Age of Kings*, in 1961. (*See also* **History in Shakespeare's Plays: England; Plays: The Histories.**)

**HENRY VI,
PART 3**

The play *Henry VI, Part 3* is part of Shakespeare's tetralogy* chronicling the English civil conflict known as the WARS OF THE ROSES. The other plays in the series are *Henry VI, Part 1; Henry VI, Part 2;* and *Richard III. Henry VI, Part 3* depicts the battles between King Henry's house of Lancaster and the rival house of York. The play ends with the assassinations of Henry and his son, Prince Edward, which mark the downfall of the Lancastrians.

SUMMARY. *Henry VI, Part 3* begins where *Henry VI, Part 2* ends: at the conclusion of the first battle of the Wars of the Roses. The victors are the

* **tetralogy** four-part series of literary or dramatic works

Yorkists—the duke of York, his sons Edward and Richard, and his ally the earl of Warwick. After York enters Parliament and seats himself on the throne, Henry arrives and offers to make York his heir if he will end the rebellion. York agrees, but Queen Margaret is furious that Henry has disinherited their son, Prince Edward. She leads the army in a second battle against York and is victorious. Although Edward and Richard escape, York is captured. Margaret and Lord Clifford taunt him—placing a paper crown on his head and offering him a handkerchief stained with his youngest son's blood—before stabbing him to death.

In Act II, Richard and Edward see three suns in the sky. Believing this to be a sign of impending success, they are undaunted by their father's death. During peace talks with the king and his supporters, Edward demands the crown. Henry says little, but Margaret and Clifford reject Edward and defy him with insults. During the ensuing battle, the king withdraws to a hillside, where he expresses his wish for a peaceful life, like that of a shepherd. His daydream is interrupted when Margaret and Prince Edward arrive in retreat from the Yorkists. Edward's victorious rebels march toward London, where they crown him King Edward IV. Warwick agrees to sail for France to arrange a marriage between Edward and the daughter of the French king Lewis.

In Act III two commoners, who are supporters of Edward IV, capture Henry. Meanwhile, Edward falls in love with a noblewoman named Lady Elizabeth Grey, and in a soliloquy* his brother Richard reveals his own ambition to be king. Shortly thereafter Margaret and Prince Edward arrive in France, where they plead for King Lewis's assistance. At first Lewis is more sympathetic to Warwick, but when news of King Edward's marriage to Lady

* *soliloquy* monologue in which a character reveals his or her private thoughts

As his army battles against rebels led by the duke of York, King Henry thinks longingly of a peaceful life in the country, untroubled by the burdens of kingship. Artist William Dyce captured the scene in his painting *Henry VI at Towton* (late 1850s).

**FROM YOUNG BRIDE
TO WOMAN WARRIOR**

The character of Queen Margaret in the *Henry VI* plays undergoes dramatic changes. In *Part 2* she is depicted as the young queen who becomes the determined enemy of York and Gloucester. In *Part 3* she shows her strength by taking control, divorcing Henry, and fighting for her son's claim to the throne. She can be astoundingly vicious, as when she offers the duke of York a handkerchief stained with the blood of his dead son. Yet her courage and ability to inspire her troops bring her respect as a warrior and leader.

Grey arrives, the French king vows to provide troops to support Margaret. Outraged by Edward's betrayal, Warwick also agrees to assist Margaret.

In Act IV, Edward's brother George is angered by the king's marriage to Lady Grey and joins forces with Warwick and other Lancastrians, who have returned from France to invade England. Warwick captures Edward, but the English monarch is soon freed with Richard's help. Next Warwick and George free Henry from his prison. Although Henry regains his crown, he invests his liberators with the power to rule the kingdom. Soon after being freed, however, he is recaptured by Edward and Richard.

In Act V, Edward and Richard besiege Coventry, the city where Warwick has taken refuge while awaiting reinforcements. When George arrives to aid Warwick, however, he is persuaded to rejoin his brothers. Warwick dies in battle, and the victorious Yorkists march to confront Margaret's army. They capture Margaret and stab Prince Edward to death. Richard then travels to London, where he enters Henry's prison cell and kills him. The play ends with Edward celebrating his resumption of the throne and the birth of his son, unaware of Richard's plans to seize the crown for himself.

DATE AND SOURCES. Shakespeare probably wrote *Henry VI, Part 3* between 1590 and 1592. As with the previous *Henry VI* plays, his main sources were Edward Halle's *The Union of the Two Noble and Illustre Famelies of Lancastre and York* (1548) and Raphael Holinshed's *Chronicles* (1587). Other material for the play came from a collection of biographies called *A Mirror for Magistrates* (1559). Shakespeare borrowed phrases and styles from literary sources, including the poet Edmund Spenser and the playwright Thomas Kyd.

COMMENTARY. In this play Shakespeare continues to develop the grand theme of *Henry VI, Part 1* and *Part 2*—that failure to maintain political and social order leads to disaster. Moreover, he suggests that earthly harmony is part of a divine plan and that God punishes those who disrupt it. In *Parts 1* and *2* conflict among the nobles has already torn England apart, and now in *Part 3* the battles and murders rage without interruption. The main characters still plot treachery and are driven by overriding ambition.

The breakdown of family relations accompanies other forms of disorder in this play. In Act I, Henry revokes his son's claim to the throne, causing Margaret to declare herself divorced and to pursue the war against the Yorkists on her own. Edward IV ignores his brothers' objections to his marriage to Lady Grey, causing George to abandon his family and join the Lancastrians. Richard, on the other hand, while pretending to be loyal to his brother, plots to seize the crown for himself. The most shocking disruption of family unity comes during a battle scene in Act II, when a son discovers that he has killed his own father and a father realizes that he has killed his own son.

Shakespeare's growing dramatic skills are demonstrated in the striking and subtle characters he has developed. King Henry is portrayed both as an ineffective leader and as a morally upright king. While the battle to save his throne rages, for example, he retires to a hillside and daydreams

about being a shepherd. Above all, he laments the tragedy of civil war, especially when he witnesses fathers and sons slaying one another.

Richard is another expertly drawn figure. Shakespeare gives him a fascinating side by mixing his violent actions with dark humor. When Richard kills Henry, for example, he raises his sword, which is dripping with blood, and says, "See how my sword weeps for the poor King's death!" (V.vi.63). Richard even offers an explanation for his wickedness. He says that because his withered arm and hunched back prevent him from enjoying any woman's affection, he will "account this world but hell, / Until my misshap'd trunk that bears this head / Be round impaled [enclosed] with a glorious crown" (III.ii.169–71).

PERFORMANCE HISTORY. Although *Henry VI, Part 3* was popular during Shakespeare's lifetime, no records of its early performances exist. Scholars have concluded from the number of published quarto* editions that the play was well received, a suggestion that was confirmed in 1612 by the poet and playwright Ben Jonson, who wrote that all the *Henry VI* plays were highly popular. The first recorded productions were Restoration* and 18th-century adaptations that greatly altered Shakespeare's original. The authentic script was staged again in 1906 at STRATFORD-UPON-AVON, and this performance revived interest in the play. Its American premiere was in 1935 in Pasadena, California. In 1961 British television incorporated the play into its acclaimed series, *An Age of Kings*. (*See also* History in Shakespeare's Plays: England; Military Life; Plays: The Histories.)

* **quarto** referring to the format of a book; to produce each gathering of such a volume, a sheet of paper is folded twice, yielding four leaves or eight pages

* **Restoration** referring to the period in English history, beginning in 1660, when Charles II was restored to the throne

HENRY VIII

A history play about England's most famous (and infamous) king, *Henry VIII* focuses on the man who broke with the Roman Catholic Church, established the Church of England, and appointed himself its head. During his reign, from 1509 to 1547, King Henry also strengthened the monarchy, built a powerful navy, and created a new ruling class determined by men's talents and ambitions rather than by their social standing. He is perhaps best remembered, however, for marrying six times and executing two of his wives.

Henry VIII is unlike Shakespeare's other histories. Rather than presenting a portrait of a great but flawed leader, as in *Henry V*, this play idealizes the king, emphasizing his virtues and largely ignoring his vices. Another element that sets the play apart is the prevailing view among scholars that it was a collaborative effort between Shakespeare and John Fletcher, who may have been the major contributor.

PLOT SUMMARY. As the action begins, Henry's meeting with the king of France is described as a "view of earthly glory" (I.i.14), but certain dukes are unimpressed. Instead, they criticize the self-serving Cardinal Wolsey, who arranged the gathering. The duke of Buckingham plans to warn the king that he suspects Wolsey of enriching himself at England's

Henry VIII

prelate high-ranking member of the clergy, such as a bishop

annul to declare legally invalid

See color plate 14, vol. 3.

heresy belief that is contrary to church doctrine

expense. Before he is able to do this, however, Wolsey has Buckingham arrested and executed for treason.

Meanwhile, Wolsey persuades Henry to question the legality of his marriage to Queen Katherine by pointing out that she had once been engaged to the king's older brother. Adding to Henry's doubts about his marriage is his romantic interest in a young Protestant woman, Anne Bullen (also spelled Boleyn). Eventually, before a court of prelates*, Katherine defends her right to be queen. Although Henry agrees that Katherine is a good wife, he expresses a concern that Mary, his child with Katherine, may not be a legitimate heir to the throne. Even worse, he notes, none of their male children have survived, a misfortune the king interprets as a sign of God's unhappiness with his marriage to Katherine. He therefore asks that his marriage to her be annulled*.

Unfortunately, Henry's decision to marry Anne Bullen spoils Cardinal Wolsey's plan to have the king wed the French duchess of Alençon. Attempting to stop the marriage, Wolsey writes letters to the pope and asks the Catholic leader to delay granting Henry a divorce. By chance the letters fall into the king's hands, and Wolsey is disgraced and overthrown. It is later reported that Henry has secretly married Anne and has named Cranmer, a religious man with Protestant leanings, the new archbishop of Canterbury.

Katherine, who is on her deathbed, learns that Wolsey has died. At first she criticizes him, but when Griffith, her attendant, reminds her of Wolsey's learning and wisdom, her anger softens and she says "Peace be with him!" (IV.ii.75). During a dream, Katherine sees six dancing figures who foretell her imminent death, give her garlands, and bid her farewell.

Meanwhile Gardiner, the bishop of Winchester, is leading an effort to convict Archbishop Cranmer of heresy* for his sympathy with Protestant beliefs. Fearing that Gardiner and his supporters will harm Cranmer, Henry gives the archbishop his ring to signify that he is under royal protection. As Cranmer leaves, a messenger enters with news that Anne has given birth to the king's daughter Elizabeth.

At the end of the play, Gardiner's efforts to imprison Cranmer in the TOWER OF LONDON fail, and the king asks the archbishop to baptize Elizabeth. As Cranmer christens the infant, he predicts that she will bring England "a thousand thousand blessings, / Which time shall bring to ripeness" (V.iv.19–20).

SOURCES AND HISTORY. Scholars believe that Shakespeare completed *Henry VIII* shortly before June 29, 1613. An unfortunate event helps them determine that date: one of the play's earliest performances, if not its first, occurred on the same day that fire destroyed the GLOBE Theater. Eyewitness accounts suggest that cannons fired onstage as part of the first act set fire to the theater's thatched roof.

Shakespeare's main source for the play was Raphael HOLINSHED'S CHRONICLES *of England, Scotland, and Ireland,* a work produced by the English historian in 1577. Shakespeare's information about Cranmer came from *Acts and Monuments,* a history of English Protestantism (often referred to as *The Book of Martyrs*) that John Foxe completed in 1563.

HENRY'S DARK SIDE

The actions of the real Henry VIII show that he was not the kindly ruler Shakespeare depicts. In contrast to what happens in the play, it was Henry, not Cardinal Wolsey, who ordered the execution of the duke of Buckingham because he feared the duke might try to seize the throne. Moreover, Shakespeare's play ignores the fate of Anne Bullen. Just three years after Henry made her queen, he falsely accused her of adultery and treason and had her beheaded.

COMMENTARY. Unlike Shakespeare's other histories, *Henry VIII* does not realistically present the king as a leader with both flaws and virtues. Instead, the play portrays Henry as a symbol of England's greatness as he changes from an easily influenced tool of Wolsey to a wise and independent ruler. Many scholars consider the play a celebration of the Tudor* dynasty, which was founded by Henry's father, Henry VII, and reached its peak during the reign of his daughter, Queen ELIZABETH I.

Henry VIII is also about England's emergence as a Protestant country. During the course of the play, Henry moves away from the Roman Catholic Church. Wolsey's attempt to use the pope to control Henry makes it clear that Henry must break with Catholicism if he is to marry an attractive young Protestant. In the end Henry rejects the "dilatory sloth and tricks of Rome" (II.iv.238) for Cranmer, a Protestant sympathizer, whom Henry calls a "learn'd and well-beloved servant" (II.iv.239). (*See also* **Church, The; Elizabeth I; History in Shakespeare's Plays: England; Plays: The Histories; Playwrights and Poets; Warfare.**)

* *Tudor* referring to the dynasty that ruled England from 1485 to 1603

HENSLOWE, PHILIP

ca. 1550–1616
Theater owner and manager

* *brothel* house of prostitution
* *bailiff* local official; mayor

Although Philip Henslowe was born to poor parents and received little education, he became one of the most prominent English businessmen of the late 1500s. Among the most successful theater owners of Shakespeare's time, he was also a moneylender and an owner of brothels*.

Henslowe began his career as the servant of a bailiff*. When the bailiff died, Henslowe married the man's wealthy widow. He worked as a dyer and then as a pawnbroker, but his early real estate investments were what actually opened the door to his financial success as a theater owner. In 1585 he leased a plot of land along the Thames River and built the Rose theater, which opened in 1588. When Henslowe's stepdaughter married the famous actor Edward Alleyn, the two men became business partners. Alleyn's company, the Admiral's Men, performed at the Rose until the turn of the century, making both men extremely wealthy. In 1600 they constructed the Fortune playhouse, and in 1613 Henslowe built the Hope.

Henslowe was a passionate and sometimes ruthless businessman who kept careful records of all his dealings. He also maintained accounts of all the plays performed in his theaters, including the names of the playwrights and the dates of the performances. In doing so he left the world an invaluable historical record of Elizabethan theater. His collected papers, usually referred to as his "Diary," cover the years 1592 to 1603. They list all the revenues he earned at his theaters, along with the loans and advances he made to various acting companies as well as to individual players. Henslowe's service as a moneylender led early scholars to speculate that he was Shakespeare's model for Shylock in *The Merchant of Venice,* but modern scholars have generally rejected that notion.

Henslowe's success was not without its problems. In 1611 he entered into an agreement with Lady Elizabeth's Men, the acting company that

eventually played at the Hope Theater. Four years later, the actors drew up legal papers charging Henslowe with dishonesty and abuse of his legal position for his own financial advantage. They also accused him of failing to keep proper records of the money he owed the actors and of buying plays and reselling them at a profit. The dispute was finally resolved by a compromise—but not until after Henslowe's death in 1616. (*See also* **Acting Companies, Elizabethan; Elizabethan Theaters.**)

HERALDRY

* *plate* dishes and utensils made of silver
* *livery* distinctive clothing worn on formal occasions

The Shakespeare family's coat of arms, granted in 1596, was a gold shield crossed by a diagonal black band with a silver-headed gold spear on it. Above the shield sits a falcon holding a spear, a pun on the family name. This copy of the escutcheon comes from a 1602 text called *The York Herald's Complaint,* in which the author, Ralph Brooke, complains about coats of arms being issued to families unworthy of them.

Since ancient times soldiers have worn markings on their armor to identify themselves as either friend or foe. The art of designing and describing the marks used on helmets, shields, and banners is called heraldry. In the Middle Ages the basic heraldic symbol—an emblem called a coat of arms—became the sign of a particular family and its status.

At first nobles and knights designed their own coats of arms. Because they eventually became too numerous to remember, however, King Richard III established the Herald's College in 1483 to oversee the distribution of arms. Heralds were responsible for keeping records of the various coats of arms. They also registered pedigrees (formal declarations of family ancestry) and supervised funerals, receiving much of their income from the latter. A herald usually led a funeral procession and announced the rank and station of the deceased at the graveside.

In Elizabethan England a family's coat of arms was an important symbol of honor and wealth, displayed on doors and on various personal items. An escutcheon, the area on which the coat of arms was displayed, was usually shaped like a shield, although a woman's coat of arms might be diamond-shaped. A gentleman's education was considered incomplete if he was unable to blazon, or explain, the symbols of his escutcheon in proper heraldic language. The surface of the escutcheon was called the field; the field's tincture (color) was the first characteristic mentioned in the blazon. Two or more coats of arms might appear on one shield, in which case the field was quartered (separated into four sections in a crisscross pattern). Above the shield appeared a symbolic figure called the crest, which might be displayed by itself on a family's plate* or livery*.

Shakespeare's works contain many heraldic references. In *The Merry Wives of Windsor,* for example, Shallow, who takes great pride in a 300-year-old coat of arms that bears a dozen white luces (freshwater fish), is satirized by Parson Evans when the Welshman says, "The dozen white louses do become an old coat well . . . it is a familiar beast to man, and signifies love" (I.i.19–21). Shakespeare occasionally used the heraldic term for red—*gules*—when describing blood. In the play within the play in *Hamlet,* for example, the First Player describes the murderous Pyrrhus as being so gory that "head to foot / Now is he total gules" (II.ii.456–57).

Around 1576 John Shakespeare designed a simple coat of arms for himself, but financial difficulties prevented him from completing an application to the Herald's College at that time. Twenty years later, no doubt with the help of his son William, who by that time had gained prominence as a poet and playwright, John Shakespeare reapplied to the college and received the grant of arms that entitled him to be known as "gentleman." The crest can be seen on William Shakespeare's tombstone at Holy Trinity Church in Stratford-upon-Avon. (*See also* **Aristocracy; Social Classes.**)

HERBS AND HERBAL REMEDIES

* *distill* to purify a liquid by evaporating and recondensing it

Herbs are plants used for medications, perfumes, and flavorings. In Shakespeare's England most people grew a variety of herbs in their own gardens, either in kitchen gardens among the vegetables or in separate herb gardens. Because of their many uses, herbs were considered to be among the most important plants in the garden.

Herbs such as pennyroyal, bloodwort, tansy, and saffron were used for flavorings in cooking. Saffron was also used as a food coloring, particularly for fancy dishes. Many herbal extracts were distilled* for use in perfumes, dyes, and alcoholic beverages. Most housewives were skilled at distilling such herbs as sea holly, thistle, valerian, and wormwood. Herbs were also made into many different types of medications, including teas, lotions, and ointments.

The woman of the house was responsible for concocting the family's herbal remedies, and most women took this responsibility very

Elizabethan healers are shown here collecting herbs to make medicines. Shakespeare observes in *Romeo and Juliet,* Act II, Scene iii, that every plant on earth has the power to do some good and some harm.

* **apothecary** pharmacist

seriously. Even in wealthy families that could easily afford a doctor's services, women treated many of their family's health problems with herbal remedies they made themselves. If the medicinal herbs needed for the remedies were not available from the home garden, they usually could be purchased from an apothecary*. Some herbal remedies were regarded as family secrets, passed down from mother to daughter for generations.

Women used herbal remedies to treat a wide variety of health problems. For example, chamomile tea was used to treat headaches, and dog fennel lotion to treat weak eyes. Other herbal remedies included lilies for liver problems, mint for colic*, parsley for toothaches, and St. John's wort for joint pain. In fact many people believed that any illness could be cured with the right herb.

* **colic** severe intestinal pain

Although many herbs actually did help specific health problems, others were probably ineffective or even harmful, such as tobacco, which when chewed was believed to ward off disease. Burning sweet rue on the hearth was thought to reduce the spread of plague*. Because unpleasant odors were associated with disease, it was common to spread sweet-smelling herbs among the rushes* that covered the floors of bedrooms and sitting areas. (*See also* **Gardens and Gardening; Medicine.**)

* **plague** highly contagious and often fatal disease; also called the Black Death

* **rushes** grasslike plants that were dried and used as a floor covering

HISTORIES, THE

See *Plays: The Histories*

HISTORY IN SHAKESPEARE'S PLAYS: ANCIENT GREECE AND ROME

Elizabethans were greatly interested in ancient history. They admired the achievements of the ancient Greeks and Romans, and perhaps more important they viewed the Roman empire as having paved the way for the establishment of Christianity. Several of Shakespeare's plays feature ancient characters, but the Greeks he depicted were significantly less accurate historically than the Roman characters.

SHAKESPEARE'S TREATMENT OF ROMAN HISTORY

Shakespeare's works based on the Roman past often focus on the philosophies and values by which these ancient people lived rather than on the details of historical events. The playwright incorporated much authentic history into his plays—including battles, rebellions, and other political events—but his greatest concern was for creating powerful drama. For this reason he often sacrificed historical accuracy for dramatic effect.

Like most Elizabethans, Shakespeare believed that the fall of Rome occurred because of certain traits inherent in the Roman character. This view lent itself to the genre* of tragedy, and Shakespeare set several of his tragedies in ancient Rome.

* **genre** literary form

PRIMARY SOURCE MATERIAL. Shakespeare's primary source for his "Roman" plays was PLUTARCH'S LIVES. Plutarch was a Greek historian who wrote a collection of biographies of famous Greek and Roman leaders. In 1579 Thomas North translated Plutarch's work into English. It is evident that Shakespeare relied heavily on North's translation. Many scenes from the plays, and sometimes even the words themselves, came from North's work.

Shakespeare also used other sources, including the works of the Roman poet OVID. A story in the poet's *Metamorphoses,* for example, was the source of Shakespeare's treatment of the rape of Lavinia in *Titus Andronicus.* In addition Ovid's *Fasti* was the principal source for Shakespeare's *The Rape of Lucrece.*

THE RAPE OF LUCRECE. A narrative poem, *The Rape of Lucrece* tells the story of a sexual assault on Lucrece, a Roman noblewoman, by Tarquin, the son of a Roman king. The poem describes the heroine's suffering and her subsequent suicide. Before dying she reveals the details of Tarquin's crime to her family. Outraged, they lead the Roman people to overthrow the monarchy and establish the Roman Republic.

Although the story on which the poem is based is a legend, one event described in the poem is historically accurate. In 510 B.C., Roman leaders rebelled against the tyrannical rule of King Lucius Tarquinius Superbus. After driving him from Rome, the rebels abolished the monarchy and replaced it with a republican government.

CORIOLANUS. The events described in *Coriolanus* occurred sometime during the early history of the Roman Republic, which lasted from 510 B.C. to 27 B.C. The play tells of the Roman general Coriolanus, who gains great honor by successfully fighting the Volscians—enemies of Rome. Despite his heroic deeds, the plebeians* refuse to support his election to consul (the highest office in Rome) because of his arrogance. Coriolanus is banished and then joins his former enemies, the Volscians, and attacks Rome. He is eventually persuaded to spare his native city, however, and the Volscians kill him for betraying them.

Several incidents described in *Coriolanus* are historically accurate. For example, the play begins with a riot by the plebeians who are angry about food shortages. To appease them, the Roman leaders allow them to elect their own officials, called tribunes. A similar event actually occurred in 494 B.C., when Roman officials accepted plebeian tribunes as legitimate officials. The dramatization of Rome's battle against the Volscians is also based on actual history. The Volscians were an ancient Italic people, who fought several wars against the Romans during the early 300s B.C.

TITUS ANDRONICUS. Shakespeare's first tragedy, *Titus Andronicus,* occurs during an unspecified time in the later history of the Roman empire. As the play begins, a Roman general named Titus Andronicus returns from war with his sons and their prisoners, among them the Gothic queen Tamora. Ignoring her pleas for mercy, Titus orders the

* *plebeian* member of the general body of Roman citizens, as distinct from the upper class

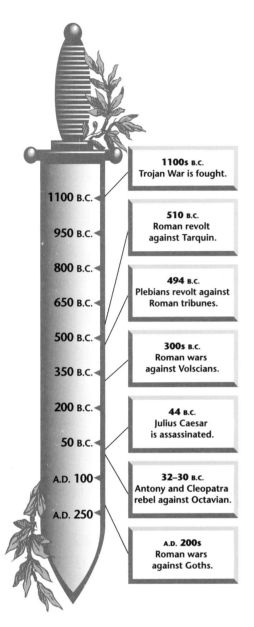

1100s B.C.
Trojan War is fought.

1100 B.C.

950 B.C.

510 B.C.
Roman revolt
against Tarquin.

800 B.C.

650 B.C.

494 B.C.
Plebians revolt against
Roman tribunes.

500 B.C.

350 B.C.

300s B.C.
Roman wars
against Volscians.

200 B.C.

50 B.C.

44 B.C.
Julius Caesar
is assassinated.

A.D. 100

A.D. 250

32–30 B.C.
Antony and Cleopatra
rebel against Octavian.

A.D. 200s
Roman wars
against Goths.

* *triumvirate* form of rule in which authority
is shared by three people

sacrifice of Alarbus (one of Tamora's sons) in accordance with Roman religious tradition. The Roman people offer Titus the crown, but he declines it in favor of Saturninus, the late emperor's eldest son. Saturninus selects Titus's daughter, Lavinia, for his wife, but her brothers oppose the union and take her back by force. During the skirmish that follows, Titus kills one of his own sons. Saturninus then decides to marry Tamora instead. Angered by the situation in which she finds herself, Tamora plots revenge against Titus. Her sons rape and mutilate Lavinia and cause the execution of two of the general's sons by framing them for murder.

Although Shakespeare does not portray actual events from Roman history in *Titus Andronicus,* he explores the forces that shaped the ancient Roman past. The play's historical value lies in its dramatization of the conflict between the Romans and the Goths, a Germanic people who began invading the Roman empire's eastern provinces during the A.D. 200s. Through the violence perpetrated by Tamora and her sons, Shakespeare portrays the eventual destruction of Rome by the Goths. He also shows Roman values as self-defeating. Titus's unquestioning obedience to tradition leads him to sacrifice Tamora's son, which in turn causes the ensuing disorder and violence. Titus also blindly supports the corrupt Saturninus simply because he is an eldest son, and even kills one of his own sons in service to the emperor. Finally, Titus's sense of honor leads him to kill his own daughter because an enemy has raped her.

JULIUS CAESAR. The events and characters depicted in *Julius Caesar* follow real history more closely than do the events in *Titus Andronicus.* Shakespeare dramatizes one of the most influential events in Western history—the assassination of Julius Caesar and the subsequest collapse of the Roman Republic. The play begins with Caesar's return to Rome after defeating the forces of Pompey, a rebellious Roman general. Concerned about Caesar's growing popularity, powerful Roman senators—among them Cassius and Brutus—plot to assassinate him because they fear that he will be crowned emperor and become a tyrant.

After Caesar's death Mark Antony and Lepidus (Caesar's friends) and Octavius (Caesar's nephew) form a triumvirate* to rule Rome. Their combined armies defeat the forces of Brutus and Cassius at the battle of Philippi. The fall of Brutus and Cassius signals the end of the republic and paves the way for the establishment of the Roman empire.

The historical events dramatized in *Julius Caesar* occurred over a period of about three years, from October 45 B.C. to October 42 B.C. Shakespeare compresses and rearranges these events for dramatic effect. In the play, for example, Antony's powerful oration at Caesar's funeral so inflames the Roman people against the assassins that Brutus and Cassius are forced to flee Rome. Historically, five months elapsed before Brutus and Cassius were driven from Rome.

The dramatization of the battle of Philippi also contains some historical inaccuracy. In the play Antony and Octavius defeat Brutus and Cassius in a daylong battle on the plains of Philippi. The actual battle, however, was fought in two parts, the first of which was won by Brutus's

forces. It was not until the second part of the battle, 20 days later, that Antony and Octavius triumphed.

ANTONY AND CLEOPATRA. One of Shakespeare's greatest love stories, *Antony and Cleopatra* dramatizes events in ancient Rome following the assassination of Julius Caesar. In the play, Antony (a member of the triumvirate that rules the Roman empire) is in love with Cleopatra, the queen of Egypt. Together, they challenge Octavius for control of the empire. After Antony and Cleopatra are defeated by Octavius at the battle of Actium, the two lovers commit suicide.

In Act I, Antony learns that his wife has died while participating in a rebellion against Octavius. His wife, Fulvia, did in fact revolt against Octavius in 42 B.C. The battle of Actium, dramatized in Act III, was an actual naval battle in Roman history. Octavius's victory over Antony and Cleopatra signaled the end of their rebellion and the beginning of a period of undisputed monarchy.

SHAKESPEARE'S TREATMENT OF GREEK HISTORY

During the Renaissance, the study of Greek history and culture was just beginning to spread to England. Although Greek characters appear in several of Shakespeare's plays, the Shakespearean play with the strongest connection to Greek traditions is *Troilus and Cressida.*

The plot of *Troilus and Cressida* is based on the Trojan War—a ten-year conflict between the armies of Greece and Troy, first narrated by the ancient Greek poet Homer in his *Iliad.* Rather than retelling the history of that war, however, Shakespeare's play comments on the ancient heroes and their values.

Shakespeare satirizes the failure of the Greeks to live up to their ideals of glory and honor. When the play begins, the war has been raging for seven years, with no end in sight. Although most of the Trojans agree that Helen is not worth dying for, they refuse to surrender her because doing so would damage their honor. Other incidents in the play reveal the corruption of the Greeks. For example, the Greek hero Achilles uses a group of thugs to help him kill a Trojan warrior named Hector, who had earlier spared Achilles' life.

Ideal love is also satirized in the play through the story of two Trojan lovers. Troilus, a prince, is infatuated with Cressida, the daughter of a priest who has joined the Greeks. The shallowness of Troilus's emotions is obvious, and although the two lovers swear fidelity, Cressida betrays Troilus almost as soon as she is taken to the Greek camp.

Shakespeare wrote several other plays that featured characters with Greek names, including *A Midsummer Night's Dream* and *Timon of Athens.* These plays have no authentic Greek history, however, and seem to say more about Elizabethan England than about ancient Greece.

ELIZABETHANS AND THE CLASSICS

The Elizabethans, like their contemporaries throughout Europe, were fascinated by the lives and ideas of the ancient Romans. They greatly admired the literature and philosophy of the period, and Latin was a key part of their education. Shakespeare's audiences were familiar with most of the stories from Roman history that he retold in his works. His audiences would have known the story of Lucrece, for example, from the works of earlier writers, and playgoers were eager to see how the playwright used these compelling tales.

INDEX

A

Academy concept of education, 2:68
Act for Regulating the Theaters (1843), 1:3
Act of Uniformity, 1:111
Acting companies, Elizabethan, **1:1–2** *(illus.)*
  acting profession and, 1:4–5
  actors of, 1:7
  censorship of, 1:46–47
  costumes of, 1:70
  court life and, 1:74–75
  directors of, 1:92–93
  Elizabeth I and, 1:112
  finances and organization, 1:1–2, 4
  friends in, 1:136–37
  Heminges and, 1:163
  Henslowe and, 1:186–87
  at Hope theater, 2:7
  King's Men, 2:36–37
  master of the revels and, 2:91–92
  patron as company's "master," 3:89
  patronage of, 2:141, 142
  performances in inn yards, 2:17
  printing and publishing manuscripts of, 2:192
  prompt book for, 2:193
Acting companies, modern, **1:2–4**, 2:35–36
  actors in, 1:8–10
  directors of, 1:95–96
  Royal Shakespeare Company, 3:25–26 *(illus.)*
  of 20th century, 3:67–68
Acting profession, **1:4–6** *(illus.)*, 1:112–14 *(map)*
Actium, battle of, 1:192
Actor-managers, 1:93–95, 96, 3:57–58, 60–63
Actors, Shakespearean, **1:7–10**
  acting profession and, 1:5
  children's companies, 1:52
  collections from, in museums and archives, 2:121, 122
  costumes of, 1:69–72 *(illus.)*
  directors and, 1:91–96
  in 18th century, 3:56–58
  in Elizabethan acting companies, 1:2
  in films, 3:50–52
  friends and contemporaries, 1:136–37
  interpretations of characters, 1:51–52
  in jigs, 2:22
  in King's Men, 2:36–37
  in 19th century, 3:60–64
  reputations based on Shakespeare's characters, 3:72

  in 17th century, 3:54, 55
  as Shylock, 2:104–5
  in 20th century, 3:67–68
  See also specific plays and actors
Acts and Monuments (Foxe), 1:183
Acts, division of plays into, 1:101, 2:151
Adaptations. *See* Shakespeare's works, adaptations of
Adelman, Janet, 1:122
Admiral's Men, 1:6
Africans, stereotypes of, 3:4. *See also* Race and ethnicity
Agincourt, battle of (1415), 1:24, 174, 175, 2:3, 4 *(illus.)*, 3:159
Agriculture, **1:11–12** *(illus.)*
  country life and, 1:72–74 *(illus.)*
  gardens and gardening, 1:143–45 *(illus.)*
  laborers in, 3:88
  land laws and, 2:46
  poverty due to changes in, 3:152
  trade and, 3:130
  village life and, 1:58
  work in, 3:168–70
Alchemist, The (Jonson), 2:79, 3:34
Alchemy, 2:78, 79–80, 3:34
Aldermen, 2:59
Aldridge, Ira Frederick, 2:134, 3:63, 126
Aldwych Theatre, 3:68
Ale, 1:130
Alexander, Peter, 1:181
Alfar, Cristina León, 3:79
All for Love (Dryden), 1:19
All Hallow's Eve (Halloween), 1:126
Allegory, 3:101, 102–3
Alleyn, Edward, 1:5 *(illus.)*, 6, 70, 92, 186
Alliteration, 2:177
All's Well That Ends Well, **1:12–15** *(illus.)*, 2:62, 164, 3:48
Alma-Tadema, Lawrence, 2:28, 3:62
American Shakespeare Festival Theater and Academy, 3:42
Americas, exploration of the, 1:116–18
Amphitryon (Plautus), 1:66
Analysis of Shakespeare's works. *See* Shakespeare's reputation; Shakespeare's works, changing views; *individual works*
Ancient influences and sources, 3:74–75
Anderson, Judith, 1:10
Anderson, Mary, 3:22, 166
Anglin, Margaret, 3:106
Animal imagery, 1:170
Anne of Denmark, Princess, 2:20
Annesley, Brian, 2:34
Annual fairs, 2:86

Antony and Cleopatra, **1:16–19** *(illus.)*, 1:192, 2:63, 167, 170, 3:37, 48, 113
Antony. *See Antony and Cleopatra*
Apocrypha, 2:60–61
Apologie for Poetrie (Sidney), 3:86
Apothecaries, 2:98
Apparel. *See* Costumes
Apparitions. *See* Ghosts and apparitions
Appian, 1:18
Apprenticeship, 1:5, 78, 2:98, 3:170
Aquinas, Thomas, 2:114–15, 149
Arcadia (Sidney), 1:32, 2:34, 162, 3:86
Archdeacons, 1:53
Archery, 1:141, 3:127, 159
Architecture, **1:19–22** *(illus.)*, 2:8–9, 58
Archives. *See* Museums and archives
Arden, Forest of, **1:22**, 1:30–32, 134, 2:126, 131, 140, 3:23, 38
Arden, Mary, 1:22
Arden of Feversham, 1:100
Arden, Robert, 3:43
Ariel, 1:118, 2:113, 166, 3:1, 116, 117, 120
Ariosto, Ludovico, 1:22, 32, 2:118, 162, 3:105
Aristarchus of Samos, 3:33
Aristocracy, **1:22–23**, 3:86–87
  in *All's Well That Ends Well*, 1:12–15
  clothing worn by, 1:60
  heraldry of, 1:187–88
  nobles incognito (in disguise), 1:99
  royalty and nobility, 3:26–28
  support of acting profession, 1:6
Aristotle, 1:63, 2:114, 115, 148, 167–68
Armin, Robert, 1:51, 2:37, 172–73
Arms and armor, **1:23–27** *(illus.)*, 1:187–88, 3:127, 128, 155, 157–58
Art inspired by Shakespeare, **1:27–30** *(illus.)*, 1:70
Artichokes, 1:143
Artificers, 3:88
Artillery, 1:25, 26
Arts, patronage of. *See* Patronage of the arts
As You Like It, **1:30–34** *(illus.)*, 2:154
  Forest of Arden in, 1:22, 2:126
  friendship in, 1:139
  Orlando in, 2:131–32
  as pastoral, 2:140
  plot of, 2:155
  ridicule of duels and feuds in, 1:107
  romantic elements in, 2:62, 163
  Rosalind in, 3:23
  setting of, 3:38
  seven ages of man in, 3:39
Ascham, Roger, 3:30
Ashcroft, Peggy, 1:10, 15, 2:120, 3:26, 72

Index

Ashe, Thomas, 1:63
Assizes, 1:82–83, 2:46
Astor Place Riot, 1:9, **1:34** *(illus.)*
Astrolabe, 2:129
Astrology, 1:119–20, 2:78–79, 3:32
Astronomy and cosmology, **1:34–36** *(illus.)*
    astrology and, 2:78–79
    fate and fortune, 1:119–20 *(illus.)*
    healthy body reflecting order of universe, 2:96
    madness and, 2:78
    philosophy of history plays and, 2:160–61
    religious beliefs and, 3:7
    science and technology and, 3:32–34
Astrophel and Stella (Sidney), 2:49, 3:86, 93
Atheist's Tragedy, The (Tourneur), 1:161
Attorneys, 2:44
Aubrey, John, 2:121
Audience, 1:8, 52, 3:53–54. *See also* Performances; Shakespearean theater: 17th century; Shakespearean theater: 18th century; Shakespearean theater: 19th century; Shakespearean theater: 20th century
Augustine of Hippo, Saint, 2:115, 149
Authorship, theories about, **1:36–38,** 1:154–55, 3:69
Autumn festivals, 1:126

B

Bachelor (student), 1:108
Bacon, Sir Francis, 1:35, 37, 2:52, 3:35, 141
Bad quartos, 1:181
Baiting, 1:142, 2:7
Bale, John, 2:18
Balks, 1:11
Ballads, 2:48
Bandello, Matteo, 2:118, 3:38
Banking and commerce, **1:38–40** *(illus.),* 1:61–62 *(illus.),* 2:21, 22, 85–86, 3:133
Bankside neighborhood, London, 2:57, 3:121
Banns, 2:88
Banquets, 1:130–31, 2:8
Baptism, 1:47–48
Barber, C. L., 2:110
Barber, Samuel, 2:124
Barbican Theatre, 3:68
Barclay, Alexander, 1:120 *(illus.)*
Barnfield, Richard, 2:181
Barnum, P. T., 3:99
Baronets, 1:23, 3:28, 87
Barons, 1:23, 3:27–28
Barristers, 2:44
Barry, Spranger, 3:57
Barrymore, John, 1:9, 159, 162
Barrymore, Maurice, 1:9
Bartholomew Fair (Jonson), 2:86
Bartolozzi, Eliza, 2:109
Barton, John, 2:67, 94, 120, 3:144
Bassano, Emilia, 1:87
Bastard, 3:27
Baths, 2:146

Battles. *See* Warfare; *specific battles*
Baylis, Lilian, 3:67
Beaumont, Francis, 2:105, 173
Beckett, Samuel, 3:69
Bedchamber, 2:9
Bedford, Brian, 3:41, 124
Bedlam beggars, 2:77, 78, 3:152. *See also* Vagabonds, beggars, and rogues
Belch, Sir Toby, 3:145, 146
Belleforest, François de, 1:161, 3:152
Belsey, Catherine, 3:81
Benefit of clergy, 1:83, 2:44
Bennett, Rodney, 3:115
Benson, Frank, 3:25, 50, 65, 119
Berlioz, Hector, 2:125
Bermuda, 1:117
Bernhardt, Sarah, 3:50
Bernstein, Leonard, 2:125
Bertram, 1:12–14, 15
Bestrafte Bruder-Mord, Der, 3:152
Bethlehem Hospital (London), 2:77
Betrothal, 1:48, 2:88
Betterton, Thomas, 1:7, 93, 166–67, 171, 3:22, 25, 55, 56, 58, 82
Bible, **1:41,** 2:21, 3:75
Bilingual editions, 3:137
Bills of exchange, 1:38
Birmingham Repertory Theater, 1:3, 3:66
Birth. *See* Childbirth
Bishop, Henry Rowley, 2:109, 3:151
Bishops, 1:53
Bishop's Bible, 1:41
Black Death. *See* Plague
Blackfriars, 1:19, **1:41–42,** 1:52, 113, 2:153, 3:55
Blake, William, 1:28
Blank verse, 2:87, 175, 3:136
Blood sports, 1:142–43, 2:7
Bloodletting, 1:97, 2:96
Bloom, Harold, 3:79
Bluing, 1:79
Blythe, Herbert. *See* Barrymore, Maurice
Board games, 1:142
Boar's Head tavern, 2:59
Boas, F. S., 2:92
Boccaccio, Giovanni, 1:14, 3:38, 149, 164
Bodleian Library, 2:121
Boece, Hector, 2:6
Boethius, 2:149
Boito, Arrigo, 2:124
Boke Called the Governour, The (Elyot), 3:75
Boleyn, Anne, 1:46, 109–10, 185, 2:5, 3:128
Bolingbroke, Henry. *See* Henry IV, Part 1; Henry IV, Part 2
Bombast, 1:59
Bonington, Richard, 1:29
Bonnefoy, Yves, 3:137
Book Titles from Shakespeare (Streamer), 2:55
Book-keepers, 1:92–93
Books. *See* Printing and publishing
Boose, Lynda, 3:105
Booth, Edwin, 1:9, 2:28, 3:64, 72

Booth, John Wilkes, 1:9, 2:28
Booth, Junius Brutus, 1:9
Booth, Junius Brutus, Jr., 1:9, 2:28
Booth's Theater (New York City), 3:64
Borck, Caspar Wilhelm von, 3:135
Boris Godunov (Pushkin), 2:54
Bourne, William, 2:129, 3:35
Bowdler, Harriet, 1:42
Bowdler, Thomas, **1:42–43**
Bowling, 1:140
Bowmer, Angus, 2:104
Bows and arrows, 3:158
Boydell, John, 1:28
Boys from Syracuse, The, 3:52
Bradley, A. C., 1:49, 3:80
Bradley, David, 2:36
Branagh, Kenneth, 1:10, 162, 176, 2:36, 67, 120, 136, 3:52, 159
Brando, Marlon, 3:51
Brave New World (Huxley), 2:55–56
Breads, 1:130
Brecht, Bertolt, 3:69
Brick building materials, 1:20
Bridges-Adams, W., 3:25, 26
Briers, Richard, 2:36
Brink, Bernhard, 2:27
Bristol Castle, 1:44–45
British Broadcasting Corporation (BBC), 3:110, 111, 112, 113, 114–16
British Library (London), 2:121–22
Britten, Benjamin, 2:125
Britton, Hutin, 3:67
Broadsides, 2:48
Brodribb, John Henry. *See* Irving, Henry
Brook, Peter, 1:51–52, 92, 2:36, 56, 67, 110, 3:36, 51, 124, 166
Brooke, Arthur, 2:170, 3:21
Brothers Karamazov, The (Dostoevsky), 2:55
Brown, Ford Madox, 1:29
Brutus, **1:43,** 2:15, 24–26, 27
Bryan, George, 2:36
Bubonic plague, 1:57, 97
Buggery, 2:6
Building materials, 1:20
Bullen, Anne. *See* Boleyn, Anne
Bum roll, 1:59 *(illus.),* 60
Burbage, Richard, 1:4, 6, 7, 41, 51, 92, 136–37, 149, 2:37, 134, 3:18, 21, 46
Burgess, Anthony, 2:55
Burgesses, 3:87
Burton, Richard, 1:171, 3:26, 106–7
Bush, Douglas, 3:95

C

Cabot, John, 1:115
Cagney, James, 2:110
Caldwell, Zoe, 3:41
Caliban, **1:43–44** *(illus.),* 2:113, 127, 166, 3:1, 116–19, 120
Caliver, 3:158
Calvin, John, 1:53, 3:8

Index

Index

Feuds. *See* Duels and feuds
Fictional settings, 3:38–39
Field, Richard, 1:136
Fielding, Henry, 2:53
Fifteen Minute Hamlet, The (film), 1:159
Figurative language, 2:42
Figures of speech, 2:174, 176–77
Films. *See* Shakespeare on screen
Financial institutions. *See* Banking and
   commerce
Finnegans Wake (Joyce), 2:56
Fiorentino, Giovanni, 2:103
Firearms, 1:25–27, 3:158
First Folio, 1:14, 17, 32, **1:127** *(illus.)*, 3:3–4,
   82
   actors listed in, 1:6
   classifications of plays in, 2:157–58
   Heminges and, 1:163
   Jonson's poetic preface to, 1:127, 2:23
   portrait of Shakespeare in, 1:29
   printing and publishing, 2:190, 191
   Shakespeare's canon and, 3:69
Fish, 1:129–30
Fishburne, Laurence, 2:136
Fitton, Mary, 1:87
Five-act structure, 1:100–101
Flatter, Rudolf, 3:137
Fletcher, John, 1:184, 2:60, 105, 158, 173,
   3:49, 69, 106, 151
Flint castle, 1:45
Flintlocks, 1:27
Florio, John, **1:128–29**, 2:20
Flower, Charles Edward, 3:25
Foakes, R. A., 2:107
Folger Shakespeare Library, 2:121
Folger Theatre Group, 3:38
Folio. *See* Quartos and folios
Folklore. *See* Magic and folklore
Food and feasts, **1:128–31** *(illus.)*
   farms products, 1:12
   festivals and holidays, 1:125, 126
   food in villages, 1:73, 74
   herbs for cooking, 1:188
   table manners, 2:84
Fools, clowns, and jesters, **1:132–33** *(illus.)*
   actors' interpretations of, 1:51
   Feste in *Twelfth Night*, 1:132, 3:146–47
   improvisation of, 1:5
   jig and, 2:22
   in *King Lear*, 2:32, 33, 35, 36
   loyalty and, 2:69
   madness feigned by, 2:77–78
   prose used by, 2:194
   as stock characters, 2:99
   in *Two Gentlemen of Verona*, 3:150
   in *As You Like It*, 1:30, 31, 33
Foot, travel by, 3:138
Football, 1:140–41
Forbes-Robertson, Johnston, 3:22
Forbidden Planet (film), 3:52, 69, 120
Foreign relations. *See* Diplomacy and foreign
   relations

Foreigners, **1:133–34**, 3:4–5
Forest and fields, **1:134–35**
Forest of Arden. *See* Arden, Forest of
Forgiveness. *See* Revenge and forgiveness
Formal garden, 1:143
Forman, Simon, 2:121
Forrest, Edwin, 1:34, 3:63
Fortune playhouse, 1:186
Fortune. *See* Fate and fortune
Foul papers, 2:190
Four-poster bed, 2:9
Fourth Folio, 3:25
Fowl, types of, 1:129
Foxe, John, 1:181, 183
Frame story, 3:104
France, diplomacy with, 1:90–91
Freehold, 1:11
French translations, 3:134–35, 136
Freud, Sigmund, 2:95
Freudian interpretation, 2:95, 110, 3:2, 80.
   See also Psychology; Shakespeare's
   works, changing views
Friday Street Club, 2:105, 172 *(illus.)*
Friends and contemporaries, **1:135–37**, 3:96
Friendship, **1:138–39**, 2:6, 63, 69, 3:23–24
Frobisher, Martin, 1:117
Fruits, 1:130
Fulke, William, 1:120
Fuller, John, 1:1
Funerals. *See* Death and funerals
*Funny Thing Happened on the Way to the
   Forum, A*, 2:156
Furnishings. *See* Households and furnishings
Fuseli, Henry, 1:28

G

Galen, 2:97, 3:34
Galileo Galilei, 3:34
Galleons, 3:84
Galleries in public playhouse, 2:152–53
Gallery in manor house, 1:21, 2:8–9
Galleys, 3:84
Games, pastimes, and sports, 1:74, 75,
   1:139–43 *(illus.)*, 2:7, 3:127–28 *(illus.)*
Garbage, 3:29
Gardens and gardening, 1:11, **1:143–45**
   (illus.), 1:188
Garnet, Father, 2:72
Garnier, Robert, 1:18, 2:141
Garrick, David, 1:7–8, 3:22, 106
   acting style, 3:56, 57
   as actor-manager, 1:93–94, 2:109, 3:57–58
   costumes of, 1:71
   paintings of, 1:28
   performances by, 1:19, 167, 2:53, 74, 120,
      3:18, 150–51
   Shakespeare festival in Stratford-upon-
      Avon and, 3:40, 99
   Shakespeare's reputation and, 3:71–72
   staging and, 3:59
Gascoigne, George, 2:49, 51, 52

Gay, Penny, 3:105
Gender and sexuality, **1:145–47** *(illus.)*
   feminist interpretations and, 1:120–23
   humor about sex, 2:12
   love and, 2:62–63, 64
   marriage and family, 2:87–89 *(illus.)*
   in *Midsummer Night's Dream*, 2:110, 111
   Miranda and, 2:113–14
   morality and ethics and, 2:115
   in *Much Ado about Nothing*, 2:119
   in *Othello*, 2:134
   premarital sex, 2:88
   sexuality in mature tragedies, 3:47–48
   Taming of the Shrew and, 3:103–7 *(illus.)*
   Twelfth Night and, 3:144–48 *(illus.)*
   work and, 3:168, 169, 170
Generals, 3:157
Geneva Bible, 1:41
Genre. *See* Plays: the comedies; Plays: the
   histories; Plays: the romances; Plays: the
   tragedies
Gentlemen, 3:87
Gentry, 1:22–23, 3:86–87
Geoffrey of Monmouth, 2:33
Geographical History of Africa, A, 1:18
Geography, 1:40, **1:147–48** *(map)*, 3:39
George II, 1:171
German clothing styles, 1:59, 60
German translations, 3:135–36
Gertrude and Claudius (Updike), 2:56
Gesta Romanorum, 2:103
Ghosts and apparitions, **1:148–49**,
   1:157–58, 160, 2:71, 80–81, 3:100–101
Gibson, Mel, 1:162
Gielgud, John, 1:3, 9–10, 162, 2:95, 120,
   3:15, 22, 26, 51, 67, 72, 120, 166
Gilbert, Miriam, 2:67
Gilbert, Sir Humphrey, 1:117
Gilbert, Sir William, 3:35
Giles, David, 3:115
Giraldi, Giambattista. *See* Cinthio
Glasheen, Adaline, 2:56
Glass windows, 1:20
Globe Shakespeare, 3:83
Globe Theater, 1:2, 112, **1:149–50** *(illus.)*,
   1:185, 2:143, 3:36
Gods and goddesses, 1:103, **1:150–52**
Goethe, Johann Wolfgang von, 2:54, 3:135
Goffe, Robert, 3:21
Gold coins, 1:61–62
"Golden mean," concept of, 2:114
Goldsmith, Oliver, 3:56
Goneril, 2:31–33
Good, Jack, 2:136
Goodfellow, Robin, 2:108
Gounod, Charles, 2:124
Government and politics, **1:152–54** *(illus.)*
   aristocracy in, 1:23
   the Church and, 1:53
   court life and, 1:74–76
   diplomacy and foreign relations, 1:89–91
      (illus.)

198

Index

Index

types of, 2:114–15
in *As You Like It*, 1:33
Love madness, 2:76–77
Love tragedies, 2:61, 170
Lover's Complaint, A, **2:65**, 2:182, 3:47
Love's Labor's Lost, **2:65–68** *(illus.)*, 3:67, 126
Love's Labor's Lost (film), 3:52
Love's Labor's Won, 2:60, 66
Love's Martyr, 2:150
Lowin, John, 2:134
Lowlands, 1:147
Loyalty, 1:138, 2:63, **2:68–70**, 2:113, 3:145
Lucy, Sir Thomas, 3:44
Lurhmann, Baz, 3:22, 81
Luther, Martin, 1:53, 2:52, 3:6
Luxury imports, 1:79
Lyceum Theatre (London), 1:3, 2:18, 19, 3:65
Lyly, John, 1:32, 2:40, 50, 52, 170–71, 3:150
Lyne, Anne, 2:150
Lyric group. *See Midsummer Night's Dream, A; Richard II; Romeo and Juliet*

M

Macbeth, **2:70–74** *(illus.)*, 3:48
adaptations of, 1:93, 3:76–77
Astor Place Riot at performance of, **1:34** *(illus.)*
castle setting in, 1:46
dreams arousing guilt in, 1:104
Lady Macbeth in, 2:74–75
loyalty theme in, 2:69
messengers in, 1:102
similarity between *Rape of Lucrece* and, 2:184–84
soliloquies in, 3:91
stage effects in, 3:37
supernatural phenomena in, 3:101
symbolism in, 3:102
television production, 3:113–14
weather in, 3:161
witches in, 3:167–68
Macbeth (film), 3:50
Macbeth, Lady, 1:104, 2:70, 71, 72, **2:74–75**, 2:74, 82, 3:79
MacDonald, Anne-Marie, 2:136
Machiavelli, Niccolo, 3:17
McKellen, Ian, 1:10, 2:136, 3:114
Macklin, Charles, 1:51, 2:104, 3:56–57
McLuskie, Kathleen, 3:81
Macready, William Charles, 1:9, 34, 171, 2:34, 36, 3:14, 18, 60–61, 72, 120
Maddermarket Theatre, 3:66
Madness, **2:75–78** *(illus.)*, 2:131, 3:2, 47
Magellan, Ferdinand, 1:91
Magic and folklore, **2:78–82** *(illus.)*
ceremonies and rituals, 1:47–48
in the comedies, 2:156–57
Oberon and, 2:130
of Prospero, 3:1
Puck and, 3:3 *(illus.)*
science and technology and, 3:34

supernatural phenomena, 3:100–101 *(illus.)*
in *Tempest*, 3:117, 119
witches and evil spirits, 3:167–68 *(illus.)*
Magna Carta, 2:5, 30
Malapropisms, 2:10–11
Malaria, 2:96
Malone, Edmond, 3:82, 83
Malvolio, **2:82–83**, 3:145, 146
Mankiewicz, Joseph L., 3:51
Manners, 2:83–84
Mannoni, Ottave, 1:96
Manorial court, 1:11–12
Manors, 1:21–22, 2:8–9
Manufactured goods, 3:130–31, 170
Maplet, John, 2:52
Marc-Antoine (Garnier), 1:18
Marcius, Caius, 1:68
Marcus Brutus. *See* Brutus
Margaret, 3:17–18
Mark Antony. *See Antony and Cleopatra; Julius Caesar*
Markets and fairs, 1:40, 57–58, **2:85–86**, 3:98, 132–33
Marlowe, Christopher, 1:33, 37, 82, 154, 2:40, 50, 51, **2:87**, 2:104, 156, 171, 3:14, 17, 97, 125
Marowitz, Charles, 2:136
Marquess or marquis, 1:23, 3:27
Marriage and family, **2:87–89** *(illus.)*
betrothal of Miranda, 2:113–14
ceremonies and rituals, 1:47–48
family as microcosm of state, 1:146
feminist interpretations and, 1:122, 123
gender roles and sexuality in, 1:145–46, 147 *(illus.)*
inheritance and, 2:16–17
love and, 2:62, 63–64
nurses and midwives and, 2:129
Petruchio and, 2:147–48 *(illus.)*
Taming of the Shrew and, 3:105
Marston, John, 2:172, 3:154, 155
Marx, Karl, 2:89, 3:73
Marxist interpretations, 1:69, **2:89–90**, 3:81
Mary Stuart (Mary, Queen of Scots), 1:46, 89, 111, 2:20, 75, 3:6, 97
Masefield, John, 2:94
Mason, James, 2:95
Masque of Oberon, The (Jonson), 3:164
Masques, 1:75, 125, 2:23, **2:90–91** *(illus.)*, 2:109, 123, 157
Mass, Catholic, 3:8
Massinger, Philip, 2:173
Master craftsmen, 1:78, 79
Master of the revels, 1:46, **2:91–92**, 2:193
Masterless men, 3:89
Masterpiece, 1:78
Matchlock gun, 1:26
May Day, 1:85 *(illus.)*, 86, 124 *(illus.)*, 125
Maypole (round) dance, 1:86
Mazursky, Paul, 3:120
Meals, 1:130–31

Measure for Measure, 1:14, 99, 2:62, **2:92–95** *(illus.)*, 2:156, 3:48
Meats, 1:128–30
Medea, legend of, 2:75
Medicine, **2:95–99** *(illus.)*
disease and, 1:97 *(illus.)*
herbal remedies, 1:188–89
madness and, 2:75–78 *(illus.)*
medical science, 3:34–35
nurses and midwives and, 2:129
Medievalism, 2:17–18, **2:99–100**, 2:137–39 *(illus.)*, 168–69
Medwall, Henry, 2:18
Meiningen Players, 1:95
Melancholia (depression), 2:76, 97
Melville, Herman, 2:54
Men of business, 1:154
Menaechmi, The (Plautus), 1:50, 66, 2:154, 155
Mendelssohn, Felix, 2:109, 125
Men's clothing, 1:59–60
Mental illness in Elizabethan psychology, 2:75–76
Mercenaries, 3:156–57
Merchant of Venice, The, **2:100–105** *(illus.)*, 2:156
disguises in, 1:98 *(illus.)*, 99
friendship in, 1:138–39
Italian setting of, 2:19
prose used in, 2:196
revenge and forgiveness in, 3:10–11
romantic elements in, 2:62, 163
Shylock in, 3:85
symbolism in, 3:102
Merchants, 1:56
Meres, Francis, 2:60, 66, 67, 3:93
Mermaid Tavern, **2:105**
Merry Wives of Windsor, The, 1:119, 187, 2:12, **2:106–7**, 2:155 *(illus.)*, 197, 3:106
Messenger, dramatic effect of, 1:102–3
Messina, Cedric, 3:114
Metamorphoses (Ovid), 2:108, 137, 3:74, 105, 153, 164
Metaphors, 2:15–16, 174, 177–78
Meter, 2:40–41, 174–76, 179
Method actors, 1:51
Michaelmas, 1:125, 126
Middle English, 2:39
Middleham Castle, 1:45
Middleton, Thomas, 3:123, 167
Midsummer Eve, 1:126
Midsummer Night's Dream, A, 1:51–52, 126, **2:107–11** *(illus.)*, 2:154
Antony and Cleopatra and, 1:18
dreams in, 1:104–5
fairies in, 1:118, 3:67
fictional setting of, 3:38
friendship in, 1:139
interlude in, 2:18
nature in, 2:126–27
Oberon in, 2:130
play within a play in, 2:108, 152, 169

Index

Index

Index

Ships, **3:83–84** *(illus.)*, 3:140, 155
  exploration and, 1:114–18 *(illus.)*
  navigation and, 2:128–29 *(illus.)*
  Spanish Armada, 3:95–96 *(illus.)*
  transport of wares by, 3:132
Shipwrecks, 2:127
Shires, 1:148
Shoreditch, 2:58
Shrewsbury, battle of, 2:2
Shrove Tuesday, 1:125
Shylock, 2:100, 101–5, 156, 3:10–11, **3:85**
  changing views of, 3:78–79
  as Elizabethan image of Jewish
    moneylender, 1:38
  English fascination with Jews and, 2:22
  interpretations of character, 1:51, 2:104–5
  prose used by, 2:196
  psychological view of, 3:2
Sicilian Usurper, The, 3:14
Sickert, Walter, 1:29
Sickness. *See* Disease; Medicine
Siddons, Sarah, 1:8, 51, 2:74, 94, 3:57, 72, 166
Sidney, Sir Philip, 1:32, 2:34, 49, 52, 140, 162, 171, **3:86**, 3:93
Sightseeing, 3:141
Signet Office, 1:153
Silent films, 3:49–50
Silver coins, 1:62
Similes, 2:177
Singers, 2:122–23
Sir Thomas More, 2:61
Slapstick, 1:132, 2:11 *(illus.)*, 12
Slave trade, 1:116
Sly, William, 2:37
Smallpox, 1:97, 2:96
Smith, Maggie, 3:41
Smiths, 1:77 *(illus.)*
Smoking tobacco, 1:131
Social classes, **3:86–89** *(illus.)*
  agriculture and, 1:11, 12
  in *All's Well That Ends Well,* 1:12–15
  architecture and, 1:20–22
  aristocracy, 1:22–23
  clothing and, 1:58–59, 60–61, 3:171
  Coriolanus and, 1:68–69 *(illus.)*
  costumes as indicators of, 1:70
  craftworkers, rank of, 1:78–79
  Elizabethan theaters and, 1:114
  food and feasts of, 1:128–31 *(illus.)*
  funeral procession and, 1:88
  games and pastimes and, 1:139, 140, 141, 142
  gardens and, 1:143–44
  heraldry of nobles, 1:187–88
  hierarchy of universe and, 1:36
  higher education and, 3:31
  marriage decision and, 2:87–88
  Marxist interpretations and, 2:90
  in *Much Ado about Nothing,* 2:119–20
  personal habits and manners and, 2:84
  poverty and wealth and, 2:186–88 *(illus.)*

  prose to reflect, 2:194–95
  royalty and nobility, 3:26–28
  urban class of London, 1:56
  village life and, 1:73–74
Soldiers, 2:112, 113, 3:156–57, 171–72. *See also* Warfare; Work
Solicitors, 2:44
Soliloquy, 1:102, **3:90–92**
Sondheim, Stephen, 2:156
Songs, 2:123–24
Sonnets, the, 2:49, 3:45, 46–47, **3:92–95**
  Dark Lady in, 1:86–87
  form and sequences, 2:182–85
  friendship in, 1:138
  iambic pentameter for, 2:174
  love in, 2:61, 64
  in *Romeo and Juliet,* 3:21
  by Sidney, 3:86
  themes in, 3:93–94
  theories of authorship and, 1:37
Sopers, 1:79
Sorcery, 2:80–81
Sound effects, 3:54
Southampton, Henry Wriothesley, earl of, 2:141, 180, 3:45
Sovereign, 1:23
Sovereigns (money), 1:61
Spain, England's relations with, 1:91, 116–17
Spanish Armada, 1:91, 111, 3:84, **3:95–96** *(illus.)*, 3:155
Spanish clothing styles, 1:59–60
Spanish Tragedy, The (Kyd), 1:161, 2:50, 168, 3:10, 152
Special effects, 3:55
Specimens of English Dramatic Poets Who Lived about the Time of Shakespeare (Lamb), 2:38
Spectacle, theater as, 1:94–95, 3:54–55, 61–63, 64–65
Spectator events, 1:142–43
Spelling, 2:191
Spencer, Theodore, 1:121
Spenser, Sir Edmund, 2:33, 49, 118, 140, 141, 171, **3:96**, 3:102
Spies, 2:87, **3:97**
Spirit conjuring (necromancy or sorcery), 2:80–81
Spondee, 2:175
Sports. *See* Games, pastimes, and sports
Spring festivals, 1:125
Squire, landholdings of, 1:11
Stage, 2:153
Stage directions, 1:93, 103, 3:54
Stage managers, 1:3
Stage practices, Elizabethan, 1:5–6
Staging methods, 3:53–55
Stanley, Henry, 2:36
Star Chamber, 1:82, 2:44, 45
Stargazing, 2:78–79
Stationers' Company, 2:189
Stationer's Guild, 1:17

Stationers, London, 2:188–90
Stationer's Register, 2:189, 3:13
Steele Glass, The (Gascoigne), 2:49
Steevens, George, 3:82–83, 94
Stereotypes of foreigners, 1:134, 3:4
Stewart, Patrick, 2:105, 135
Stock characters, 1:50, 2:99, 154, 3:74, 154
Stocks, 1:82
Stoicism, 2:148
Stoker, Bram, 2:18
Stone building materials, 1:20
Stoppard, Tom, 2:56, 3:21, 24, 69
Stourbridge Fair, 2:86
Stow, John, 1:170
Strange's Men, 2:36
Stratford Shakespeare Festival (Ontario), 3:41, 124
Stratford-upon-Avon, **3:97–99**
  Anne Hathaway in, 1:162–63
  cycles of history plays at, 1:171
  family background in, 3:42–43
  friends in, 1:135–36
  Royal Shakespeare Company of, 3:25–26 *(illus.)*
  Shakespeare festival in, 3:40–41
Streamer, Volney, 2:55
Stride, John, 3:22
Structure of Shakespeare's plays. *See* Play structure
Stubbs, Imogen, 2:136
Subplots, 1:101
Suburbs, 1:57
Summer festivals, 1:125–26
Sumptuary laws, 1:60–61, 70, 147, 3:89, 170–71
Supernatural phenomena, **3:100–101** *(illus.)*
  fate and fortune, 1:119–20 *(illus.)*
  ghosts and apparitions, 1:148–49
  in *Macbeth,* 2:73
  magic and folklore, 2:78–82
  Oberon and, 2:130
  Titania and, 3:124
  witches and evil spirits, 3:167–68 *(illus.)*
Superstitions about death, 2:81–82
Superstructure, 2:153
Suppositi, I (Ariosto), 3:105
Surgeons, 2:97 *(illus.)*, 98
Surrey, Henry Howard, earl of, 2:48–49
Suzman, Janet, 2:136, 197
"Sweating sickness," 2:96
Sweets, 1:130
Swords, 1:24, 3:158
Symbolism and allegory, 1:150–51, **3:101–3** *(illus.)*, 3:120, 159
Syphilis, 2:96

T

Table manners, 2:84
Tailors. *See* Craftworkers
Tale of Gamelyn, The, 1:32
Tales from Shakespeare (Lamb and Lamb), 2:38

Index

Iago as, 2:14, 133–34
influence on tragedies, 2:169
in morality plays, 2:138–39
Richard III as, 3:17
Shylock in tradition of, 2:104
as stock character, 2:99
villainous characters and, 1:49–50
Village life, 1:72–74
Virgil, 3:118
Viscounts, 1:23, 3:27
Vision through madness, 2:77–78
Visual effects, 1:92
Vogel, Paula, 2:136
Voltaire, 2:55, 3:134–35
Voss, Johann Heinrich, 3:136

W

Wages, 1:62
Wake, 1:48, 87
Walker, William, 1:136
Walking, 3:138
Walsingham, Sir Francis, 3:97
Walsingham, Thomas, 2:87
Wanamaker, Sam, 1:150
War games, 1:141
War of the Theaters, 2:152, **3:154–55**
Warburton, William, 3:58
Ward, John, 3:49
Wardle, Irving, 2:95
Warfare, **3:155–60** *(illus.)*
    arms and armor for, 1:23–27 *(illus.)*
    foreign relations and, 1:91
    military life, 2:112
    naval, 3:84, 95–96 *(illus.)*
    Spanish Armada and, 3:95–96 *(illus.)*
    tournaments and, 3:127
Warhorses, 3:158
Warkworth Castle, 1:45
Warner, David, 3:15
Warner, Deborah, 2:36
Warning signs, 2:82
Wars of the Roses, **3:160**
    castles during, 1:44, 45–46
    Henry VI, Part 1 on, 1:176–79 *(illus.)*
    Henry VI, Part 2 on, 1:179–81
    Henry VI, Part 3 on, 1:181–84 *(illus.)*
    Richard III and final events of, 3:15–18
        (illus.)
    sources on, 3:75
    television production on, 3:112

Washington Shakespeare Company, 3:107
Watchword to England, A (Munday), 2:139
Water supply for London, 2:59
Water transport, 3:132, 139–40
Watteau, Antoine, 3:115
Wealth. *See* Poverty and wealth
Weaponry. *See* Arms and armor
Weather and the seasons, 1:124–26 *(illus.)*,
    2:126–28, **3:160–61**, 3:165
Weddings, 1:48
Welles, Orson, 1:167, 2:28, 74, 135,
    3:50–51
West, Benjamin, 1:28
West Side Story, 3:52, 69
Westminster, 2:58
Wet nurses, 2:129
Wheel of fortune, 2:100, 168–69
Wheeled vehicles, 3:139, 140
Whetstone, George, 2:92
Whipping, 1:82
White Tower, 3:128
White, Willard, 2:136
Whitehall Palace, 1:57
Whitsunday, 1:125–26
Wieland, Christoph Martin, 3:135
Wilhelm Meister (Goethe), 2:54
Will. *See* Shakespeare's will
William Shakespeare's Romeo + Juliet, 3:52
William the Conqueror, 1:46, 3:128
Windsor Castle, 1:75
Wine, 1:130
Winter festivals, 1:124–25
Winter's Tale, The, 2:156–57, 165–66, 3:48,
    3:161–66 *(illus.)*, 3:161
Witches and evil spirits, 3:100–101, **3:167–68**
    (illus.)
    dangers after childbirth from fairies, 1:47
    ghosts and apparitions, 1:149
    in *Henry VI, Part 1*, 1:178
    in *Henry VI, Part 2*, 1:179
    in *Macbeth*, 2:70, 71, 72
    spirit conjuring, 2:80–81
Woman's Prize, or The Tamer Tamed, The
    (Fletcher), 3:106
Women
    boys in roles of, 1:5–6
    clothing for, 1:60
    in comedies, 2:156
    death during childbirth, 1:87
    disguised as men, 1:98–99
    education of, 1:108–9

friendship between, 1:139
healers (wise women), 2:98
herbal remedies concocted by, 1:188–89
    (illus.)
place in family, 2:88
roles in Elizabethan society, 1:145
roles in plays for, 1:121–23
on stage, 1:2, 8, 9, 10, 93, 3:55, 57
work of, 1:73, 78, 3:168, 169, 170
See also Feminist interpretations; Gender
    and sexuality; Marriage and family
*Women's Part: Feminist Criticism of Shakespeare,
    The* (Lenz, Greene, and Neely), 1:120,
    121
Woodlands, 1:134–35
Woodward, Henry, 1:14
Wool industry, 1:12, 39, 40, 3:130–31,
    169–70, 170–71
Woolf, Virginia, 1:95
Word abuse and misuse, 2:10–11
Wordplay, 2:42, 119, 174, 176–77, 3:150
Wordsworth, William, 3:94
Work, **3:168–72** *(illus.)*
    country life and, 1:72, 73–74
    craftworkers and, 1:76–80 *(illus.)*
    farm labor and products, 1:11–12
    guilds and, 1:155–56 *(illus.)*
    in medicine, 2:96–98
    unemployment with agricultural changes,
        1:73
World Shakespeare Bibliography, 3:74
Wriothesley, Henry, 2:141, 180, 3:45
Writ, 2:45
Writers inspired by Shakespeare. *See*
    Literature inspired by Shakespeare
Writers. *See* Playwrights and poets
Wyatt, Sir Thomas, 2:48, 3:92

Y

Yeomen, 1:11, 23, 3:87–88
Yong, Bartholomew, 3:149
Yorkist tetralogy, 2:2, 3–5. *See also Henry VI,
    Part 1; Henry VI, Part 2; Henry VI, Part 3;
    Richard III*

Z

Zeffirelli, Franco, 1:162, 3:22, 51, 69, 106
Zelauto (Munday), 2:139
Zoffany, John, 1:28